THE BIG YIN

The Life & Times Of

BILLY CONNOLLY

also by Jonathan Margolis

Cleese Encounters

THE BIG YIN

The Life & Times Of
BILLY CONNOLLY

Jonathan Margolis

CHAPMANS

First published in Great Britain in 1994 by
Chapmans
An imprint of Orion Books Ltd
Orion House, 5 Upper St Martin's Lane, London WC2H 9EA

This Orion edition published in 1995

A CIP catalogue record for this book is available
from the British Library

ISBN 0 75280 069 8

Typeset by Selwood Systems, Midsomer Norton
Printed in Great Britain by Butler & Tanner Ltd, Frome and London

For the usual lot

INTRODUCTION

Billy Connolly is the most successful and popular British stand-up comedian of modern times, but he provokes a peculiar reaction in Scotland, in England, in America, Canada, New Zealand and Australia. Young people think he is a has-been, the middle aged that he is a never-was. The elderly still think he is too filthy, alternative comedy fans, that he is too clean, while hippies insist he is a sell-out. Journalists have a distinct downer on him, as do churchmen, local politicians in Glasgow, posh Edinburgh-ites, TV critics in the USA ... I could go on. But I shall simply repeat: Billy Connolly is the most successful and popular British stand-up comedian of modern times, wherein lies a lot of stories, anecdotes, recollections and theories.

This book would have been impossible without the Olympian research work of Bryony Coleman and Claire Coakley. Eternal thanks also to: Radio Clyde, the *Glasgow Herald* and *Evening Times*, the Associated Newspapers Library, the New York Public Library, the Motion Picture Academy Library and the American Film Institute Library, Los Angeles. I am hugely grateful to all the individuals who agreed to be interviewed and quoted by name, as I am to those who were keen to contribute to the book, but asked not to be identified. Gabrielle Morris, my assistant, put up with a lot; and Graham McOwan of The Lighter Side Bookshop, Upper Richmond Road West, London SW14, deserves special credit for giving me the idea of writing the first biography of one of my all-time heroes.

Jonathan Margolis
London, Glasgow, and Los Angeles, 1994

PREFACE

'I always knew I could get to the top. I've known it since I was a small boy. I knew I was a wee bit special.'
Billy Connolly, talking to the Daily Mail, *6 May 1976*

From the outside, the Great American Music Hall, as it is called with a hint of fashionable irony, is a scruffy theatre on a scuzzy street at the wrong end of San Francisco's theatre district. Billy Connolly's name was up in lights this December evening in 1993, but they were not the world's biggest or brightest lights, considering that the turn they were advertising was a prime-time TV star doing stand-up comedy for fun. The letters were spelled out in a crooked line, on a placard surrounded by revolving white torchbulbs.

Connolly's advance billing on the San Francisco theatre's forthcoming events pamphlet had been little more impressive, the name in letters one eighth of an inch high, the same size as those afforded to a group of Finnish folk artists, Varttina, and the Nate Ginsberg Big Band. But it was not a sign of failure at all. Billy Connolly had no need whatsoever to be here other than a love of his craft and a burning need for a live, intelligent audience.

Inside, the theatre was surprisingly grand, an Edwardian relic with marble columns, ornate balconies, mirrored walls and plenty of slightly smoke-stained gilt work on its intricate ceiling. When it was built in 1907, Blanco's, as it was known, was an exclusive restaurant and high-class bordello. It later became a posh cabaret venue. The Music Box.

Billy Connolly's show was a sellout, if only at the last minute, ticket sales having quickened in the final few hours before his opening night of three in San Francisco. The audience, mostly young and, although with a fair proportion of Scottish expatriates, principally American, sat drinking at round tables in the area that would once have been the stalls. When the tall Scotsman bounded onto the stage, beardless and wearing a black T-shirt and jeans, the applause, whistling and whooping was prolonged and rapturous. Billy Connolly may not be a *big* big name in the USA, but Connolly fans comprise an enthusiastic cult several times larger than the entire population of Scotland.

The comic paced the stage like a huge bear as the greeting noise showed no sign of abating, and indeed grew in volume. 'Oh. Oh, woah, woah,' he shouted, the most familiar Glasgow accent in Britain sounding at once welcome and incongruous here on the West coast of America. 'Oh, shit, yeah,' he went on. The racket began to die. 'I never know what to fucking do in this bit.' The first laughter came, ten seconds after Connolly first opened his mouth, albeit aided by the strategic use of the word fuck.

He got eleven fucks and fuckings into the first minute and a half of his act, which warmed up the Americans, but seemed fractionally to embarrass some of the Scots. Perhaps some of the more out-of-touch expats had seen, in even tinier letters than 'Billy Connolly' on the playbill, the words 'Scottish comedian', and had come expecting someone tame and harmless in a kilt. Although he is a teetotal vegetarian who avoids coffee, Billy Connolly is anything but tame and harmless, and, more important still, has never as far as the most detailed research can discover, either worn or confessed to wearing a kilt other than in the severest jest.

To the Big Yin, now in his early fifties and, despite an inner seriousness, miraculously still in touch with the childlike humour that finds farting an inexhaustible source of humour, fate must seem even more amusing – having signposted his route from Partick to a home and a public on the West coast of the USA, via Buckingham Palace.

In 1952, aged ten, Connolly was amongst a crowd lining Glasgow's Kelvin Way with his schoolmates, waiting to wave at the newly crowned Queen. He and his friends delighted at being let out of St Peter's primary school for the occasion, and Billy was already standing out from the crowd – in this case, in the sad sense of being the only child there without a Union Jack to wave.

'She was coming up the road in the limo,' he remembers, 'and all the kids were waving flags. And I didn't have one! But I had my dinner ticket for school, this bloody dinner ticket, so I drew a Union Jack on the back of this wee rectangular dinner ticket. I drew the lines in, just like a Union Jack. And there were a lot of bushes and trees and things in Kelvin Way, so I got a wee branch and poked it through my dinner ticket and waved it at the Queen, thinking I was being a great patriot.'

Thirty-five years on, the young patriot from Partick was not just waving at the Queen, but helping direct her son and daughter-in-law away from protocol and towards celebrity partying, the late 1980s court jester, out on the town with the Duke of York, as his wife, Pamela Stephenson, persuades Fergie and the Princess of Wales to visit Annabel's nightclub dressed in disguise.

Connolly's path – from flag-waving to frolicking with the young royals and living an LA lifestyle – is one of the best examples of rags to riches stories in the history of comedy. If it were made into a Hollywood film, Sean Connery would be roped in to star, given a highly implausible wig and beard, and even then criticized for a storyline beyond the realms of realism.

The reality is the true yarn of the Big Yin – a tale of comic talent triumphing over class, adversity and a Glasgow accent that would once have made him unacceptable south of Gretna Green, never mind in America. Connolly's is a story begun in Glasgow tenements, developed in a Clydebank shipyard and folk clubs, taken on a world tour and currently based in Los Angeles, where its hero is engaged in the Sisyphean task of trying to succeed in the States when, despite five appearances on the David Letterman show, his name stubbornly remains a little unfamiliar to the public. It is not that Billy Connolly is *unknown* to Americans, but just that even after he has by any standards hit the big time, people there still need prompting to remember who he is. Whether it is the American next to you on a commuter flight, or the showbusiness types gathered round a Hollywood restaurant table, the response to Connolly's name is the same – a furrow of the brow, followed by an awakening ... 'Oh, yeah, I really like him.'

Connolly is probably the most famous Scot in Britain, but his is not the twee, shortbread-for-the-tourists Scotland, or even the contemporary 'cool' of the Edinburgh Festival. As a mid-1970s review in *The Times* of his London Palladium show put it: 'For him the Scottish national dress is not the kilt, but a pair of wellingtons, and the mark of class distinction is a childhood spent wearing "wellies" in summertime.' Asked when he started to become famous in England, about the sense of community in Glasgow tenements, he replied, 'Sure, when there's sixty-five of ye sharing the toilet, it never has a cold seat.'

The man who now lives next door to David Hockney in LA spent his childhood in the Glasgow of the 1940s and 50s, climatically and culturally every inch of its 5,500 miles away from the sunshine state. Glasgow has undergone some change in the fifty-one years since Connolly was born there, both cosmetic and considerable. The European City of Culture in one recent year has seen a kind of trendiness tagged to its name, and now has a plethora of clubs and designer shops; but it has also, since the late 1970s seen the tide finally turn against its shipbuilding industry and gutsy working-class culture.

It is an area from which many, like Billy, have moved on, but it is also one in which Connolly's childhood contemporaries carry on as they have for the last thirty-five years, with or more often without those big, manly shipbuilding jobs. Duncan Campbell, in a foreword to an early collection of Connolly jokes and stories, *Gullible's Travels*, eloquently described what remains of the Glasgow of Connolly's youth: 'The people he grew up with work in the shipyards, as welders or platers or "sparks", or go to sea, or drive lorries or serve their time in the Army or in jail. They support Glasgow Celtic or Partick Thistle, drink in the pubs at nights, perhaps go to Spain or Majorca for their holidays, though their parents would have taken them to Rothesay, read the *Daily Record* and vote Labour.'

Connolly himself describes his Glasgow as 'a living, working, singing and laughing culture, a culture of a city renowned for toughness born of adversity . . .' Although 'singing and laughing' is an integral part of that culture, it is adversity that is more characteristic of Connolly's formative years – although not the destitute 'we had to walk fifteen miles to school with only one shoe on' cliché'd kind; adversity for Connolly was not something to complain about, but a fact of life, an integral part of his background, and hence his character. No wonder it is still the core of his stage storytelling even half a century on.

But this was not merely social deprivation, the poverty that leaves a young boy wanting to wave at the fleeting sight of a visiting royal but lacking a flag to do the waving with; Billy Connolly's childhood was, by his own account – an account which, understandably, can be different depending on when he describes it and to whom – an emotional nightmare, fundamentally lacking in love, lonely and often brutal. Connolly's upbringing was the very kind that can be almost relied upon to send children spiralling down into crime, self-loathing and nihilism. Although Scots of Connolly's age will often point out that they, too, were abandoned by their mother and brought up by relatives – for all kinds of reasons, it became an alarmingly common scenario – the danger inherent in the psychological brew that was Billy Connolly's upbringing cannot be overemphasized. It is a tribute to both father and son that Billy was kept on the rails, a point often raised by some relatives and friends from way back, who are puzzled, and even offended, by some of the harder words the adult Connolly has had to say about his father over the years.

Billy Connolly skated on thin ice at times, spending one night in police custody after a fight, developing more than a nodding acquaintanceship with alcoholism and, even when he was a famous and established performer, finding himself convicted in the sheriff court for beating up a journalist. But, with the help of a prodigious intelligence, a roaring ambition, an attractive personality – and the occasional stroke of luck – he overcame these disadvantages to become a kind of social hybrid. He is an ex-shipyard worker who has a keen interest in the spiritual, a man whose stature and bearing suggest he would give you a Glasgow kiss as soon as shake your hand, but was recently seen on BBC2 wearing a linen suit and impersonating a royal wave as he pontificated on the history of Scottish art.

Most ironic of all, the man who made his living from outrage and on occasion poking fun at the Pope was once a Child of Mary. Aesthetically at least, Connolly was a model member of this youth élite of the Catholic Church; with his blond hair and cherubic face, the boy Connolly looked as if he had been assembled from a DIY altar boy kit.

But in matters of ritual or belief, Connolly's Catholic faith is among the childish things he has put aside, as he explained in *Gullible's Travels*: 'It's a funny feeling now that you don't believe any more when you look back on yourself as a person that did believe. Because it was dead cosy, I must admit. Everything fell into place in those days: the comforting things around you – like your favourite pencil and ruler – which would have a special taste to it: and you would write your name in big letters on one side and your address – always ending in The World, The Universe – on the other side.'

It is this ability to summon up memories of the minutiae of life and to communicate them in such a way as to afford them every ounce of their due importance, whilst at the same time making them funny, that makes Connolly's talent more than some gimmick dependent on banana boots.

But the Billy Connolly of today no longer needs gimmicks to enhance his appeal. Connolly's 1994 in particular was an extraordinary year, a period of virtual rebirth of his reputation in Britain, and even more so, in Scotland. In January, when he started a long tour of Scotland, Connolly was in grave danger of becoming yesterday's man. His move to the USA, the showing of his competent but not brilliant American sitcoms on British TV, and his settling down happily with Pamela Stephenson, who for a variety of reasons has never been very popular in Britain, had all combined to make him almost the epitome of Mrs Patrick Campbell's joke about the performer who was once a tour de force and now was forced to tour.

That Billy Connolly was no longer popular was the received wisdom, but fortunately for Connolly, no one seemed to have told the Scottish public this in January and February 1994. Every show in Scotland was a sellout before it had even been advertised. Rave reviews followed Connolly around his home country, and he went on to do an extended season at the old Hammersmith Odeon in London. During that show, an advertising hoarding went up opposite the theatre, showing a beaming Connolly, with a can of non alcoholic Kaliber lager and the giant caption, 'Hello, girls!'

The ad seemed like a cheeky riposte to a controversial Wonderbra hoarding that was appearing in Britain, in which a pneumatic-looking model almost bursting out of her bra, was accompanied by the caption, 'Hello, boys!' Within weeks, and long after Connolly's Hammersmith season had ended, the two posters were to be seen side by side all over Britain. It was one of the most profuse and sustained poster campaigns ever seen, and yet it was doubtful whether, a year earlier, Connolly's modern, beardless face would have been popular, or even well-known enough to star in such a huge way.

While the poster campaign was at its height, yet another boost to his soaring new reputation was appearing, a six-part BBC TV series, 'Billy Connolly's World Tour of Scotland.' The series, in which Connolly explored Scotland and told stories about his life, made friends for Connolly among both TV critics who had never been fond of him, and among a new generation with no memory of the boozy, bearded, raucous folk hero Connolly had been to their parents.

In the summer of 1994, at the Edinburgh Festival, Connolly's presence at a variety of shows, merely as a member of the audience, struck awe into young comedians who spotted him. Although he did nothing particularly star-like to fan the flames of adoration, Connolly's progression round Edinburgh was something akin to a royal one.

After decades of ups and downs, at the age of 52, it seemed that once and for all Billy Connolly had become what he had wanted to be since he was a boy – loved, admired, respected and rich.

But getting to this point entailed a very long journey indeed.

CHAPTER I

'Mrs MacLean Loved You'

'Son of an engineer and a homemaker'
From Billy Connolly's entry in the American publication,
Contemporary Theatre, Film and Television, *Vol. 11*

Billy Connolly's royal connection begins at birth. He was born to the
regal pairing of William and Mary on 24 November 1942, although the
room in which he made his debut, at 65 Dover Street in Anderston,
Glasgow, was more practical than palatial, and has since been demolished.
Anderston was by no means the bottom of the heap in Glasgow. It was
not strictly speaking a slum district, but an area of red sandstone buildings
in a city where most working people lived in yellow tenements that
pollution had stained a miserable, blackish grey.

Billy's father, William Connolly, was the son of an Irish immigrant
to Partick, and worked as an optical instrument technician, making
rangefinders for military use. A short, stocky, quiet man with a round
head, and little like Billy was to look in adulthood, William married
Mary MacLean, a sixteen-year-old he worked alongside. It was 1940 and
Mary was four months pregnant at the wedding. William went off to
serve in the RAF when Florence, the baby, was born. Mary was eighteen
when she had Billy and only twenty-three when the marriage broke up,
leaving William in 1946 to bring up Billy, and his sister Florence. A
Catholic, William never remarried, and only divorced in 1976, but he
did move in with a nurse called Monica in the late 1940s. They lived at
a house in Stewartville Road, Partick and in May 1949 had a son,
Michael, Billy's half-brother, who today works as a postman.

In the absence of his mother, the formative female figures in Billy's boyhood were his two aunts, Mona and Margaret. Billy and Florence were taken by William to live with the aunts in the dockside area of Glasgow's Partick district in their two-room tenement flat. White Street today is a road being hauled up by its neighbours – rose-red brick properties being claimed by Habitat hoarders and university students, who enjoy an area with plenty of pubs, clubs, restaurants and the nearby Art Gallery. But in the postwar years, the stonework was black, the future, though not bleak (postwar shipyard industry provided secure employment if not aspirations), synonymous with the shipyards for Connolly and his contemporaries.

And in the meantime, there was a childhood to endure, although under the circumstances it wasn't all bad – only most of it. Little cameos from his first four years remain with Connolly like pieces of treasure – the drawer his mother kept the sweets in, the way his sister used to frighten him in bed with a mirror, reflecting a circle of light onto his face, which he thought was some kind of beast that was going to eat him.

When he first became a public figure, Connolly was adamant, at least in press interviews, that he had a happy childhood. This 1976 comment on Glasgow's Radio Clyde is typical of what he had to say about his childhood at that time. 'I think we all got on quite jolly. I think you'll find that most marriages that break up, should. I think it's the best thing that could happen to most of them. My father and my two aunts brought me up so I suppose it was OK. There were three wages coming in. It was quite jolly.'

Asked if it had a terrible effect when his mother left, he replied, 'Not at all. I think we were all the better for it. She was better as well. She created a nice life for herself and we got on with it down in Partick.

'Coming from a one-parent family is OK if you don't know what a two-parent family is like,' he continued. 'That becomes the norm, you just get on with it. It probably affected me mentally, but you don't weigh yourself up against the mummy's boys and the guys who've obviously got happy families.'

With increasing maturity, with finding happiness in his second marriage, with the onset of an interest in psychotherapy, with a few readings of the Californian writer John Bradshaw (who believes we carry childhood psychological damage around as so much baggage until it is acknowledged and unloaded) – you take your pick – his view of child-hood changed dramatically. 'I didn't enjoy it at all, it was awful because my aunts began to regret it,' he said in 1994. 'They were both single and in their twenties, I guess, then, and one was just out of the Wrens in Portsmouth and the other one was a career nurse, and I think they deeply regretted it. Especially the older one who took the real mother place in my life – Mona. She deeply regretted it because it kind of cost her marriage and happiness and stuff, and she kind of took it out on me. I don't blame the woman, it's just the whole thing was uncomfortable and awful and dreadful. I didn't like my childhood at all.

'I felt a bit inadequate. All the other kids had fathers and mothers, you know. And most comedians and performers I've met are like that. They've got a wee skeleton in the cupboard which is nothing to be hidden once you're an adult but which as a kid seems enormous. I just wanted freedom. I wanted out of jail. I was hit a lot and there were other ... bits and pieces that were happening.' He did not elaborate. 'When I say these things my relatives get upset,' he would comment. It was not only the aunts who hit the young Connolly. 'I remember a woman called Mrs Cumberland in Dover Street. She used to babysit me. She used to batter me. I used to pee myself all the time,' he says.

These days, Billy brings an aunt out of the closet and onto the stage with him. Agnes is her name in his act, and she serves his comic talent well. He mimics her octopus-like ability to talk to her friends, watch TV, scold her nephew, cook crumpets and knit, simultaneously.

In the act, Billy's matriarchal figure holding court in the home is not, perhaps understandably, reminisced over in the golden light of childhood memories. Connolly attributes a scolding sketch to an 'Agnes'. He enacts the rhythmic pattern of slapping in time with a scold which runs along the lines of, 'Don't you ever do that again, you filthy, filthy ...', each syllable spat out in staccato time as each slap makes contact with the 'young Billy'. Funny in its familiarity – his audience is in stitches, recognizing the character which, if they have not seen in their own families, is familiar in the great comic (and not wholly unmisogynous) tradition of the interfering old bag – but, in terms of Life imitating Art, Connolly is probably underplaying it here.

During his childhood, his own scoldings appear to have been more serious. He was to tell Melvyn Bragg on 'The South Bank Show' in October 1992 that: 'My childhood was deeply violent ... I was beaten up a lot by my aunt. It had a profound influence on me – I am still working on the stuff she did to me ... There are other things which disturb me greatly. I will get around to it eventually.' He described this aunt to Bragg as 'psychopathic', and, over the years, his reminiscences gradually recall more than the obligatory childhood cuff round the ear. 'They hit me a bit, but everybody got hit then, it wasn't such a bad thing being hit,' Connolly will say when he is feeling strong and phlegmatic about it. It is a coincidence, if not a consolation, to Connolly that he grew up to find most comedians have unhappy childhoods and that, as he has put it, 'You don't find many cosy mammy's boys in the trade.'

What undermined him more importantly was that he was also repeatedly and systematically told over a period of years that he was stupid and useless, a slander which still haunts him today as a deeply held belief – even though at the same time, as he said in one of his first interviews as a national figure (in the *Guardian* in 1974), 'I always knew it was going to be all right. Even when I was a wee boy I knew I'd be all right.'

'It's just I believe that I'm not quite as good as everybody else,' he told a surprised Michael Parkinson. 'Oh, yes, it gets worse as you get older. I mean I'm a very happy man now, but I still have the scars of that, very much so. It shows up when I'm asked to prepare something. Suppose you said, "I want to do a film on Glasgow and I'd like you to write some nice, funny stuff about it for next year." I'd say, "Great, great I'll do that." And then when I was on my own I would panic and I would believe that I couldn't do it. And I'd be scared to start it in case I couldn't do it very well, and then a week before the film I would write it and it'd be OK. But for the eleven months and three weeks leading up to that I would have a profound belief that I couldn't do it. And that's how it's manifested itself for me.'

Connolly went on to restate his persistent belief that the bad things about his childhood stood him in good stead. 'I've got no complaints at all. When I talk about the Glasgow of my childhood I can paint the whole room because everything is indelibly etched in my mind, whereas people who are happy, it all becomes one big amorphous mass, and they carry on, and I'm deeply envious of it ... people who got kisses from their parents, and stuff. I was never kissed as a child, and I remember at school talking to guys, and they would complain, "Oh, my mother kissed me outside the school," and how awful it had been. I was deeply jealous, and said, "You lucky swine." '

He also speaks generously often of his father and even his 'mad auntie' Mona, and of the whole nature of his upbringing. 'My Aunt Mona could be really funny at times. When she saw somebody who was eleven pence ha'penny short of a shilling, sort of howling at the moon, she always called them Happy Harry. The way my father and the people who brought me up used to talk to me. And you never understood all those expressions, like, "You'll smile on the other side of your face," and one they use in Scotland which has always made me laugh, "I'll take my hand off your face." You'd think if you wanted to tell someone you were going to slap them you'd say, "I'll put my hand on your face." It's a wee cultural Glaswegian thing.'

Billy has also said his father was 'unhappy'; both his father and grandfather were '. . . piss artists and drunks, poor guys who didn't know they were alcoholics'. But Billy's relationship with his father has remained important, if never reaching anything near idyllic. In the mid 1970s he was to admit: 'I love my father. Apart from loving him and the emotional tie, he is my friend. About once a week I'll say: "I must nip down and have a drink with father." He doesn't tell jokes, but he's funny. I sell my honesty – he's just a warm, generous, honest man. He wouldn't sit in a room listening to anything nasty about anybody.'

And his father is also brought into the spotlight on stage, even now. He is the brutal figure berating the young Billy for not being able to work the camera for the holiday beach snapshot; he is the judge and jury for the Billy in his fifties who went on holiday and took close-up shots of concrete, two inches away from its surface. Back home, Billy would present these to his elderly father as 'The Statue of Liberty', or 'The Sydney Opera House', and would be incredulous that his father did not find them funny. It is touching that he still tried as an adult to make him laugh, especially when he continues to nurse the memory of being thumped so hard by William that it was like 'being hit by a building' or, alternatively, 'having a Volkswagen dropped on you'.

Billy's relationship with his father must have been hard for both parties, with William left by his wife to bring up his bairns, and Billy conveniently placed to be the brunt of his frustration. Matters weren't helped by the fact that William was liable to forget Billy's existence at the most inopportune moments – such as when they were together. 'My poor dad once took me to the zoo in Glasgow and went off for a jar and came back and couldn't find me and thought I'd got lost. It was the day that Sheila the Tiger escaped. He thought I'd been eaten by her. Another time he lost me in the Barrowlands and a policewoman found me and took me to the police station and I got a sultana cake and sympathy.'

Still, William would remember to pick up Billy's comics every Friday, a touching routine Connolly still remembers, and did his best at the father/son lessons in life. 'He told me one wonderful thing, my dad: "We all make mistakes – that's why you have a rubber on the end of your pencil." Wonderful! Fuck all that "Alas, poor Yorick!" stuff, it's much overrated.'

Another time, Connolly senior came upon Billy wandering the streets kicking his leg out in a strange way. Billy had been reading a football book full of how-to-play-better tips, and it said that you had to learn to crack your leg like a whip. His puzzled father asked Billy what he was up to, to which he replied, 'Oh, trying to crack my leg like a whip, Dad.' 'He told me not to be so daft,' says Billy.

Poignant and touching scenes from Connolly's childhood memory; but what was the big picture? What sort of place was the Glasgow Billy Connolly was born and brought up in?

Lurking in the Glasgow Central Library, unborrowed in decades, is a book called *The Glasgow Story*, by one Colm Brogan. Published in 1952, when Connolly was ten, and clearly by a rather brutally anthropological, middle-class writer, it nevertheless paints a useful picture of the world that was going on immediately around the young Billy, an account no less down to earth for being from the opposite end of the telescope from Connolly's.

Brogan noted, for example, that the Glasgow working man changed enormously, in the physical sense. 'Over forty years ago, one of the most common proletarian types was locally known as the 'wee bauchle', a man little over five feet with features that had been assembled in careless haste, and shambling legs that bore eloquent testimony to the lifelong effects of rickets.' Such men were frequently underestimated in bar room fights in wartime France, when their (not un-Connolly-esqe) warcry was, 'Gie him the crust.'

The wee bauchle was the product of the worst slum conditions in Europe, Brogan contended – a Cowcaddens or Gorbals childhood was a quite literal survival of the fittest. By the time of Connolly's childhood, however, the contrast between the slum-hardened proletarian and the next up the ladder (which would have included Connolly's family) was diminishing. Rickets was conquered, and average body weights had shot up. But still there was a visible distinction between the skilled men in heavy engineering and the shipyards, with their broad shoulders and massive strong hands, and the undersized, underweight wee men.

The character of the 'wee man', with his combination of cleverness and unworldliness, his violence, his disregard for the law, his eccentricity – not to mention his funniness – is the star of much of Billy Connolly's humour, as well as that of other Glasgow comics. But as with most points of folklore, it is hard to get agreement on even the most basic tenets. In the comedian Stanley Baxter's 1986 *Bedside Book of Glasgow Humour*, the subject of height is brought up almost at the start. 'Glaswegians are intensely interested in the physical aspects of their fellow citizens,' Baxter wrote. 'Any male approaching six feet in height has "big" before his name, as in Big Hughie and Big Wullie. A female of five feet is "wee" as in Wee Samantha and Wee Polly.'

So far, so good, but Baxter then went on to the question of the wee bauchle, whom he describes as a small, unkempt individual and calls a 'bachle'. A bachle, he says, is known for being self-effacing; an *aggressive* wee unkempt individual, is a 'nyaff'. A *bauchle*, as Colm Brogan would call a bachle, is nothing more than a worn-out shoe, which a bachle might well wear, and be described as a 'shachly bachle'. (A shabby tall man, Baxter adds, could never be a bachle, but 'a big dreep'.)

At the same time as all this class-divisive folklore was in operation, however, for Brogan, Glasgow was perhaps the most democratic city in Britain, a place where there was very little snobbery. 'If a Glasgow publican wants to make his place select, it never occurs to him to add a saloon bar. He shuts out women instead.' He mentions a pub near the BBC in Glasgow that was shared equally by broadcasters and coalheavers.

'The coalmen would frequently make comments on the radio pro-grammes, but there was nothing self-conscious about the social mixing.'

However, in describing the Glasgow Scottish accent at the time, Brogan seemed temporarily to lapse into something near to the class snobbery he had just discounted. 'The medial and final T are never pronounced, and articulation does not exist. Shapeless words come slithering out in a slovenly jumble known as a 'slush'. Some of the most distinguished experts in communication by slush ought to make good ventriloquists, for they can indulge in the exercise they call speech without moving their lips at all.'

In the Glasgow family of this era, men were entirely the boss. The wife's main role sometimes seemed to be as a supplier of caustic com-ments. 'But a husband would no sooner tell his wife what he earned than she would ask ... One Glasgow man, home on leave from the Army, confided to a friend that he had been compelled to fetch his wife a weighty clump on the ear. He was not a man of domineering nature or rash brutality, but he felt that some emphatic action was demanded when he found his wife reading a book. Not a newspaper, mark you, but a real book, with covers. This has to be stopped by the simplest and most direct method.'

As for the women: 'Brought up in grim and barely civilized conditions, the lower grades of proletarian females are hardly more capable of running a well-ordered house than they are of conducting an orchestra ... privacy was negligible, and the quality most admired was not to be superior in any way. Doors were left open, and women would talk 'hinging oot' of neighbouring tenement windows.

But, as Brogan conceded with some pride, amazing feats of upbringing were accomplished. 'The foulest mouthed slum mother of my acquaint-ance cared for her children in a manner that was literally heroic. The words that came trippingly off her tongue would have shaken a police-man, but the teachers and the school nurse regarded her children as the cleanest, the best cared for and also the best behaved in the school. Considering that she brought them up in a house that would hardly pass inspection for a stable, it took a highly exceptional character and devotion to do what she did.'

For the men, working in the shipyards took both skill and hardiness.

There was little protection from the wet bitter winter, and a good deal of danger. Riveters, well down from welders in the aristocracy of the yard, stood on high scaffolding picking up red-hot rivets chucked up to them. At the top of the yard pecking order were engineers, the fitters and turners, whose skills were unmatched anywhere in the world. Many of these men had served on ships around the world as junior officers, and ended their working days living in suburban houses, effectively members of the bourgeoisie.

The pay differential in the early days of the yards was great, the skilled men earning at least double the unskilled. But by Connolly's time, the conventional wisdom was that the differential made serving an apprenticeship barely worth the trouble. That degree of cynicism was exacerbated by unemployment in the 1930s, during which skilled men thought themselves lucky to get work as a cinema usher, and tens of thousands of Glaswegians emigrated to Canada and the US.

'When work was stopped on the *Queen Mary*,' recalled Colm Brogan, 'a blight descended on Clydebank and farther afield. Men felt and said the Clyde was finished. The great cranes, like Meccano storks, stood over yards where grass was growing. Unemployment was miserable everywhere, but on Clydeside it was spectacular; it brought the hopeless and stricken silence of the plague.' The war, he added, brought back full employment, and this was still the position when Brogan wrote his book – but the experience of unemployment left the artisans of Clydeside with a lingering hatred for Tories – by which they meant any industrialist.

The shipyard humour that Billy Connolly turned into a world commodity was always abundantly in evidence in Glasgow. It was, and to an extent still is, a cousin of Liverpool humour, with its strong Irish input – Billy Connolly calls Glasgow 'Liverpool without deodorant' – but has a surreal element that is exclusive to Glasgow, and exists in a slightly more self-reliant and self-confident culture than Liverpool's. It is less, perhaps, a culture of mournful complaint, and more of staunchness and steadfastness, as if the ambient Scottish Presbyterian culture had its influence even on devoutly Catholic Glaswegians whose emotional homeland was Ireland.

The ironic, clever, self-deprecating, Liverpudlian type of Glasgow humour leads Connolly to echo an English friend who, on hearing the football result Partick Thistle 2, Motherwell 1 (Partick being Connolly's famously erratic team) commented, 'My goodness, I always thought that they were called Partick Thistle Nil.'

Brogan illustrates the peculiar nature of Glasgow shipyard humour – and, as it turned out, much of Billy Connolly's output – with a tradition from the prosperous days before the First World War, when shipyard workers were expected to return to work on the Monday that marked the end of the Summer Fair holidays. They used, he relates, to gather solemnly outside the yard gates and go through the ceremony of 'tossing the brick'. This involved throwing a brick in the air. If it came down again, they stayed off for a day or two more. If it stayed up in the air, they would go back to work.

It could not be said that the Glasgow deprivation of Billy Connolly's childhood is no more. Even in 1994, there was a ten-year life expectancy difference between Drumchapel, the bleak, Soviet-style estate he moved to in 1953, when he was eleven, and the pretty suburb of Bearsden, which is within sight of 'The Drum'. Glasgow women today have the poorest health in Europe. The core of Glasgow's health problem remains housing. Although it is forty years since the greater part of slums in areas like Anderston were pulled down, repaying interest on the loans taken out to fund rebuilding still accounts for sixty-six pence of every pound raised by taxation.

Yet although official statistics on recorded crime fail to confirm it, there is a strong feeling in the city today that Glasgow has become far less violent over the years; this would seem to be a reverse of the conventional wisdom that where unemployment and poverty increase, so, inevitably, will violence. Locally it is thought that the relaxation in drinking laws brought about this decrease in violent crime. Pubs used to close at 10 p.m., and it would be common to try to down six or seven pints in the final fifteen minutes. Fights and flying glasses were the norm every night of the week when employment was still more or less full. Today, such pub fracas are rare enough to merit an Arts Council grant.

The shipyards whose noise pervaded Billy Connolly's childhood have not quite been silenced, but as a relic of another life, might equally rate some kind of preservation order. Stephen's, where Connolly was an apprentice and later a qualified welder ('But I was a funny welder') is now vacant flat land covered in grass, but John Brown's yard is still in place. A handful of men build oil platforms and small naval frigates there. Even if central Glasgow has a clean air of sophistication (it seems a curiously European city), the overwhelming belief in the city and further down the Clyde in towns such as Port Glasgow (where at Scott Lithgow until recently, supertankers under construction were so big they had to be built in two halves) is that this is a desperately sad end. Although his family was not overly keen on Connolly going into the yards, Billy himself says they had always fascinated him and likens the 'thing' Clyders have about working in the yards to miners in Yorkshire and Durham, and fishermen in Peterhead and Fraserburgh.

The life and development of cities over the centuries is a fascinating thing. The four-storey pink stone tenements of Billy Connolly's youth are now sought after and fashionable. Instead of being the part of town nearest the Clydebank shipyards, Byres Road, and even White Street, where Connolly lived with his aunts, are today better known as the backyard of Glasgow University and the Art Gallery. It is now pretty well the trendiest bit of trendy Glasgow.

Within a few hundred yards of Billy's childhood home, indeed, is a pub in whose name can be traced a mixture of the long-established Glasgow humour, the influence of foreign cultures on this cosmopolitan city, and the archness of undergraduate wit. The pub is called Murphy's Pakora Bar, an affectionate joke based on at least three ethnic groups, and one that Billy Connolly, both then and now, might well approve of.

Back in Partick in the late 1940s, home life in the extended Connolly family was tense and prone to be a little gloomy. The Celts may be renowned for throwing a party even without the obligatory occasion, but *chez* Connolly was not a party kind of place. 'New Year was never a big thing in our family. Christmas was the thing, Christmas was nice. It was never ever a party thing, never even a Christmas dinner, it was just a happy time, a happy atmosphere. We very rarely had parties in our family for anything, and I don't even recall having a birthday party ever. We just weren't a party kind of family.'

Outside home, Billy's wider boyhood world was set in St Peter's primary school, in reading the *Beano* and the *Dandy* (later, *Wizard, Rover* and *Hotspur*) and in a playworld of middens — the rubbish dumps between tenements — where he would pass time with schoolmates to a Glasgow–

Catholic soundtrack of hymns and the clatter of the shipyards which (in their day) could be heard from his classroom. The vivid picture Connolly evokes of his childhood is very much like the literary award-winning material Roddy Doyle later found in Dublin; it would have been fascinating to see what Connolly could have produced had he used the same material as a source for novels rather than comedy.

What you did in a midden, of course, was hunt for treasures, the prime hunting ground being 'The Lucky Middens' where all the posh people lived. 'They would throw out really nice things sometimes. I got a great primus stove once, a real beauty, made of chrome, which I used for years when I was cycling around. And I found a beautiful stainless steel Spitfire – which my father threw out.'

Setting fire to middens was another excellent pastime. When he got home from an afternoon of so doing, Billy's shoes would be grey with ash, a point his aunts would perceptively pick up on, and thump him accordingly. 'I used to wonder how my parents had this amazing psychic ability to tell where I had been playing. And of course all the time I must have smelt exactly like a bloody midden.'

Billy was to use the relative qualities of middens as a measure of success for quite a while. When he later lived in Hyndland Road in the West End of Glasgow with his first wife Iris, he told her: '. . . we had a Lucky Midden. It was just a rented house that we'd moved to from Maryhill Road, but it was a really nice area and I was actually living in a house whose midden I had raided when I was a wee boy.'

The playground code of conduct at school was not as macho as might be expected. Being caught playing skipping with the girls was not the heinous crime against manliness you might expect. 'Some of the guys were very good at skipping and no one ever called you a pansy for doing it; they'd call you a pansy if you were bad at it,' Connolly recalls.

Connolly was no pansy; in fact he was something of a protagonist when he was still quite young, with the initiative to form his own gang, and the arrogance to name it The Connollys. 'We used to fight with The Sinclairs, who came from round the corner. We made tomahawks with tin cans and sticks; you bashed the can over a stick with a brick and made a sort of hatchet affair. And we would fill a tin can full of ashes, shove it in a nylon stocking, whirl it round our heads and hurl it into the enemy camp, leaving this big smoky trail behind it. I can't recall anyone being hurt, though there was a fair bit of walloping going on; but no slashing or anything like that.'

When he was six or seven, Billy was the grateful recipient of a first kiss, courtesy of one Gracie McLintock, in some bushes in a local park. 'There was about five or six of us guys and Gracie. It was like confession, we were all sitting in a row and one went in at a time and got a kiss and came out. And I had never been kissed in my life by anyone. I'm sure my mother kissed me as a wee boy, but I don't remember. It changed my entire life. It was brilliant. A light went on inside me which has never really gone out. And I can feel it today, that kiss.'

St Peter's was a typical Catholic primary school then, the interior painted corporation pastel green, an enormous crucifix prominent and a curriculum centred on songs about Jesus, taught by men and women Connolly calls 'the pterodactyls'.

Still a primary school, St Peter's is only a few yards up the road from Billy's aunts' house – a proximity which was to prove problematic for the young Connolly, who had no escape from the eagle eye of the school caretaker, the jannie (janitor) who, as he recalls, had no compunction about landing him in the soup in the holidays as well as during the school term, or thwarting every conceivable schoolboy rite of passage. Billy and his mates would, for example, smoke cinnamon sticks – until the caretaker came along. 'One time he even came into the lavvie when we were all puffing away, got a light off us and then went and told the teacher.'

Although St Peter's had prison potential, the source of Connolly's frustration was also a place from which he could mine material. A playground, after all, is a place where toilet humour is revered and, as Connolly explains, he listened attentively. 'Of course, I got lots of material from my schooldays: all the snotters and peeing in my pants and the lying that went on about the size of people's willies. I learnt how to insult people then, too. The worst you could call someone was "smelly". Or you would say, "Your ma's a darkie." When I first came across swearing, I thought it was a great thing to do so I swore like a trooper for ages. In one sentence I would put in every swear word I knew – and didn't have a clue what any of them meant.'

It was 1947 when Billy started school and, interestingly, he has a particularly vivid recall of all the children without fathers, the ones with crippled fathers (the War had just ended, aside from the normal attrition rate of a tough area) and the children who were themselves deformed, injured or otherwise misfits.

Billy hated school, after a honeymoon period of about six months, during which he was thought of as promising and was taken round the school to show how he could write on the blackboard; he was given a little prize for this, a card with a horse on it. Over in her class in the girls' department, Billy's sister could read and stood up to do so to everyone; the pair were quite celebrated at St Peter's at the start. But Billy soon fell into the clutches of a psychopathic teacher called Big Rosie MacDonald, who made his and the other children's lives a misery. He still feels he could summon up the outrage to kick Miss MacDonald even today – she used to call people with glasses 'four eyes'. The other classes, taught by nuns, were as violent, with regular strapping for the children.

The violence was not all physical; there was also the brutal shouting and noise – from the adults. 'There was this big woman that was in charge of the school dinners. To get silence she used to batter the table with a ladle, and I remember the delight on the face of every boy in that class when she walloped the end of the table with her ladle, and it flew through the window. Can you imagine all the wee faces?'

It was at St Peter's that Billy heard his first ever joke, a rhyme that sounds like nonsense, but actually makes sense if you know a 'skelf' is a splinter; the rhyme ran Pat and Mick/Went up a stick/And couldnae get down/For skelfs. 'I thought it was hysterical. What it means, I'll never know, but it was my first joke and I was very proud of it.' He also claims to remember the first moment he made others laugh. It happened when he was seven or eight and fell in a puddle. He found that sitting there amid the laughter of others was not terribly uncomfortable, so stayed longer than necessary because he enjoyed the laughing. He simply did not hear laughter at home; this was the antidote to the misery of life with mad Aunt Mona, and, like so many comedians (at least when they look back at their lives) it was the spark of something close to a planned campaign of attacking life by being funny.

Circumstances beyond his control occasionally conspired to add to

Billy's comedy potential. He was unfortunate (or perhaps fortunate) enough to be born with the initials W.C., and seems to recall people peeing on his leg. His aunt once embroidered the dreaded letters on the top pocket of his blazer, which led to people trying to pee in his pockets. In its unpleasant way, it was still heady stuff for a child trying to forget his unhappy home for a few hours a day.

The cultural came into his life by virtue of other assets at first, as Billy explained when profiling Glasgow for the *Sunday Times* in 1986. 'At the front of Kelvingrove Park in Partick is the Kelvingrove Art Gallery and Museum where, on many a Sunday, my sister Flo and I would go for an afternoon's cultural absorption and a slide on the highly polished floor. Some talented buyer in the Glasgow council had purchased Salvador Dali's *Christ of St John on the Cross*, causing quite a furore at the time. I have always been grateful to that person, for I spent many happy hours looking at that painting.'

It is Connolly's ability to encapsulate a childhood and, despite the particulars of his accent and background, to communicate it to a varied audience, regressing each to their own memories, which makes audiences almost vibrate with him. Innocent childhood inspiration Connolly's background gave him, yet it was of the very kind that could easily have served as an apprenticeship for a Glaswegian 'hard man', the type of man who would belt you as soon as take a pint off you if you picked the wrong team to praise when discussing Celtic or Rangers. Going from school (where 'aspirations' weren't high on the agenda), to home in the evenings where a feeling of being in the way was supplemented with being belted by anyone half an inch taller than you, could fan the flames of feuding.

But without wanting to put too romantic a slant on it (and Connolly does not), these were the days of the Basics politicians urge us today to return to, the era of old-fashioned law and order, where communities were watched over morally by the extended family and disciplinary wallops would be dispensed by family, neighbours and public authorities alike without fear of a visit from Esther Rantzen. And although later on, Billy was to find himself very briefly in prison, his youthful dealings with the Law – the *Po*-lice – were amicable.

'The Partick police when I was a boy were terrific,' he recalls. 'They were magic big guys. Talk about "finger on the pulse" – they knew exactly what was going on. It was the end of the kick-in-the-arse era, just before the beginning of, "If I catch you I'm goin' tae tell yer faither" . . . many's the time I got a smack on the lug from a policeman. Not that it changed my ways, but I'm really thankful that he didn't run upstairs like a big lassie and tell my father.'

It was not just the police that were different, or at least perceived differently, from how they would be by a 1990s version of young Billy. There is no question that social workers would have been a major part of such an unfortunate boy's life today. In the Glasgow of the late 1940s, outsiders would intervene in another family's problems, but on a strictly untrained and informal basis. Connolly remembers with affection a woman called 'Mrs Smith', who lived round the corner. A fat woman with enormous breasts, and a big, black cardigan, she would see him playing, give him a cuddle and say, 'Oh, it's wee Billy Connolly. Your mother ran away and left you.'

'And I disappeared into these huge breasts. I remember it to this day. It was brilliant . . . I felt lovely, because she was telling me the truth as she saw it.' It is interesting that such behaviour would be seen as the height of interfering old biddy-dom today; Billy would probably tell his social worker about such things happening.

Billy saw Mary, his mother, only twice during his childhood. She moved thirty miles and a ferry ride away from Glasgow, to Dunoon, where she spent twenty-six years working in a hospital canteen and had four children with a William Adams. Billy explained in the 1970s, 'I don't like her much, but I don't blame her for going. I don't feel any malice. There was a war raging. She was twenty-one, living in a real slum area with two kids. At any given moment she didn't know whether her husband was alive or dead.'

'I feel,' he once said, 'more malice against the war, and what it did to millions of people's lives, than I do against her. I suppose she was getting offers from all over.' Mary supported this general angle on events by telling the *Sunday People* in 1991, 'There was no bitterness when the marriage ended. We kept in touch for the first few years but I did not see Billy between the ages of nine and eighteen. When we met again he whirled me off my feet and gave me a big hug.'

Billy's account of these reunions are less Hollywood by a considerable factor, however. Of the meeting at nine, he has no recall. He went to Dunoon to look for his mother when he was sixteen. 'She was very nice; we had a wee chat. The feeling was strange. There was no feeling of belonging. I think there was on her part because she remembered me obviously an awful lot better than I remembered her,' he says of this encounter.

The next time Connolly met his mother, he was twenty-five, and already a well-known performer in Scotland, with the trademark long hair and beard. He was doing a show in a hotel in Dunoon, so it would have been surprising had his mother not turned up backstage. 'I thought she wanted an autograph,' he explains. 'Then she said: "I think I'm your mother."'

'There's no answer to that, so I said: "Can I buy you a drink?" But she turned out to be a rigid non-drinker. It's odd being faced with your mother when you are a grown man, and she's a stranger. It's not as it happens in plays. You stand around looking at each other, you fidget, you cough. I said, "Well, do you want to come into the lounge here, this bar?" And she said, "Oh, you don't drink too much, do you?" I thought, what? Are you worried about me? A Christmas card would have been nice.'

Hamish Imlach, the Scottish folk singer, happened to be backstage in Dunoon at the crucial moment of Mary Adams' reappearance. As with all recollections of the great small moments of history, his memory of this one is slightly different from the main protagonist's. 'Billy was in the toilet,' he says. 'She came to the door and said, "Is Billy Connolly here?" and although he could hear, he didn't say anything, so I said, "I don't know where he is. If you'd like to wait at the bar. Who is it?" "I'm his mother." Well, still nothing from Billy. Then he said, "Tell her I'm not here," and I said, "But you're going on stage in fifteen minutes." So he went out, and it was private, I don't know what they said, but obviously they didn't make up or become bosom buddies or anything like that.'

Billy Connolly's mother's response to the meeting is, perhaps, one for the psychoanalysts' textbooks. Not only did she bridle when her son invited her for a drink, which, as he explains, is what he always does if he is stuck, but, so passionate was her hatred of drinking that she

27

complained bitterly in later years when he recounted this particular snippet of their conversation.

The 'discovery' of Mary Adams by the Glasgow tabloid the *Sunday Mail* in 1990 was to end any semblance of good relations between Billy Connolly and the Scottish press. The story, from the limited point of view of a newspaper, was a perfectly true and valid one, even if running it on Mothering Sunday was a mite corny. Press agents often deliberately leak similar stories to newspapers on behalf of their showbusiness stars. But this non-leaked 'revelation' of his mother's whereabouts desperately hurt Connolly and angered his oldest friends beyond belief – Imlach still describes it as 'obscene' – for several reasons. Just one was the implication, in the headline 'Billy's secret mother', that he had somehow been *secreting* the old lady, when the truth was more the converse.

Mary Adams' self-piteous outpourings to the press at this late stage in the Mother and Child Reunion distressed Billy almost as much as her original act of leaving him all those years before. His mother's abandoning him was the central event of his life, the mainspring of his personality. It was not the invasion of privacy that devastated him – he invades his own on a daily basis on stage – so much as the sheer stupidity and meanness of his mother's reported ranting. If he tended on balance to blame the messenger (a nosey and prurient tabloid messenger, it has to be said) more than his mother for her sentiments, it was understandable; the crude treatment the *Mail* afforded the story sent him reeling. But the real pain lay in the fact that it was sadly obvious that Mary would be pushed to get out the Rich Teas, never mind killing calves, for the return of this prodigal son.

'I am quite happy sitting here in my wee house the rag man would not give me a balloon for,' she said in the interviews after the discovery of her existence. I don't watch his TV shows and have never seen any of his films. If he was your son, would you? I just feel his material could be embarrassing. But as long as he's happy that's the main thing. We live in two very different worlds after all.'

Once in full – if inconsistent – flood, Mary was even scathing in her allegations about her son's generosity. 'The only present I ever got from Billy was three hankies wrapped in cellophane. And that was only because he was dossing down on the living-room floor after busking around the local pubs with his pals ... If Billy was a ghost, he wouldn't even give you a fright. But he knows I don't want anything so he never offers. It's as simple as that. Billy did offer to lend me money to buy my council house but I would not borrow money from him, or anyone. Although I have to watch my pennies, I'm quite happy as I am.

'I am an anti-royalist,' Mary plunged on, twisting the knife almost unbearably for Connolly. 'He's welcome to mansions and palaces. When I hear that side of him I think to myself, "What the hell is he playing at?" ... I'm not one for that lifestyle. I don't drink and I'm easily pleased. I worked hard for what I have and I owe nobody a penny, not even Billy. We get on fine in our way. He phones me now and again and we have a good laugh.'

The *Sunday Mail*'s Mother's Day special was accompanied by photos of Mrs Adams looking at photos of Billy's children. According to Imlach, the photos had been sent to her secretly by Billy's then wife, Iris. 'Iris felt very sorry for her mother-in-law not seeing her grandchildren, so unknown to Billy had sent some photographs of the kids to his mother, and these are the ones she sold to the press. Tearfully looking at the grandchildren – Billy's on holiday and she's in a council house in Dunoon.' Like Iris, Pamela Stephenson, too, sent photos to Billy's mother, of her and Connolly's wedding in Fiji in 1988.

Connolly's own response to both the real and the press rediscovery of his mother was not to slip even an inch into sentimentality. In 1991, Mary was still living in £27-a-week terraced council house in Dunoon, while Billy was pointedly not building a 'granny flat' at his £2 million English home, Grunt Futtock Hall, in Windsor. Even if Mary were asked to be closer to Connolly (and not just in the geographical sense) it is doubtful that she would accept.

As the months went by, the startling words Connolly's mother used about him, even if they were teased out of her by skilful reporters dabbling dangerously in the Connolly family psyche, devastated the comedian increasingly. 'She said she was disappointed in me and it hurt,' he told his friend Michael Parkinson in a 1991 interview on local radio in London. 'It hurt deeply. I thought I wanted a reconciliation but I changed my mind.'

Periodically, Connolly has downplayed his mother's early departure from his life. 'It was very odd when my mother went, but not a shock,' he had said. 'It was very strange and very exciting, I thought at the time. My sister Florence was more shocked by it because I think she knew more about it, because I was only four. And she was my guardian, my sister. And she kind of looked after me.'

Billy was luckier than some children of one-parent families in as far as he had living grandparents, the MacLeans, to be close to. Grandfather Angus MacLean was originally a Highland man, from the island of Coll, and had the characteristic restraint and formality of the Highlanders, even though by the time Billy knew his grandparents, they were living in Anderston. His granny Jessie worked as an office cleaner, and had a passion for boxing. 'She was a wonderful person, my granny. I'll always remember her fur coat and the smell of her perfume, and she had lovely big red lips. She was a smashing granny who did incredibly well for herself.'

The day Billy's sister Florence told their granny he was going professional as a folk singer, she could be relied upon to say what grannies are expected to say in such circumstances – 'What, he's going to give up the welding? He's going to play the banj-oh?' The Glasgow pronunciation of banjo made his career move sound especially silly. Granny had a wonderfully granny-esque, if untranslatable response: 'His heed's full of dabbities,' was her judgement. 'And no doubt, if she were here today she would say the same,' Connolly says. 'My father thought my head was full of dabbities. My relatives think my head's full of dabbities, and they're all absolutely correct. And the trick is to let your dabbities come to the front. Some people have dormant dabbities which they should lick from time to time.' (A dabbity, for non-lowland Scots, is a facetious or silly idea.)

In 1986, Billy brought Pamela Stephenson and his children by her to meet their great grandfather. The meeting was a touching one, and delighted Billy, who was taken aside by his grandfather at one stage during the visit. 'He said, "You know, your granny loved you." And it was such an incredible buzz. No, do you know what he said? "Mrs MacLean", this is his wife, my grandmother. "Mrs MacLean loved you." And I said, "I know, I remember."'

CHAPTER 2

The Gabalunzie Boy

'The more you know, the less the better.'
Incomprehensible Scottish saying taught to
Billy Connolly at his grandfather's knee

When Billy Connolly says he was convinced that he was different from other boys, was marked out to be special, that it would 'be all right in the end', it sounds as if he speaks with the benefit of hindsight. Yet the sense of otherness is so marked in all his own accounts that it is no surprise when it is reflected by those who knew him. Childhood memories of other children are notoriously unreliable, but Billy is not recalled at all by several of his contemporaries; he was not all that far from being one of those quiet, anonymous schoolboys who are forgotten with ease by children and teachers. When he went back to both his junior and secondary schools for a London Weekend Television 'South Bank Show', he was distressed to find that he had somehow disappeared from all the records.

In his teens, he was known as being borderline odd, with a penchant for being on his own and wandering around graveyards. While his pals would go to the pictures when they played truant from school, he would sometimes go to a crematorium and watch funerals. Billy also developed a tendency, that was to reappear in different forms over the next several years, to look after himself by not getting too dangerously close to real bad boys. But had he taken on board too heartily the lessons in life he was to learn when he went to his secondary school, St Gerard's in Govan, it could have been a disaster. He might have been initiated into the

Glaswegian hard nut stereotype club, but, as he says: 'The really heavy guys and me never really had that much in common, even at school.' The Connollys gang of his former years could have turned into something more threatening than innocent catapult wielders and midden experts, but they did not.

Similarly, had Billy been born forty years later, his chances of making it through to the success of his adulthood would have been far more limited. Glasgow was a relatively hard place in the mid-1950s, but no one then could have envisaged the narcotic disaster that was to befall the city's youth by the 1990s. A shocking report by the all-party Scottish Affairs Committee in May 1994 showed, as an illustration of the Scottish drug problem, almost fifty per cent of the teenagers in one Strathclyde secondary school was *injecting* drugs. As a result of the report, urgent advice was going out to primary schools to start anti-drug education even for little children.

Back in 1956, a move from Partick to the Drumchapel estate outside Glasgow for a fourteen-year-old Billy Connolly did little more than change the geography a little, giving him a lengthy bus (or bike) and ferry ride to school in Govan. His circle of friends did not alter in nature as much as it might; today, if he had not been initiated into shooting up in Partick, moving to a rough overspill estate would doubtless have done the trick.

Drumchapel is set in rolling countryside and, while not obviously in the country, it is one stop further out from middle-class Bearsden on the bus from Glasgow. It is also on the course of the Antonine Wall, eloquent evidence that even as far back as the Roman occupation, the area was considered the back of beyond, a suitable site for a cheap, hastily built turf overspill wall for the better known and sturdier Hadrian's job down on the border with England. Although Drumchapel is only about a square mile on the furthest northwest edge of the city, it seems larger and further out. The estate looks quite different from anything in London or the north of England. Walking about Drumchapel is curiously like going up a down-escalator – everywhere is a longer trek than it seems. 'The Drum' is a smaller version of Soviet estates, built after the War by a Labour council with a political mission not dissimilar to that of the Soviets, even if its tower block socialism took a more well-meaning form.

Today, as you enter Drumchapel from Bearsden, rows of very attractive new, low-rise flats are the first thing you encounter. The peeling, Siberia-style blocks are back a few hundred yards; how unsurprising, you think, that the renovations to Drumchapel should start at the most immediately visible, Glasgow end of the estate. As these places go, however, Drum-chapel does not look too bad. All the same, the highly improved state of White Street, Partick, where Connolly was moved from by the council, shows just what a mistake shipping poor families out to Drumchapel was. What was considered a slum then now looks highly desirable, and not just to students and the middle class.

Connolly has not been kind to Drumchapel, especially in his early comedy routines, when he would refer scathingly to it as a 'reservation' for deprived Glasgow former slum dwellers. But in 1976, in a late-night conversation on local radio with the presenter Tom Ferrie – who was a boyhood friend of Connolly on the estate – he relented a little. 'To be quite honest I liked it when I lived there. When I moved to Drumchapel I was fourteen and there was a bluebell wood there and it was in great condition then – I don't think it's in quite so good condition now – but it was lovely then. We had rabbits and pheasants' odds and ends and I really quite liked it. I just started to dislike it when I got older, into my teens and things. In my late teens when I was stuck out there, it cost me a lot of money to go any place. It was a kind of cowboy town, but I liked that aspect of it, buying stuff out of vans, a ragman coming in a wee green van.'

Even when Billy finally escaped the Partick house for Drumchapel, he explains, 'I never really got involved in the local gang thing, the wee fly men doing things to one another. I had to start to make a whole lot of new friends, which was quite strange; at that age you should have forged most of your friendships. But I had to break them off and start again. So my friends were boys I knew from school in Govan, who lived at the Drum.'

But he was not exactly walking with the angels, either. At St Peter's, he was doing very nicely indeed. When he started at St Gerard's senior secondary on the other side of the Clyde in Govan, after having failed the eleven plus, then been allowed to retake it and done well, he was rated at a highly creditable seventh in a class of forty-three. He then, however, fell into bad company, even though St Gerard's was a school regarded as being for the *crème de la crème* of working-class boys, right down to having green blazers as uniform. Billy's social and intellectual fall (apart from reading his one proper book, *The Lord of the Flies*) was, all the same, a descent he has always been thankful for.

It was a slow decline. At the end of the first year, he still managed to come tenth out of thirty-five. 'And then I stopped. I fell in with a bad crowd, I think. The baddies seemed more interesting and funny. Baddies are all funny. Gangsters are funnier than professors. And I just enjoyed their company and started plonking school and going to the pictures. And in a funny way, I held on there. I didn't pass the exams, but I still enjoyed English and French, not maths – I was always rotten – I always enjoyed science immensely. I hung on, the message went in although I didn't pass the exams. I didn't come out as a dodo. And in those days there was full employment, so you swanned out and into a job anyway, and who cares. I don't think I had a lack of education. I had a pretty good one really. I didn't win. I didn't get the paper at the end. I liked not so much the rough part of being a working-class kid but the funny part, having a laugh as opposed to everything else, the adventures, jumping out and doing stupid things and not paying attention.'

While his sister Florence was well on her highflying way at the posh Notre Dame school to her destiny as a schoolteacher – a great ambition then for a working-class girl – Billy was mentally elsewhere while nominally at school. At St Gerard's, he would watch pigeons all day, gaze past a group of single storey temporary buildings (which, in the way these things invariably happen at school, had long since become a permanent fixture) towards the shipyards, and the sound of the cokers working. When called upon to work at school, he would go to some pains to do imaginary, rather than real, sums or whatever. He claims at one stage to have done no homework for two years. 'I got belted every day for it, but when I weighed it up I would much rather have the belt than do the homework.

'I started to develop this way of thinking: be your individual self and just forget the rest. Not so much that I thought school was wrong, I just knew I wasn't happy in what I was doing. And I was doing my own wee rebellious bit. The dreamy kind of bit. I would much rather sit and dream. As a matter of fact, I would much rather sit and spend the same time doing homework kidding on I was doing homework.'

At least once, he was caught dodging school, when he went to the Royal Concert Hall to see a lunchtime television show called the 'One O'Clock Gang', which was shown before a live audience. He volunteered to be one of the audience participants, and was found out after one of his relatives saw him on TV.

Billy won only one accolade at St Gerard's. 'It was a pair of swimming trunks and I won it for five-a-side football. You'd think they'd give you a football or boots or something, but they gave me a pair of swimming trunks which faded. They were like knickers. It was awful. They had elastic on the legs and elastic on the waist and they were dark blue – they were like lasses' schoolknickers. And after a while they faded to a funny browny colour. They were hellish. I couldn't even get a decent prize.'

The not-so-latent urge to make people laugh was still an issue, long after that first, seminal incident in the puddle in the St Peter's school playground. He was now quite certain he wanted to become a comedian, but had no idea how to do so. He told his father what he wanted to do, and he told the science teacher, Bill Sheridan. Mr Sheridan made fun of Billy, but later he came up to him discreetly and said, 'That's great', and went on to talk to him about the giants of Glasgow comedy.

But comedy was not the only interest that was awakening the young Connolly. A burgeoning love for rock and roll was growing in him – nothing unusual for a teenage boy, but in Billy Connolly it took on a characteristically focussed intensity. 'I've always liked Chuck Berry and Jerry Lee Lewis, and even Bill Haley and Little Richard. I was about fourteen when that all started to happen,' he told his old friend Tom Ferrie in an interview on Glasgow's Radio Clyde in 1976. 'I used to go on holiday with the school to Aberdeen and Carnoustie and all sorts of other exotic places, and get those records in Woolworths. Somebody always brought a record player. We never had rock records at home, because it was a wee bit sinful, rock and roll, at that point. Woolworths used to sell sort of copies, cover versions of rock songs with rotten singers, and guys doing Little Richard impersonations.'

He was, or at least he claims he was, introduced inadvertently to country music, an even more significant departure as things were to unfold. His father apparently bought him a Slim Whitman record, 'Dear Mary', believing it to be a Catholic hymn. ('I'm writing this letter,' runs the lyric, 'Dear Mary, to let you know how I feel/I'm lonesome and so weary I can hardly eat a meal.' An idealized self-image began to form in Connolly's mind, he explains, of himself as a 'a big skinny guy with cowboy boots who just wandered around . . . there's a tramp in Scottish mythology called the gabalunzie man, who brings you good luck when you see him. And I thought maybe that would be a good thing to do, be a tramp, because of the freedom.'

Connolly left school at fifteen. The only careers he had ever contemplated were that of vet and priest, but, by the time he left St Gerard's, he neither wanted nor was cut out academically for either. His departure was unceremonious, attracting as much attention as he implies was usual for his school career – none. Although school folklore told of the existence of a careers master, Connolly never met him – and in fact remembers not knowing any pupil who ever even glimpsed him. Armed with no qualifications other than two engineering certificates, known as J1 and J2, Billy claims he graduated from St Gerard's without even saying goodbye.

'I left school totally ignorant,' he recounted to Radio Clyde in the 1970s. 'And apart from the engineering course that I did rather well, I didn't have any certificates that I could recall, and somebody said, "Do you have any school certificates?" And I said, "No, I've left them in the house." And he said, "Well, if you being them tomorrow . . ." And I said, "Well, I can't make it tomorrow, I could come on Monday." So I went up to the school, and I said, "Look, did I get any certificates here?" And they said, "Well, I'll just go and have a look. What's your name?" And I said, "Connolly." So the secretary went away, and lo and behold, I was blessed. She brought this one out and it was a different guy called Connell, and I got his. But he was rubbish as well. It was things like PT and music and geography. What do you do? I thought. A long-distance athletic fiddler, you're going to get no place. So she typed it out with my name on it.'

CHAPTER 3

Work

'He was the right man in the right time in the right place.'
Retired shipyard worker Jimmy Lucas
on his one-time colleague, Billy Connolly

Billy Connolly wandered into his first job aged fifteen, in 1957, delivering books by bike for John Smith's Bookshop, of St Vincent Street, Glasgow. Connolly describes his pre-1960 self-image as that of 'failed teddy boy'. Humble an occupation though it was, Billy made the most of the merchandise and continued his reading, which had begun with *The Lord of the Flies* and by now was directed towards the likes of Nevil Shute and P.G. Wodehouse. He was also once knocked down by a trolley bus in West Nile Street. His cycle basket was crushed.

For a few months, the dispatch door in the alley at the back of the shop was his world. His duties started with sweeping the floor, after which he would deliver brown paper-wrapped parcels all day to offices and the more upmarket homes in the town. The shop was dominated by rather overbearing middle-class women of a type he had not really encountered before, and he did not take to them.

Anyway, Billy did not last long in the book business. He was sacked after an incident involving missing books. 'I was the lowest common denominator, the buck stopped at me, the newest message boy, and I got the heave-ho,' he insists even today. 'I can swear it wasn't me. I have a completely clear conscience. I got sacked in the nicest way you could imagine. I got sent up to the head office and this man – I think his name was Curlyfeather – who was in charge of the thing, and he had a big oil painting of a tram car behind him, it was all very impressive. And I was swearing my innocence at that time, and he said waffle waffle, flannel, flannel and he shook my hand and away I went with my stamp album into the distance.'

So, in 1958, he swapped books for buns, getting a job as a baker's van delivery boy for Bilsland's Bread, armed with the PT, music and geography qualifications of the hapless boy Connell. 'The guy looked at it and he said, "Aye, fine." So PT and geography must be the requisite of the van boy of Bilsland's. So away we went, and I delivered bread.' He enjoyed early mornings hopping over garden walls in the suburbs of Glasgow and chatting to housewives and café owners. It was a job he loved, and stayed at until he was just over sixteen.

Reaching sixteen in any working-class boy's life was a turning point, because it opened up the world of men's jobs. Being a Clydesider offered the constant lure of going to sea, and Connolly felt it strongly. During his year or so of commuting from Drumchapel to Govan via the Govan ferry, the ships plying the Clyde began to attract him; for some reason, they all seemed to him to be registered in Baltimore, and a fascination with such places began to form. 'I went to join the Merchant Navy, and they said the only thing I could be was a steward; and my father said, "They're all homosexuals. Don't do that"', Connolly told the journalist Mick Brown of the *Daily Telegraph* in 1993. 'Then I said, "I'd like to be an actor", and he said, "Well, they're all homosexuals as well." So I thought, maybe the world's this huge place just full of homosexuals who'll get you unless you're a welder. The only hedge against homosexuality was to become a welder.'

A welding apprenticeship was not quite what Connolly or his father had in mind initially. He desperately wanted to be a marine engineer, to see Shanghai and Valparaiso, and, especially, Baltimore. But the J1 and J2 engineering certificates he genuinely did hold were qualifications boys were supposed to get at night school *while* they were apprenticed, not before.

'It was like Catch 22. All dressed up and nowhere to go. I'd all the certificates and no work. And I went to Stephen's shipyard. My father used to write me letters for jobs and I would copy them out. He knew the language to put down and I would write away to personnel men – I kept putting "personal" instead of "personnel". So I got sent for, and I genuinely thought I was going to be an engineer and I became a welder. Because I think they've got a list, these guys, and they say, "How many welders do we need?" And they were choosing middle-class guys, guys who'd obviously come from grammar-type schools, and they were becoming engineers. But I became a welder and I'm glad. Because I think if I'd become an engineer I would have gone to sea and that would have been the end of that, or I'd probably now be working up on the oil rigs as an engineer. But I became a welder and I loved it, because they called us the Black Squad, the welders, cokers, platers, riveters and other guys that get dirty. I loved their company and their patter was great. And I loved working in the shipyards very much. And that's what I became.'

There is little doubt that this choice of career, fifty per cent of which was made for him by circumstances outside his control, led directly to the stage, and to the fame he always believed he was bound for. The job and the culture that went with it was to become a major part of his act, giving him inspiration to create sketches that would not only paint a sociologically accurate picture of a section of Scottish life, but would also provide a gag or two. 'I remember at one point, when I was a welder,' he has said, 'sitting in the shipyard designing my first album sleeve though I couldn't even play a mouthie.'

The shipyards were, at that time, the epitome of Glasgow culture. The mainstay of the industrial workforce – six ships were being built at Stephen's alone the day Billy Connolly started work there – they represented another institution waiting to provide the 'rest of their lives' for the children who could hear the yard sounds from their classrooms. So in 1960, aged sixteen, Billy took up a five-year welder's apprenticeship in a Govan shipyard, Stephen's at Lindhouse. He started bringing back to his Drumchapel home a very welcome £20 a week, and continued living at home until he completed his apprenticeship at twenty-one.

But the yards were to prove more than a source of security for Connolly; the people he encountered there became a cast of characters for the blond, acne-ridden boy to grow up among, as well as a (if not *the*) source of inspiration for his comedy. However, the importance of this vacillates over the years, depending on Connolly's waxing and waning accounts of the shipyard's influence. His one consistent assertion is that the crack was mighty. 'I loved working as a shipyard welder. I was good at it and was proud of what I was doing. I liked the crack and the work, and seeing what I had done go sailing past. I had the time of my life. There was a lot of good patter among the lads. I think it is because the shipyards are so grim. I'm sure miners are funny people as well.'

Connolly's accounts of the Stephen's era tell of another world within the shipyard walls. 'I was so happy there. I fell right into it. Loved it,' he enthused to the *Sunday Times* in 1975. 'As soon as that gate shuts, a shipyard becomes a complete wee town. You could buy shoes, cigarettes, transistor radios, cheap booze. It was an amazing place ... It's an uncomfortable job at times, wet, damp, cold. You weren't allowed a fire because the heat might buckle the metal. And the guys were forever peeing over the side so there was piss everywhere.'

In most ways, conditions at the yard were grim, as dangerous as those in a mine, and more like a prison or barracks than of a place of work. In the winter, you made a point of wearing two pairs of socks and still got freezing feet, but what Connolly remembers more clearly than discomfort is laughter, even when dangerous things were happening, such as workers getting bad shocks from electrical equipment or sliding on ice-covered decks. The humour was cruel and merciless and made an indelible mark on Connolly from day one. From the welders, cokers, platers, burners, joiners, engineers and electricians, he learnt the combative, competitive, funny way men talk to one another. Life as an apprentice consisted largely of lessons in the major life task of generally wising up – and in learning to be the uncomplaining butt of jokes.

Running gags in the yard did not do anything so namby pamby as to stop to pay respects to the afflicted. Connolly fondly remembers the Player of the Year trophy they made for the simpleton colleague whose contribution to the welders' dinner-time football matches consisted solely of running around waving his arms in the air.

Then there was the macho cult of, for want of a better word, dishonesty. Shipyard scams included making metal coins to the right weight that would fit into cigarette machines. Connolly recalls the entrepreneurial spirit being extended in this endeavour to making a mould of a coin and freezing water in it. Speedy insertion of this devious device in a cigarette machine would result in the worker getting the fags and the mysterious appearance, beneath the machine, of a puddle the next day – a small-scale extension of that crime writer's favourite, the evidence-less murder-by-icicle. You could buy anything you wanted in the yards – workers' lockers bulged with everything from brassieres to whisky, cigarettes to records. The more adventurous executed grander larcenies. Among Billy's collection of yard yarns is the tale of the men who stole a grand piano. They spotted it on a boat, winched it out and drove off with it. Even when stopped at the yard gates they kept their cool, using the solve-all-phrase: 'Off for repairs', and got their booty out without being bothered at all.

At the beginning, to the young Connolly, it was quite terrifying to encounter the hard old hands, who would continually send him and the other apprentices up – often right up – the garden path. Among the unofficial initiation tests for the young lads was the Stowaway's Locker trick. Connolly would be asked by one of the older blokes to fetch what they wanted from the Stowaway's Locker. Off he would go, asking other workers the location of the Locker. One would 'help' with directions to go 'doon there, turn right, keep on past the paint shop and you'll see it'. And when Connolly would arrive at the end of this suggested path to enquire politely: 'Is this the Stowaway's Locker, please?' he'd be told, 'Naw, son – doon past thae benches there, turn left and ask again.' He'd arrive to be told once more, 'Naw ...'

There was, of course, no such place, and Connolly soon realized the folly of this wild goose exercise. So wary did he become that, a few months later, when he was asked to fetch some Carborundum, he thought such an unlikely sounding name could not possibly exist, and must be some other mythical substance. After repeatedly insisting that he couldn't be fooled this time, he had to be convinced that there really was such a product, and it was quite good for sanding surfaces down, too.

Apart from the apprentices' rites of passage, there was plenty more to keep Connolly amused as he learnt his trade. The shipyard contained more characters than a Dickens novel. 'I always wondered why the guys in the shipyard made me laugh more than the comedians at the theatre, with their jokes about honeymoons, Pakistanis and the Irish,' he says. 'The yard talk was always about human beings and their functions and malfunctions. So I went off and took that kind of talk to the stage.'

In 1975, he recalled for the *Sunday Telegraph* some of the shipyard characters that dominated his new world: 'There was the blacksmith who kept his fag bobbing about in front of his face on a wire attached to his helmet. And "The Great Voltaine", a labourer who used to entertain the troops at dinner time dressed up in a silver-painted welder's helmet, and a cape decked out with light bulbs. He had a helper who walked about behind him with a battery, lighting the bulbs up. "Think of a number," Voltaine would shout. "Thirteen," somebody would say. "Correct" ... He was bloody great.' Connolly still delights in the repartee of the yards, albeit from a safe distance in Hollywood. There was, for instance, the manager who tried to discipline a man caught with an illicit can of tea, and who was told to piss off. 'So the manager says, "Do you know who I am?" And Wullie McInnes turns to his mate and says, "Hey Jimmy ... here's a fucker disnae ken who he is."'

Billy's immediate foreman was a man called Sammy Boyd. Boyd was always trying to shoo Billy away. 'Oan ye go, son, awa' tae the lavvie,' the older man would insist. The lavvies in question were prehistoric, evil-smelling and daubed in obscene drawings that were mostly gouged into the wall so that occasional repainting only served to make them a little harder to make out. One day, on being sent away to the lavvies yet again by Boyd, Connolly complained that they were disgusting. 'Luxury, son, luxury,' came the reply. 'Ye should have seen them when I was a boy...'

The most influential, however, of the gurus Connolly came into contact with were another pair he worked with, a plater and a joiner called by the music hall names of Lucas and Dalgleish. 'They were so funny I'd have my dinner and rush back to my job to hear them. Productivity zoomed. I was always the funny man but I was schoolboy funny then. I learnt a lot off them,' he said in 1974, and has continued to pay tribute to the two men consistently, even if at times he has denied that he owes the shipyards anything as a comedy training ground. ('I get fed up with people, especially English journalists, asking, "Do you owe your humour to the shipyards?" Quite genuinely I don't owe it to anybody. I was always a funny kind of guy,' he grumbled in 1976.)

However, in his 1990s routine he attributes credit for at least one joke to the fast-talking partners, and when he did a show nearby in Greenock in January 1994 and met them for the first time in more than thirty years, he gave them the best seats in the house, paid tribute to them during the show and took them out for a Chinese dinner afterwards. At the time of researching this book, the pair were writing Billy a long monologue entitled 'Wee Davie Darra', the story of a shipyard worker and his 5ft 8ins turd.

Some of the time back in the yards, according to Connolly, Lucas and Dalgleish would tell jokes, while at others, their humour would lie simply in behaving in a bizarre – dare one say surreal? – way, such as stopping work in the middle of a complex operation, running to the other end of the half-finished liner, putting their arms round one another and singing, 'We'll meet again.'

Jimmy Lucas and Bobby Dalgleish now sixty-four and fifty-nine respectively, live in retirement at Gourock, twenty-five miles up the Clyde, near Port Glasgow. And they are still cracking jokes – in fact trying to stop them is about as easy as getting Connolly to decide whether his success is attributable to the yards or whether it's simply the way *he* tells them.

Connolly's acknowledged debt to Lucas and Dalgleish – along with his understandable oversight in failing to keep in touch with them – led to a sublime moment (at least for Billy) during a 1979 'This Is Your Life' show. The Thames TV researchers sent to Glasgow to find Lucas and Dalgleish succeeded insofar as they came back with an elderly ex-employee of Stephen's shipyard named Dalgleish. Sadly, the old boy wheeled on to the show by Eamon Andrews as 'one half of the comical duo who were your inspiration back in those days' was entirely the wrong Dalgleish. Before he was introduced in the studio in London, we saw this surprisingly dour elderly funster filmed on the derelict Stephen's site, describing his long-standing relationship with his old mate Billy. Connolly, to his great credit, gave away nothing other than a brief double take when this Dalgleish came from backstage, and gamely hugged him as if he had been the one man on the show with whom he truly wanted to be reunited. As Connolly's lifelong friend – the folk singer and broadcaster, Danny Kyle, who comes from Paisley and worked in shipyards with him – has remarked, 'You know, you could fill the Kelvin Hall in Glasgow three times over with people who claim to have worked with Billy back in the yards.' Kyle's point is borne out by the evidence of Billy Connolly's press cuttings over the years, in which the status of his unnamed but liberally quoted friends is about as suspect as the 'friends' of the royal family who seem to have little in life to do but comment about them.

Lucas and Dalgleish are almost like an updated Vladimir and Estagon from *Waiting for Godot*. The real Bobby Dalgleish looks like Mikhail Gorbachev, Jimmy has a comedian's face with a couple of Doddy-style teeth and a big beak of a nose. Lucas and Dalgleish's pranksterism has not been muted by the passing years. When their long-discussed whereabouts were discovered by the local Greenock *Telegraph* in 1993, the national press in the form of a TV listings magazine got to hear about it, and sent an American reporter to interview them. After an afternoon chatting with them, as she was leaving, they asked her for the money for her cup of tea. She was fishing in her purse before they explained that this was an ironic Scottish joke.

'There were plenty of double acts in the yard,' says one. 'Pig McKendall and his mate Billy Cleary, Bob Boyle and Baldy McGregor, us. Pig was a wee guy who would gamble on anything; two flies on the wall, he would bet you that that fly would beat that one. If you were paddling in the stream he would say that your paddle beat that paddle in the stream. Now a chap in the shipyard started in the morning and he fell down a tunnel and he was killed, and the shop steward says, "This is the part I don't like, telling a woman that her husband has died in the yard." So McKendall, who would gamble on anything, says, "I'll go up. I don't mind telling these people." So he knocks on this woman's door, and the woman comes to the door, and he says, "Are you the widow Brown?" And the woman says, "I beg your pardon, I'm Mrs Brown." And McKendall says, "I bet you a fiver you're not." '

Lucas and Dalgleish remember the young Billy as being tall and spotty and untidy, so they called him a beatnik. 'He did what he was told because in those days if they didn't do what they were told to they got a cuffed ear. He liked to hear the humour and eventually he used the humour he heard in the shipyards. A lot of Glaswegians have a natural sense of humour. Everyone joked all the time. Someone would come in and say, "I did a silly thing last night." And someone would say, "What was her name?" Someone says to me, "D'you think priests should marry?" I says, "Aye, if they love each other." Billy was good at making up stories. He made a joke about being in the erection squad.' (Erection squads comprised four men who lifted a unit while the tack welder, of which Connolly was one, welded.)

As the delightful jokesters relentlessly and exhaustingly recount examples of the shipyard humour of the 1950s, it is easy to see how, with the best will in the world, Billy Connolly finds it easy to resist the notion that he is nothing more than a smoothed-down, internationalized retailer of unadapted, native Glasgow wit; it is clear that over the years, Connolly has done some work on the material. 'What would it take to paint a forty-eight-foot mast?' they ask. 'A forty-eight-foot brush.'

'When you were young in the shipyards they sent you to the store for a long stand – but they called it a long stond in Scottish – or you went to the store for spotted paint (white with black spots), or for a left-handed screwdriver, a rubber hammer, a bubble for a water level,' says Lucas. 'I remember sending Billy on those missions. I once told an apprentice to get a piece of chalk. "How big?" he said. "A big bit," I said, and we nicknamed him Vera Lynn because I sent him for a piece of chalk and he came back with the white cliffs of Dover.'

When they met again, Lucas and Dalgleish were delighted at the depth of Connolly's memory of the yards. 'Billy remember names,' Bobby Dalgleish recounts. 'I hadn't seen him for thirty years. He even told a story in the rest room. He said, "Do you remember Colin MacLean?" His daughter was married to Harry Lauder's nephew. Colin used to say, "I bought a new pair of gabardine shoelaces, a double-breasted simmit (vest), I bought a pair of them Harris tweed underpants. By God they were awful itchy." Billy uses this. I've heard him using it.'

If Lucas and Dalgleish came as close as anyone at Stephen's Yard to tutoring Billy Connolly, their influence was still minor compared to that of the culture of unconscious humour that the yards, and working-class Glasgow generally, fostered. It was as if he were not merely observing acutely but systematically picking up and analysing whole styles of communication for some mysterious future use.

45

He gave an example of this acute observation in another local radio interview in Glasgow in 1976. 'I think only Glasgow and Liverpool people do this thing. They get all angry when they're arguing, and they try to make up certain quotes that they've heard before and they get them all wrong because they're all flustered. There's a very well-known one of the shop steward saying, "There's been allegations made here, and if I catch the alligators, I'll sort them out." I was at a union meeting, the Boilermakers' Union, a strike meeting as a matter of fact, in the Borough Hall in Partick, and all the officials of the union were on the stage – a big row of tables and their wee glasses and their wee jugs of water. And there was a guy who wasn't quite sober – it doesnae normally happen at union meetings – but there was this guy – he wasnae terrible sober, he'd been doing sort of sober impersonations to the audience and had slipped – and he stood up and said, "You're a liar, you." And the official said, "I beg your pardon." He said, "See yous people, yous want to preach what you're talking about." '

Of course, another Glasgow tradition that Billy had yet to become acquainted with – and was later to become positively friendly with – was drinking. The shipyard years signalled the start of a long and fruitful relationship with alcohol, and that combined with music signalled the start of a grown-up social life. Although he was quite partial to cold milk from a machine, it was a time of experimenting with alcohol – the term experimenting loosely translated as drinking a lot of it.

Connolly was always something of the outsider, and he remained individualistically immune to peer pressure to drink. 'I didn't go through the Partick pre-pub age drinking thing, the wine-drinking, the vino collapso number – though a lot of my friends did. So I didn't get involved at all until I was eighteen or nineteen.' When he did, it was at the Portland Arms in Troon, which he visited on his bike. 'It wasn't what I looked on as a good time. I knew that I would drink in later years and I looked forward to being in pubs and being adult.'

He certainly fulfilled that ambition. Twenty-two years later, and minus several liver cells, he pretty well gave up boozing. 'I've always been a great beer man. I like pints of beers and stories and lies, and spending hours and hours drinking beer and telling stories, and I was just spending too much of my life doing it. I certainly didn't have a drink problem. I don't. So I stopped drinking because I needed to be on guard all the time.'

He restricted his drinking to the odd pint and wine with dinner. But Billy retained an enormous, even over-romanticized, affection for the culture that went with real drinking. Already a huge star, and living in London with his lover Pamela Stephenson, he was seized one night in Glasgow with the desire for a pint of heavy and a fish supper, in that order. 'To be quite frank,' he confessed on local radio, 'I didn't enjoy the pint very much.

'But I went and got a fish supper in Byres Road, and it was great, extraordinary, plus it was made even better because it was the last fish in the shop. It was sitting there in that wee thing itself, and it was wonderful. And there was a drunk, he was the best, a real music hall drunk coming down Byres Road swearing at the traffic. I love them. We were eating the fish supper sitting in the car watching this man. He was beautiful; he was about six feet and hairy and broad, a big guy, and he had a sort of rucksack and he was out to lunch. There was nobody home, his big body was making its way home alone. And there was cars trying to get round him and he was shouting, "Yah, shaddup, on yer bike." A big Glasgow hardcase. And he got to the pavement, into the same chip shop as I'd been in, got his whatever it was, his haggis and chips, and he stood in a doorway like a half-shut knife ramming this stuff into his face ... And that was the cabaret. It was lovely. I'd forgotten about guys like him. The munchies after the drinkies. It's great.'

Like a lot of tough young working-class men then or now, Billy Connolly also got himself a criminal record, although he does not mention this in interviews. It started in piffling terms, but was to build up to something close to serious. First, as he recounts, he was fined 2s. 6d. by a police court at Partick for playing football on private ground. Soon after that, he was caught syphoning petrol. He had run out while riding his bike, and had no money on him, so went from garage to garage offering to leave his licence in exchange for a gallon of petrol, and to bring the money later. None of the garages would agree to this, nor even let him leave his bike overnight on their premises. He was too far from Drumchapel to wheel the bike home, so, as he relates it, 'I got myself a wee hose and a can. And got caught.'

Billy's third brush with the law (although he has also confessed additionally to being fined £15 for relieving himself in an unauthorized place) was when he was eighteen, and resulted in him being arrested, spending a night in a police cell, and receiving a year's suspended sentence.

By his account, it was a highly unfair rap. He had been out in Bearsden with a girl, when a man came across and hit her in the mouth. He says he was frightened, but felt he had to hit him; the man hit him back, and Connolly, with the help of another man, thumped the assailant a second time. It was probably a tribute to Billy's punching power that the police came to Drumchapel later, as he was going to bed, to arrest him. He was already in his pyjamas, and as he heard the police coming, put jeans and a shirt on over them. Later, in the cells for the night, a policeman noticed prisoner Connolly had taken his clothes off and was settling down in his pyjamas – a rarity even in the theatre of life that was Milngavie police station. Both Connolly and his colleague were fined £15 and given a year suspended – but the other man stole a motorbike during the sentence, and ended up in a young offenders' institution. Billy kept clean, and was simply admonished. 'The guy I beat up was a real animal, but his father was quite a wealthy bloke,' Connolly said later. 'Nobody deserved a smack in the mouth as much as he did, ever. If I ever see him again, I'd be delighted to do the same, absolutely delighted. And I'm not a very violent person. I just detested the guy.'

The folk music that was to be the next great development in his life after joining the shipyard was not part of Billy's scene at the start of his adulthood. Along with rock and roll, riding various decrepit motorbikes, hanging out at a youth club called the 41 at a school in Milngavie (where the girls were reputed to be sensational), and mooching around the Partick Thistle football ground at Firhill Road, *the* great activity was dancing, the glittering delights of the Barrowland Locarno, the F and F in Partick, and every other dance hall in Glasgow, and along with that, Billy's initiation into the delights of women. He was a regular dancer at the age of sixteen. Coming home from the yard 'the black sheep of the family' ('My father was in clean engineering – he came home the same colour he left'), Connolly would clean up and get dressed before going out to a ballroom. He would head off out of the house smiling at his aunt's farewell comment: 'Ye're away daein' that moondancin', are ye?'

Danny Kyle is fond of describing the sartorial elegance the young Connolly now affected: 'At that time, Billy wore Italian suits. He had no beard, no moustache, a Perry Como haircut, bumfreezer jacket and pointed shoes. We used to sneak away from the yards to go to jiving school in Glasgow. We both had gold medals for jivemanship, and danced in the team at the Rooftop Dance Show. You know, Billy was once on "Come Dancing".'

The soundtrack at the Barrowland Locarno was pre-The Twist and came courtesy of big bands such as Billy McGregor's Band and George MacCallum's Metronomes. One of the chart toppers at the time, 'Please Help Me, I'm Falling' by Hank Locklin, was a Connolly favourite, and he greatly enjoyed actually touring with him later on – although he concedes that his chatty homages about how much Hank's music had affected him may have 'bored the arse off' his hero. To this style of music, Connolly and his crowd would dance the Moony, a none too sophisticated technique requiring the women to hang onto the man's neck and the man to hold on equally tightly to the woman's buttocks, a step Billy would delicately refer to as a sensible form of dancing cheek-to-cheek.

Despite this talent for dancing and enjoyment of the ballroom life, Connolly denied, however, in a late-night radio interview with Tom Ferrie that he was ever much of a ladies' man. 'I've never been successful with women in my life,' he said, with a touch of wryness, one fancies. Connolly and his mates would stock up on Dutch courage before proposing a dance (initially) to a woman – having a few bevvies at the bar before retiring to the Barrowland's loo to consume a half-bottle of wine in between jostling for preening space.

'My trouble was I was like a broken radio. I was stuck on transmit, I wasn't on receive. I never knew when I was winning when I was chatting up women; I didn't know when to shut up. I'd talk to women and they'd be laughing and say, "Oh you're a terrible man," and laugh, "oh what a guy." And then they would shoot me the line and it would go right past me because I was on my next, and I was looking for signs and couldn't see them. And other guys who were dull as ditchwater were away with their girlfriends to somewhere else. And I'm sitting there talking and they're all laughing when the whole point of the exercise was something else altogether. So I wasn't very successful.

'I fell in love a lot of times,' Connolly continued, 'but I wasn't a ladykiller; I didn't score very well. I didn't have many notches on my belt, scalps on my pole, but I fell in love a lot. I tended to either have no women in my life or to be deeply, madly head–over–heels in love with one. I did have some success but I wasn't like your sexual cowboy; I wasn't remarkable in that department. But I fell in love a lot, and I know them all now and I love them still. Like me they're getting old, but they're still very attractive and it's still a gas meeting them. I met one last year, and it was deeply moving.'

He described a touching meeting with an unnamed old flame, who was now working in a shop in Glasgow. As Connolly and his daughter were leaving the shop, she stopped him. 'Oh by the way,' she said, and produced a small plastic wallet. In it was her school blazer badge – and his Parachute Regiment wings. She asked if he wanted them. Embarrassed at first, he replied, 'Well, sure. I want them if you don't want them.' Connolly says she replied, 'Well, I kinda want them.'

'It was a lovely moment,' Connolly says. 'It really lives in my heart. It's a very important moment to me, because I love her and I'd like her to love me back. I love her in a very clean and honest way and I treasure her, as I do all my girlfriends – they did me immense good. Because I don't remember being loved very much myself as a child, and so I learnt to love from being loved by these people.'

Connolly went on to reflect on a subject one might not have expected him to have strong views on – the reduction in the number of public lavatories in Glasgow. 'This is a shame,' he philosophized, 'because if, like myself, you've experienced being in town having had a few pints, and then miss your last bus or can't find it, and you've a young lady on your arm and have to walk home to Partick with six or seven pints inside you, it's no joy, because you'll be walking along a girl's street and start to wiggle around because it gets a bit painful. And the young lady's saying, "That's funny, that. I could have swore he looked all right when I met him." A mile further along the street, you're on your knees walking sideways with your hands in your pockets kidding on you're looking for small change. Peeping up closes, looking for one without a back door.

'Eventually you find one, shoot up the close, the legs just a blur, hand against the wall ... keeping an eye open for neighbours, peeping out the windows. Now you can do all sorts of things. If there's two of you, you can play at wee trains in the gutter, wee subways. And if you're artistically minded, you can leave some artwork in the wall, or if it's snowing you can sign it. But just where you're at the good bit, you hear a stamping of feet coming closer and closer, and then they grab you, two arms ... it's two big policemen. They take you down to the station and do you for wee-weeing on the Queen's property. And the reason they knew you were there is because a month before they were down the street with a police cadet having filled him with six or seven pints of water, led him down the street, saying, "Yes officer, I think if I needed a wee-wee I would do it here." So they're all waiting for you behind the midden, they know exactly where you're going to pee. So please, please don't do it. Because I did it and it cost me fifteen quid.'

Very late in his teens, by his own account, it wasn't only the women who were catching Connolly's eye. The strange business of his fleeting homosexual phase was to unsettle Connolly back in 1962, and to come back to haunt him in 1993, when he, perhaps ill-advisedly, revealed it to the tape recorder of the *Radio Times* writer Andrew Duncan – not only revealed it, but brought it up and kept referring to it over lunch with Duncan. On his American tour in late 1993, he was still, as a part of his stage routine, railing against the press in general, and Duncan implicitly, for making it public.

What he said to the *Radio Times* was this: 'I went through a phase, at about twenty, when I fancied men as well. There was a kind of androgyny going on – high heels and perfume for men – and I thought it was a bit of OK. I was a chrysalis on the point of becoming a moth. I had an actor friend whose feelings were much stronger than mine and he put me right about a few things. I thought, "What's happening? This isn't my department at all." '

It was the only reference, before or since, to such a phase, and raises the prospect that Connolly may have 'outed' such a latent and chronologically distant ghost of a feeling in psychotherapy back in California. The news of the revelation, insofar as it went, certainly did not play well back in Scotland, where the newspapers, milking the issue for the little it was worth, reported the statement pretty much as an admission by Connolly that he was gay. It would not be unfair to say that many Scots have a profound and nationalist-tinged thing about sex and the 'norms' of manly behaviour. Just one sample edition of the Glasgow *Daily Record* on the January 1994 day of Billy Connolly's return to play in Glasgow after a five-year absence contained the following stories cheek by jowl: one, that the American magazine *Complete Woman*, in a 'Tour d'Amour' survey of the world's men, found the Scots ('tartan tigers') the world's best, most tireless and unreserved lovers; two, next to that, a photo and caption depicting the Russian fascist leader Vladimir Zhirinovsky cuddling another man in a sauna; third, a couple of pages on, a story under the enormous and alarming headline QUEEN BILLY!, a report that a gay Boston history professor, William Percy, had evidence that William of Orange was a rampant homosexual who enjoyed the services of rent boys. The *Record*'s fine story was mischievously rounded off by a priceless quote from 'a red-faced former Grand Master of the Orange Lodge, Magnus Bain'. Mr Bain fumed, 'I have absolutely no comment to make about this, and I don't wish to continue the conversation.'

At the time of these mild homosexual feelings, when Connolly was nearing the end of his apprenticeship, he was simultaneously beginning to wonder what exactly was his department in many areas of life. He was still convinced its limits were not confined to the shipyard, and the 'special' feeling he'd had as a child hadn't quite left him. Although he '... had these notions of escape, of being Hank Williams or Luke the Drifter, even before I could play an instrument', in reality, the nearest he got to dream destinations such as Australia was building a ship called the *City of Melbourne*; and the only respite from the daily grind of apprenticeship came in the form of humour and giving blood at the Southern General Hospital, a routine that at once made him feel heroic and got him an afternoon off work.

But the humour was to prove more profitable. Connolly continued to hone his own funniness, which had effortlessly amused his classmates, but now had to pass muster with grown men who needed a much stronger punchline to fall down laughing in the shipyard canteen. 'They didn't *need* to laugh any more; they were funny themselves and they were men. But being funny was just an everyday thing in the shipyards. If you were funny they called you a patter-merchant, and that's what I wanted to be,' he explains.

But the key to Connolly is that really he always wanted to be more than that and, more importantly, he was prepared to take (and make) the opportunities to ensure that his patter was to find an audience beyond the shipyard walls. And although Connolly's life at this time was not focussed on comic stardom, the feeling that there must be something more spurred him on. The folk singer Hamish Imlach has told (although he confesses to being a little uncertain if he has the details right) of an enlightening episode for the young Connolly: 'Billy and a girl were walking through Glasgow and there was this guy coming along in cowboy boots and hat, leather jacket, tailored denims. The girl pointed and said: "There's Alex Campbell, the folk singer." And Billy went into a bar and sat looking at a pint and thought: "Nobody ever says, there's Billy Connolly, the welder." '

The fact that, in the first instance, Connolly's determination to expand his horizons gave him the impetus to do nothing more radical than join the Territorial Army because, as he put it, 'Life was dull. I thought jumping out of planes would make a change,' was just one of destiny's wrong (but by no means disastrously wrong) turnings. Connolly joined the Parachute Regiment of the TA when he was a welder – it was around the time of the Suez Crisis – and stayed for three years. The appeal was '. . . to make myself more exotic', with the main attraction being the red beret. 'I thought, Christ, I'm guaranteed a woman in this gear.' He was to be slightly disappointed in this respect: 'I got my red beret and looked like acne.' Apart from the experience of doing seventeen parachute jumps, his TA time was to prove something of a farce from day one.

The doctor at his medical, he claims, commented, 'You're not very big downstairs, are you?', to which he alleges he replied, 'I thought we were only going to fight them.' Whether Connolly's account of this episode is verbatim or not hardly matters; like dozens of funny men before him – Spike Milligan springs notably to mind – the military (if only in its part-time, hobbyist version) provided Connolly with ample new material, from the very first moment he encountered it.

Still, the action and adventure appealed to him. On active duty in Cyprus (after twelve jumps) for the battalion's annual two-week training exercise, he remembers, 'It was great. It was all bayonets down the trousers stuff . . . everyone looked like Rambo.' Shortly after arriving on the island, he was waiting to jump, the doors of the Beverley aircraft open for a 1,000-foot night jump. Billy was sixth in line. Behind him, his best TA mate Eddie McCandless did what friends are for, and yelled above the engine noise, 'Hey Billy, do you realize this is our thirteenth jump?' Later, after this helpful morale-booster, Billy saved McCandless's life by telling him the static line was caught round his arm. His life-saving advice almost went unheeded, because until that point, Connolly had been doing nothing but crack jokes.

'If I had jumped out of that door that night it would have taken the arm right off me but he saw it before – he checked me out – before we started moving towards the door and shouted to me,' says McCandless, who is now sixty-four and living in Calgary, Alberta, where he moved in 1980, leaving his job as quartermaster's stores orderly for the battalion (15 Para) and taking up a job as a dustman. 'I thought that he was clowning again because he was always having a white hanky and was pulling this white hanky out of my chute and saying, "Oh Eddie, your chute has got a fucking hole in it," or something like that. That's what he used to do, pull the white handkerchief out of the boys' parachutes and say, "Eh, there's something the matter with your chute because there's a bit of it there," and it would be this hanky. He was always up to mischief, you know. In fact he was really funnier then than he is now. He used to do great turns; he used to have us all in stitches with his antics. But I can assure you that he saved my life that night I went out the door with him, because he was right at my back.

'I'm a bit older than Billy, and he used call me feither,' McCandless continues. 'I met him in 1962. We both went to Abingdon on a parachute course. We definitely hit it off immediately – he was a great lad and very smart, very well groomed. When I used to look at him with his beard later on, I used to say, "Jesus Christ what has come over him?" I couldn't believe that it was the same Billy; he was always very well groomed and always a very smart-looking soldier, believe it or not, even though we were only TA. He immediately struck me as being very, very funny ·

when I first knew him. He used to have all the battalion boys choking with laughter with his antics. Jokes and physical stuff, whatever.

'One night we were up north in Scotland and we were in a wee fishing village and they all jumped off the pier into the water. They'd had a couple of beers and I think they were going crazy. Billy wasn't quite the ringleader but he wasn't far from it. When we were in Abingdon that time, we had a night off to go into the town, and we had this RSM Campbell, a Scot himself. He turned to Billy and said, "Connolly, remember you and your boys from Glasgow, you're only sightseeing. You're not attacking it." Billy replied with all his hand on heart stuff. But he was a good soldier. He was always to the fore if you were down and out; he was always there to cheer you up. He was a great backer up.

'One of the first jumps we made at Abingdon, Billy was number two and I was number four, so I was about a hundred feet above Billy when he hit the deck. The RAF instructor had been shouting at us to get our knees up, but Billy didn't, and I heard the sergeant shouting at Billy, "Connolly, you made a bad descent!" Billy said to him, "Ach, sarge, if you want to get your own back, just kick me up the arse." And he bent over in front of him and the sergeant did just that and kicked him.'

Fine soldier he may have been, but it was on that trip to Cyprus that the pointlessness for him of this form of military life finally sunk in. In the Kyrenia Mountains he recalls how, 'We were supposed to be chasing the Green Howards. After about a fortnight we captured one. It turned out he worked in the same shipyard as me. So I said to myself, Christ, I could have got him any day in the canteen. What the hell am I doin' in the Kyrenia Mountains wi' nae arse in my trousers?' But the time was not entirely wasted. On a night training exercise on Buddon Ness, near Dundee, Connolly stood up in the back room of a Carnoustie pub and lustily sang 'The Wild Side of Life' ... 'And I thought to myself, hey this is the game ...'

'One night,' recalls McCandless, 'we went down to Nicosia. We had been down there a couple of nights having a drink, and Billy kept telling the manager of this nightclub that he could do a better performance on the stage than any of the stage hands that he had. He kept nagging him about it. So this time, the person who had come to do a turn on the stage didn't turn up and the manager asked Billy if he would go up and perform, so he went up and did a turn and it was bloody great. He did a couple of songs and he was really good. I think he had taken his banjo over to Cyprus with him. He was a great turn, a great singer, a great performer. The outstanding thing I remember about Billy was that he said, and he kept saying over and over again, that he knew he would make the big time. He had that aggression that he was going to do it.'

Even though we need to be careful about successful people who 'always knew they were going to be big' (we never, after all, hear a peep from the thousands who thought they would make it but never did), Connolly's self-belief even at this early stage of his life deserves to be given credence, if only because what he always claims to have been his emphatic inner conviction that he would triumph is backed up to the hilt by the memories of friends from his distant past like McCandless.

The thought of showbusiness, or at least of giving up conventional work to wander around the country playing the banjo, was by now paramount in his mind. It was an instrument he had lately taken an almost inexplicable liking to, even though until that point he could only play the mouth organ. 'I enjoyed seeing my mates fall about at my jokes,' he says. 'There was just something deep down in me that kept making me want to entertain anyone I was with. One day an older man who worked in the yard came up to me and said: "Billy, if you want to become someone on the stage now's the time to do it. Not tomorrow. But now. Otherwise you'll wake up one morning, find yourself sweating away in the bowels of some ship – a man of fifty – with a life full of regrets to show for yourself. It's the things we never do in life," he said, "that we always regret." Suddenly I had this vision of myself still working in the yard in twenty years' time. I was only eighteen then, and it frightened the life out of me. And that's when I decided to go into showbusiness.'

The decision to swap blowtorch for microphone may have germinated at eighteen, but in the meantime there was work to be done. Firstly, there was the small business of completing his apprenticeship. Then he had to make his appearance, as a now ex-Territorial, a little more exotic. He grew a splendid beard, which became less splendid when he burned it welding, with a splash of molten metal. The hair singed off, and a patch formed on the right-hand side of his face where no hair would grow. He then set about adapting the design of the beard, and hit upon the face-lengthening notion of taking the sides off. The next time he was to see his own face properly was twenty-six years later.

Completing the apprenticeship was a process not without its poignancy. His official qualification document was handed over in a black leather case, and he noticed the secretary had spelt his name wrongly, ending it -e-l-l-y. Although he found the office people at Stephen's rather intimidating, and (as at the bookshop seven years previously) none more so than the middle-aged women 'with pointy glasses', he querulously raised the misspelling. 'Oh, for goodness sake,' she grumbled. 'We don't have time to do this sort of thing.' 'You had five years!' Connolly very reasonably replied as she retyped it.

Showbusiness ambition or not, Connolly was now a journeyman welder, albeit a slightly eccentric-looking one, and very soon, after answering a newspaper advertisement, Connolly received a letter from one William Hillhouse offering a lucrative, ten-week contract in Biafra, southern Nigeria, helping to build an oil rig.

Dramatic as its possibilities sound, going to Africa was not a particularly seminal experience for Connolly. Although he has spent a lot of time performing to expatriates in Middle East and Commonwealth venues, the expat scene has never been a thing that has enchanted him. 'You meet a welder from Govan,' he commented in his early book *Gullible's Travels*, 'and he calls himself "an engineering consultant". And a Brit! "Hi – I'm one of the Brits." Just off the plane from Govan and he's suddenly become a "Brit". Plumbers become "hydraulic advisers".'

'There were three legs on this oil rig,' he recalled on Radio Clyde of his Nigerian episode, 'and there was about forty men on each leg, and we were finished at night. You're not allowed drink on an oil rig, no booze at all, but the local guys from a little town called Port Harcourt would row up the river in this rowing boat with big carry-outs of Heineken beer, and we would sit on a barge at the side of the oil rig and drink it. So one night, we were all sitting around, it was great – one of those black warm Africa nights – sitting drinking the beer with the squad, and the other leg had finished. It was very rare for two legs to finish at the same time, and this other crowd had come down for a drink, and we were all well smashed and I was singing a song about Glasgow.

And a guy come over and says, "You come from Glasgow?" And I says, "Sure." And he says, "So do I." I says, "That's great, where?" "Partick." "Oh, I live in Partick." He says, "You're kidding." I says, "No." "Which street?" "White Street." He says, "Och, now I know you're kidding." Because he lived in White Street, and do you know, he lived in the next close to me. And I'd never seen him in my life. And we came back from Africa and I saw him in the street, and I've never seen him since.

'Another time, I remember a guy from Motherwell took exception to the fact that I was from Irish Catholic stock. He kept asking me my religion, and I said, "Don't be daft, we're up a river in Africa, for Christ's sake. What you talking about?" He kept hinting, and eventually hit me a smack in the mouth. So I hit him even harder and he fell down.'

When he returned from Nigeria, long before the civil war that devastated Biafra, Connolly went to Jersey to work in a power station. Then he returned to Glasgow. 'I had some money – about £700 – and just didn't work any more. I went back to the Clyde but walked out of my job on a Fair Friday. Just walked out: I didn't even lift my books. I was single. I played the banjo and guitar and I sang. I thought, "To hell with it. I'll give it a try." After that, I wandered around having a great time and then formed a group called the Humblebums.'

For the historical record, it is worth noting that Billy Connolly was a very good welder indeed. Several years later, in 1970, he received a letter from Mr Hillhouse offering him the post of supervising welder on a contract coming up in Saudi Arabia. Mr Hillhouse had never connected Connolly, W. with the Big Yin. Billy sent him two albums and said no thanks.

CHAPTER 4

Folk

'Why Don't You Go to Dunoon?'
Title of the song Billy Connolly's folk friends believe was his first, Dunoon
being where his mother lived after abandoning him as a child

Before the late 1950s, folk songs were something Scots learnt at school
and quickly forgot. But in the 1950s, a generation of folkies began to
revive old songs and write new, all for live performance. This revival
started in England, but was especially pronounced in Glasgow, where
folk clubs, pubs and parties were all settings for singing of a type that
was earnest and ribald in just about equal parts. Some of the keenest
folkies were refugees from skiffle, and the songs did not often have rigidly
set lyrics, the words being subject to continuous organic change. Boring
verses were lost, sometimes fine phrases reduced to rubbish. Most
importantly, the songs did not exist on radio or TV, which gave the folk
scene an engagingly subversive feel.

Drugs were, of course, rampant, in the folk explosion, as was fairly
indiscriminate sex. But folk audiences, however, were very well
behaved – much better than drunken students. Folk rapidly developed a
political side, with the Communists and the Labour Party – and even
organizations like the Workers' Musical Association – getting in on the
act. The word 'alternative' was first used with something like its modern
meaning to describe this growing folk scene; neither the media nor the
concert booking agencies nor the concert halls were involved. Performers
would simply take a room in a pub or a hotel and get on with it.
Prototype hippies also gravitated towards folk; they would dream of

going to busk in Paris, until De Gaulle cracked down on them and encouraged the police to beat them up. Edinburgh then became an overspill from Paris.

Billy Connolly's musical education and his timing were perfect to ride the crest of the folk boom. He was first introduced to country music as a small boy, when his father used to buy big MGM 78s of Slim Whitman and Hank Williams. He could warble his way through all Hank Williams' songs as a child, and differentiate between 'good country', with as many acoustic guitars as possible, and 'Nashville trash', but had no great inclination to perform. His was not a musical family. 'I was like Les Dawson, every Sunday the family would gather round the piano, wishing one of us could play it. Nobody even sang at parties.

'My father once sent my sister to piano lessons, and he asked me if I wanted to learn the banjo, but he was talking about the guitar. The guitar wasn't very popular when I was a wee boy and everybody called them banjos. And I wanted to say yes but I was embarrassed and I said, "no, no I don't fancy that." And every time I passed Jack's Doll Hospital which was down in Trongate, and where they used to sell guitars and banjos, I'd look and really wish that I'd said yes.'

So his sister would nose around the dolls section of the shop, and he would affect disinterest. But there was unquestionably a deep frozen ability, as well as desire, waiting to be warmed through. The first instrument he bought as a teenager was a mouth organ, on which he learned to blow 'I'm off to Alabama'. 'Come on Billy,' he recalls saying to himself. 'You're showing promise. You taught yourself that, you can't be a dumpling.'

He started watching folk programmes on television, but called folk 'campfire music' because it came out of acoustic banjos and guitars. But, as he recalls it, it was when the Beverly Hillbillies appeared on television that he focussed on the desire to hear, and to play, the bluegrass banjo like they did in the opening music to his favourite show. 'So I went and bought one in the Barras for £2, for fun and because I wanted to make that picking sound, and went to lessons.'

Motivated by no one but himself, this was a remarkable enough thing to do, but playing the banjo was particularly difficult for the young man. He had injured the index finger of his left hand in a minor accident at the shipyard, and did not have quite the rigid strength in the finger to play bar chords, where that finger is required to bridge and hold down all five strings of the instrument. From the start, Billy had to adapt conventional technique, on both banjo and guitar, by using the usually weaker middle finger of his left hand for bar chords.

The effects of the accident aside, his banjo playing soon developed a distinctive style. 'I found great banjo players were getting very little applause while I could go on with the very basic banjo playing and bring the house down by making it funny and giving it a bit of character, and so I just developed my own dynamic style of playing as opposed to the pretty banjo picking. I gave it "laldy", as they say in the business.'

But taking up music was not simply a matter of technicalities; there was a whole new culture to learn, and Billy was a willing, determined pupil. 'I went to George Square, to that wee hut, the information place, and I said, "Are there any folk song clubs in Glasgow?" And they sent me to the folk centre on Montrose Street, which is now closed down unfortunately, and they did banjo lessons. And I ended up as the banjo teacher in there. I wasn't very good but everybody else was rubbish, and so I was the teacher. I had to own up once. I was teaching this guy, and in three weeks he learnt everything I could teach him and I got a bit embarrassed and so did he and he left the class and the following week I left.'

Throughout the early 1960s Billy Connolly continued to be a contradictory soul. Sometimes a loner – he would get on a bicycle and ride round Scotland, a pastime he still enjoys even as a permanent resident of Los Angeles – at other times, he went quite purposefully seeking a pack he could run with.

Before he fell in with the folk scene, he was in a gang which went by the imaginative moniker of The Men. Its members were all (unsurprisingly) men, and had motorbikes, except that Billy's was a puny version of the others' monster models. The machines may have been mean, but the gang itself was relatively placid. They had no desire to get involved with biker subculture and simply spent their time riding around on the bikes, stopping for a cuppa (yes really) and then coming home again to mam, or similar. Of course, there were some rollicking good parties but nothing Meatloaf would have wanted an invitation to.

However, they got noticed, and, although news cuttings and photographs have long since disappeared, Connolly insists that the Scottish tabloid *Sunday Mail* once featured the gang when The Wild One was playing in Glasgow. The photo, he recalls, showed him among a group of leather-clad Glaswegians standing beside a road sign which read: 'Jesus Died For Our Sins.'

But it was when Billy found the folk culture that he really felt here was a club he wanted to be a member of. Alan Cherry, one of the new folk crowd – a loose group of about thirty people – Billy was veering towards, recalls: 'There was just a great crowd of us who all went about together. And we used to go away for weekends, very spontaneous. We'd be in a pub on the Saturday morning, and just decide to go to Devon. We went two or three times up there. We stayed in a youth hostel, or a caravan. We used to have a good tune in the pub up there.'

Cherry, now a quiet, bearded lab technician at Glasgow University, continues: 'We were all hippies. We felt a bit different. We had long hair back in the days when nobody had long hair. You were different, and you knew you were different, and you liked being different. Especially when you were in the crowd. Like kids today do, you felt you were part of something. I knew we were in a great minority then. Nobody bothered about what people did for work or what religion you were, and religion was quite a big thing back then in Glasgow. You could see all the fights in clubs because of religion. But amongst the crowd nobody ever bothered.'

Free love came as part of the hippy package among Glasgow folkies as everywhere else, and Connolly partook of it as much as everyone in the gang. 'I like sex. I think it's great, but I'm not into promiscuity for its own sake. I never pull women or anything,' he said in 1976. 'In my early playing days, before I got married, I was a raver. Every night I'd wake up in a different house. I wouldn't know where I was. But then I got very concerned about being the best, the most original, the most famous, and I knew it had to stop. I'm a very strict father.'

Neither hippies nor folkies were known as sparklingly humorous people, and this is where the Connolly set (being Glaswegians) differed. 'Billy was funny then, but there was such a crowd of us and everybody had such a sense of humour that he didn't shine or stand out to us then,' says Cherry. 'It was the same with the banjo. There were maybe three or four guys who played the banjo a lot better than Billy, but then again you learnt off each other because it wasn't competitive. You were just enjoying yourselves. Now Billy has this charisma, but he wasn't really the guy you'd have expected it all to have happened to. Then he was just one of the boys. Everybody was very quick, very sharp, especially his cousin John Connolly, who was exceptionally so. He's away down in England now, and totally totally changed. He came up for Billy's father's funeral and just did not want to know any of the old crowd . . . married, settled down. He used to be the really wild man. I remember once, John got stopped on the train when he couldn't find his ticket and Billy was laughing, and John said, "I don't know why you're laughing, I gave them your name and address." '

Billy's horizons were expanding thanks to his new friends. One year, he joined Cherry, John McDermott and John Connolly on holiday in France. 'We were there for two or three weeks,' recalls Cherry. 'We'd done wee jobs here or there and lots of drinking, and then Billy arrived, and we spent two or three days with him. We went back with Billy on the boat. From Dover we hitched to London to meet up with folk, but Billy had bought himself a ticket to London. He just jumped on the train.'

The gang, Cherry recalls, hung out in London for weeks, but Billy suddenly announced he was going back to Glasgow. 'I am quite suspicious that he was just on his annual vacation from the shipyards at the time, as opposed to giving it all up and doing his stuff with the boys,' Cherry says. Neither was Billy Connolly in the hitchhiking league even for the long haul back to Scotland. 'You'd put your thumb out in the Finchley Road,' Cherry laughs, 'and he'd say: "I have a ticket." '

Danny Kyle, who was the leading light in guiding Billy round the folk circuit, confirms Cherry's view of Connolly at the time as someone more in the background than the fore. Kyle describes him then as 'a shy welder, a very, very shy young chap'. This hesitancy may have been due to the ultimate seriousness of Connolly's purpose at this time. His banjo tuition – which few of his friends, curiously, even knew he was taking – was to become a much more serious process, both technically and in social terms. In 1964, he went to the Atlantic Folk Club on Clydebank.

'I thought, Oh-ho, this is it. All the women looked like Joan Baez, and all the guys were hairy. All I'd known was suits, ties and Perry Como haircuts.' At the Atlantic, he saw a part-time entertainer, an Englishman called Ron Duff, playing the banjo. Billy told him he had recently bought a banjo and wanted to learn from him. Duff, now an engineering designer, remembers: 'He was a natural. Within weeks he was playing the clubs.''

'When I became a welder in a shipyard I thought everyone else was much the same as I was,' Connolly expounded in an interview in the *Sun* in 1982. 'But they thought I was a loony. It was only when I went into music that a whole new vista opened up because everyone else in folk music was loony too.'

He was enchanted by his hairy new pals; just as he had always tried to find something outside the shipyard to divert and develop him, turning to dancing lessons or the TA, so he saw the folk scene as both an attractive alternative to everyday monotony and as an escape route – one he deeply desired – from his less than satisfying background. All the characters that were to have leading roles in the next chapter in Billy Connolly's life were now forming out of the fog – including his first wife, Iris, whom he met early on and married much later. He became friendly, for example, with a short, dark, thirty-one-year-old man with dark glasses; Billy Johnston was later to be his roadie and general fac-totum – 'The Wee Yin', as he became known. Coincidentally, this other Billy was an electrician at Stephen's Yard, but Connolly first noticed him in the Marland Bar, a decrepit folk venue in Glasgow, and only later recognized him at the yard.

Rapidly becoming a folkie he may have been, but Billy Connolly was by no means some peaceable hippie; he was still a Glasgow shipyard worker in many significant ways. The first time his friend Hugh Jordan, then a teenager, now a journalist and radio personality in Belfast, met Connolly, the singer made something of an impression on him. 'We met in a hotel about twenty-five miles from Glasgow. It had a wee folk club and Billy was in the Skillet-Lickers. I was walking up the stairs and in front of me was a guy who was at school with me, but not a friend of mine, called Brian Donnachie. Billy had long hair at that time, before long hair was kind of normal, and Brian Donnachie walked past him, and as he walked past he stupidly said out of the side of his mouth, "Poof". And Billy turned round and punched him, the hardest fucking punch I have ever seen and he knocked him right down the flight of stairs – bang, whack – and he had a massive bruise on his face. What I found funny about that was ten years later, Brian Donnachie actually looked like Connolly because he had shoulder-length hair and a wee beard like Billy.

'Billy would punch in the jaw very quickly: he was no slouch,' Jordan explains. 'The other incident I remember was in the Green Gate Asian restaurant in Gibson Street in Glasgow. Billy would arrive back in Glasgow very late after a gig and these Indian guys, if they knew you, got you something to eat and allowed you beer, because they wouldn't be licensed. Anyway Billy was very conscious of socialist values and these kind of things and one day they were in for a meal after being out and there were some drunken Glasgow guys in being cheeky to the waiters, and Billy is listening and getting very uneasy with the kinda talk of these guys, and then he can't take it anymore because they were being totally racist in their talk, and Billy just jumped up across the table and in the course of doing so shoved the face of Billy Johnston, who was by now his roadie, in a curry just to get leverage to jump across the table. And he just punched these guys right out of the door. Then, of course, the Indian guys loved him and used to send him Christmas cards and things after that.'

Music, people and unconventional behaviour were obviously the essence of the folk scene, but there were also fascinating new places to explore, right there under Connolly's nose in his home city. The Marland Bar, a peeling, leaning, insanitary structure in George Street, with mushrooms growing up the toilet walls, was just one such. 'I loved it there and learnt a lot about music and playing from the guys there,' Connolly says. The Marland has long since been demolished to make way for a car park. The Scotia Bar was another of these musty folk haunts. This more than 200-year-old pub – the oldest in Glasgow – still stands on Stockwell Street, next to a wholesale fishmongers, and the former site of the music hall that Stan Laurel's father ran. A serious, dark Celtic sort of place, the clone of a thousand Dublin pubs, the Scotia has a beautiful wooden interior, and is full of literary-looking men with beards and woolly hats. The Scotia has done its time as a roughhouse, when it became a Hell's Angel hangout, but is now firmly a folky and literary haunt, with plenty of Billy Connolly memorabilia on its walls. It still holds folk evenings, with instruments available for the asking at the bar.

The plethora of long-haired, beatnik punters in the 1960s folk boom made the Scotia a regular stop-off point for the Drugs Squad. It was they, however, not the folkies who tended to come off worse from visiting the Scotia. Billy remembers how the whole pub would start whistling the 'Z-Cars' theme when the plainclothes policemen came in. Occasionally, the cry from would go up, 'Anyone who can't tap-dance is a poof!', starting a foot-tapping frenzy among the drinkers. In an attempt not to look conspicuous the short-haired straight-looking coppers would tap-dance along too.

But there were other dim, dark subterranean dives that attracted Connolly like a moth in reverse. The folk legend Hamish Imlach founded Glasgow's first all-night club with a friend, Clive Palmer (who played banjo in The Incredible String Band) in 1964. 'It was at a time where you couldn't play music in pubs if you didn't have a licence,' Imlach explains, 'but you could bring your own carry-outs in, which irritated the police no end – we read the small print. We used it from eleven o'clock on a Saturday night till five or six in the morning. People didn't have to leave till the first buses. And there was a coffee bar next door, and everybody would bring a half bottle or a few beers in with them.'

Connolly's own attitude to alcohol tended, in a Glasgow sort of way, towards moderation. He claimed not to be an *enormously* heavy drinker and had a definite distaste for the confirmed alcoholics on the folk circuit, 'who spend all their time on the bottle and you have to peel back the layers of skin to see their eyes'. In his cleaned-up, 1990s incarnation, when he drank no alcohol and would only break his vegetarian diet to eat a little chicken if his daughter made fun of him by saying he was scared of chickens, he said he could barely remember half of his adult life because of drink.

At the time, however, he made a habit of never being drunk on stage. He had a reputation for appearing drunk, but explains that he would sometimes pretend to be, or on one famous occasion, when he was staggering around the stage at the Ashfield Club, was stone cold sober, but had a bad dose of flu.

But that was when he was already a solo performer. Early in the 1960s, before he had even finished his apprenticeship, Connolly was forming and reforming bands. With Ron Duff, Billy and two others, Mick Broderick and Jimmy Swankey, put together a loose combo without a name; then Connolly moved on to play with another banjo player he had met, called Jimmy Steel, who added to his skills. Then Billy took the lead as he had done at school with The Connollys gang, and formed a trio, The Skillet-Lickers, with Jim Carey and George McGovern.

Those who think of Connolly as more an imitator than an innovator might find evidence in The Skillet-Lickers: Billy did not even come up with his own name for the band, and took the name from Gud Tanner's Skillet-Lickers – Billy's attitude being, what would he need the name for anyway, he's dead. And it was with this group that Connolly first found that singing for your supper in clubs could yield more than a complimentary packet of nuts. A friend called Matt McGinn had invited them to play at a gig he had been booked for, and so they took the stuff they had been rehearsing on stage. It was a success: they went down well and were paid a quid (between them). But the scene of their first real professional gig together was in the Paisley Attic (with Jim Steel); it was the first time Billy had performed in front of genuine folky people, and it was obvious that he was a natural. His reputation began to grow.

Although the band ventured down to England to perform ('I slept a fortnight in Preston railway station, which was dead central for getting to gigs,' recalls Connolly), it was Billy who decided to disband The Skillet-Lickers and become a member of The Acme Brush Company – a group defined by its lack of definition. 'They were about twelve complete lunatics, kazoo players and assorted loonies, lonely people and manic depressives from all over the globe, hairies and drop-outs,' Connolly says. 'They had no sort of format. If somebody knew a song, he sang it and everybody stood around. If you knew the tune, you played it. If you knew the chords, you just got on with it. And if you had a kazoo you could hum the tune along. And if you had a harmony, well good on you, you're a permanent member of the band. So I joined this loony outfit, and it gave me a lot of nice bizarre attitudes. It took me away from the serious bit.'

It was still a time of loose, fluid groupings, *ad hoc* bands, *pro tem* travel arrangements, a happy-go-lucky life. Billy regularly called on Michael, his younger half-brother, to get him to drive him to places sixty or seventy miles away in his dilapidated car. They often would not get back until early the next morning. 'Billy would collapse into his bed and I would collapse into work at the Post Office thoroughly knackered,' recalls Michael.

'Billy's first paid booking outside Scotland was at the Black Bull in Cockermouth,' Hamish Imlach says. 'He did the first half and tried to Anglicize his accent which is the only time I've ever heard him doing that. It sounded totally ridiculous, and later I remember saying to him, "What are you doing?" He said, "Nobody will understand what I'm saying." I said, "Well, nobody understands you now." I said, if they get one word in three they'll get it. And he went on the second half and did a normal act and went down a storm.'

The lack of wholemeal-ish seriousness that the Acme Brush Company represented for Billy was crucial; it was his initial reaction to the implicit earnestness of folk, and even though he was many years away from abandoning folk music for comedy, the die was cast. 'By that time I had gone into the silly bands,' he recounted in another of his late-night marathons on Radio Clyde, the radio station he has used through the years almost as a confessional. 'I was just having a laugh, going round the folk festivals, creating hell. I used to go round in a sleeping bag with the bottom just lightly sewn. And when I got up in the morning I would just push my feet through the bottom and walk around the festival in my bag until I completely woke up. And then I would shed my bag like a cocoon and a butterfly would emerge.'

It was the funniness and oddness of the folk crowd that appealed to him now. Clive Palmer, for example, was a Billy sort of man. He had hair down to his waist with a red ribbon in it, a limp from polio and a dachshund he took everywhere. Billy, as keeper of a fairly impressive but notoriously hedge-like head of locks himself, once asked Palmer how he kept his hair so shiny. 'And he said, "I put paraffin on it, I find it keeps the lice down." And I thought, oh my god, who are these people?'

Connolly asked Palmer if he would teach him a bit of banjo, and immediately gained an invitation to 'the weirdest house in the world.

'He lived in this room – the ceilings were about twenty foot high – but he lived in a tent, in the room, because he couldn't heat the place. And I was sitting in this tent, and I thought, what have I done here? Playing the banjo with this loony. A man I really grew to love and respect very deeply. Still do. I believe he's a schoolteacher now somewhere in London, married, gave his banjo away. He makes rolling pins as a hobby. He's a most beautiful loony. He gave Wes Jones, the guitarist, a shoe for his birthday. One shoe. That's what happens when you get stoned at lunchtime.'

The folk scene changed Billy's life in every conceivable way; it even introduced him to a pretty, hippyfied wife, Iris Pressagh, an interior designer from Springburn, Clydebank. It was Ron Duff, Billy's banjo teacher who was, you might say, instrumental in introducing him to his first wife. 'One night in one of the clubs, very early on, a couple of girls asked us back to a party. One of them was Iris, and the other was her best friend in those days, Eileen.' Duff married Eileen.

It was Eileen who initially fancied Billy, and persuaded Iris to ask him to the party. 'But as soon as I saw Iris that was it. It's funny how people fall in love, but right away, I thought: "That's for me." I thought about all the other girls before her and wondered what I'd been doing and suddenly all I wanted was right there. We came from two different worlds, different towns, backgrounds, and yet it worked right from the start.'

Billy's friends thoroughly approved of Iris as well. 'I liked her very much,' says Imlach. 'She was very quiet and withdrawn, but very, very nice. She was a very pretty girl, very tall, very slim, and very shy. She was very, very well liked by everybody. I've never heard anybody putting her down . . . She was really outside it all. I met her at parties, but I don't think she was very interested in coming to the gigs.'

'It was so hard for us before success started happening, but Iris was always right behind me,' Connolly acknowledges. She could have told me to get a regular job, aim for some sort of security. I told her, "I'm going to crack it. It may take a wee time, but just you see." And she hung in there and encouraged and supported me. I was always broke.

Wherever we went she was paying for both of us. She had a good job as an interior designer so that's where any money came from.'

Billy and Iris lived together for four of their eventual sixteen years as a couple, but were in a succession of rented flats before they bought their lochside mansion at Drymen. In 1968, hippy Iris and Connolly had a major row, and she decided to go to France to pick grapes. After about four months, she got a letter saying, 'Come home now or don't bother coming home at all.' As she said on 'This Is Your Life', 'I quit the job and hitchhiked home.' She also proposed to him. 'I remember the moment,' jokes Connolly. 'The test was positive.' Or perhaps he was not joking; they married at Glasgow's Martha Street Register Office on 27 June 1969 and Jamie, named after James Maxton, was born later, in December.

It was in 1965 that events led Billy to a destiny that bore the name 'Humblebums'. First, he took his ten-week welding job in Biafra, returning with a pocketful of money and no desire to work again in the shipyards. Then, he hooked up with a man whose hair was even longer than his own, an ex-rock guitarist, Tam Harvey. The time had come for a change of luck (and, second nature to Connolly, a change of clothes). He put on pink striped trousers and a purple shirt and with Tam, formed a duo called the Humblebums.

'When Billy first started with the Humblebums with Tam Harvey, and they got this gig in Glasgow, we were awed and right jealous,' Alan Cherry says. 'It took the audience about ten minutes to stop laughing at his hair and things.' The new group were big news in Glasgow. They were referred to by the press and disc jockeys as anything from the Bumblebees to the Humble Ones. The misnomers were sometimes deliberate, as the contentious 'bums' element of the name was deemed too *risqué* by some DJs for the listening public – although Billy himself saw it as a reference to tramps. The group looked like making it big. After a meeting with Tom Scott of Major Minor records, Connolly went to London with his self-penned wares but without success – Tam was after a purer country sound, a continual tension between the two. Billy was told to try Transatlantic, but quickly found he had had enough of the record company pass-the-performer game, and did not bother. He didn't have to. Weeks later, a man from the company, Bill Leader, was sent from London to see Connolly and asked him to join Transatlantic. He did.

Providence also stepped in in Paisley. After performing in a charity show, Connolly was approached by a young man who said he wrote songs, too. 'Not another one,' thought Billy, who had been approached by hopeless hopefuls before, but agreed to go to a get-together later that night with him. Connolly was in for a surprise. Whereas his own song-writing was pedestrian bordering on the pretentious (Billy's collection of songs include such singularly uninspiring titles as 'Looking into Your Eyes'), the stranger's songs were impressive (songs spawned from a couple of years spent sitting at home, doing nothing but writing them) and professionally performed on his guitar.

Billy went to Tam with tales of this man's talent and suggested he would be of value to them. So the hopeful, whose name was Gerry Rafferty, joined up with them to make the Humblebums a trio. Although for a while they were joined by Ally Bain on fiddle (who later went on to have a success with bands like Boys of the Lough), these three were the core Humblebums.

They started as they meant to go on, making an impression. In 1965, they played at the Metropole in Glasgow in a folk week which was part of the Commonwealth Festival. What caught the public's ear, however, about the trio, was the funny patter between songs that was rapidly becoming Billy Connolly's trademark. Could it even be, some of the Glasgow folkies wondered, that this bizarre-looking bearded man could be a comedian in his own right? On balance, the prevailing view was, this was unlikely.

The tide of favour started to turn against Tam as Gerry began to make his mark on the group with his obvious talent. Tam Harvey's guitar playing was, according to the other two, not moving on with the developing music. After a short time, Tam Harvey left ('one of those unfortunate things', according to Connolly), leaving Connolly and Rafferty to make a couple of successful LPs and become, probably, the most popular folk duo in Scotland.

Folk musicians at work rival rabbits in their ability to propagate. Although some songs begin with a pair of performers, by the time the final chord is struck it's not surprising to find another fifteen people on stage, contributing to the cacophony. It was in this tradition that the Humblebums duo eventually expanded, recruiting four more members, including a woman organist and a man who worked in the Transatlantic stockroom on guitar. There was also a window cleaner, although no Formby-style ukelele. It was a motley six-piece crew, but they had a ball on their travels, the tour transport not a luxury coach but a minivan in which fights over who got to sit in the front passenger seat were a kind of irritating tradition.

Connolly's career had its ups and downs. It is a popular youth dream at some time to grow up to enjoy a wild lifestyle; Connolly had dreamt it earlier than most, and was now living it – just because they were folkies, his band did not forego the traditional rock traditions in favour of camomile tea and friendship bracelets – they were, after all, Glaswegians. Billy took great pleasure in gigging around and partying through the night, but it was to take its toll on even this toughest of nuts. In 1967 the exhausting on-the-road routine caught up with Connolly, when he contracted pleurisy and pneumonia. 'I had just run myself right into the snow, down on my hands and knees, being the Wild Raver,' he later rued. 'The light went out. And I had this uncanny feeling that I was going to die, because I was coughing blood all over the place, couldn't breathe properly, my legs wouldn't work.'

There was some astonishing success to come before the band broke up in 1971. The Humblebums had several hits, and even an appearance on the Royal Command Performance. But the Rafferty/Connolly partnership was never a match made in music heaven. It was more a battle of ideals: Rafferty's to hone his song-writing craft in search of a quiet life, and Billy's to wait for the song to finish so he could start on the funnies. As Michael McDonagh, then the band's manager, told the Glasgow *Evening Times*: 'He was always exceedingly funny, although actually quite shy in terms of the audience, but his relationship with Gerry was less than comfortable. It was magical when it worked well but the chemistry wasn't quite right. Billy had very funny songs and Gerry was trying to be Paul McCartney and sing poetic love songs.'

Rafferty was a painfully shy man who often played with his back to the audience and, ideally, would play songs without a break to avoid the need to speak to the public. He pleaded with Billy to shut up, but the gaps between the songs gradually grew longer than the numbers themselves.

Just when Connolly finally realized his audience appreciated the quips more than his quick-fingered banjo prowess is disputed. The development was most likely gradual and organic, creeping up on the Humblebums without the band's truly noticing it. Connolly puts it down to a specific moment long before the Humblebums, at the first folk club gig he did, at a club called The Attic in Paisley, where he was playing a set of Irish songs with another of his banjo gurus, Jimmy Steel. The first two numbers went without a hitch, although Connolly was shaking with nerves.

'But the third thing I did was called St Brendan's Isle. It was about sailors on a sailing ship way back coming to an island and all stepping on it and they think the ship is sailing away from them but they're on the back of a whale and it's swimming away. I'd done about a verse and a half and I forgot the words. I just sat there, and Jimmy was going diddley-dum-de-dum-de-dum, de-diddley-dum-de-dum-de-dum, waiting for me to come in, so I'm going rickelty-tickelty, rickelty-tickelty on the banjo and staring at everybody in a cold panic. And I couldn't stop going rickelty-tickelty, rickelty-tickelty and I said, "I've forgotten the words," and everybody burst out laughing.

'So then I said, "It'll come back in a minute. Hang about, just talk among yourselves. It's something about a monster or something," and they all started to laugh. And something inside my brain must have gone click, you've missed your vocation in life, this is it. So I flanneled about, just chatting while the diddley-dum was going on, and when it came back I waited for the right diddley-dum and came back into the song and they applauded, and I finished my song, and we brought the house down, more for my bravery and my cheek than my capabilities in the pop music scene.'

But however it happened, once the realization set in that it was comedy rather than music at which Connolly would ultimately shine, he seemed quite consciously to set about turning Rafferty's serious presentation of his songs into the musical interlude for his comedy. 'Gerry was a better musician than me, but I was better at stage craft. It just couldn't work any more. I just had to get funny. You can't go on singing about dead sailors forever. You have to own up after a while,' was how Connolly put it later. Elsewhere he spoke about tiring of being one of 'four pullovers singing songs about dead sailors'. In the end, it was no surprise that Rafferty, with minor celebrity status and a classic song, 'Baker Street', behind him, eventually went off to form Stealers' Wheel, while Connolly bit the bullet and went it alone as a broke comedian living on a diet of booze and grilled porridge. As soon as the record company stopped their retainer, Billy slipped back to his not-so-distant impoverished days, so broke he had to borrow the train fares and rely on friends for lifts.

Yet not everyone on the scene believed Connolly was as keen as he appeared to 'graduate' from music to comedy. Hamish Imlach, who knew him intimately at the time, says: 'The key to Billy, I think, is that he always wanted to be a musician and song-writer and never a comedian. He fought against that, and he really gave his best shot with Gerry Rafferty, and it was inevitable the songs he wrote were compared to the ones Gerry wrote. Gerry as a song-writer was in a different league to Billy, and Billy as an entertainer is in a different league to Gerry, but I don't think Billy thought that way at the time.'

The split with Rafferty signalled anything but instant stardom. Billy stayed with a friend in Finchley, in the suburbs of north London, and readjusted to living the hard life. His first solo effort was to try to make it in London as folk singer, and he failed. He returned to Glasgow, Iris and Jamie, £500 in debt. 'I didn't know how I was going to pay for my next meal. I didn't even have enough money to buy a decent pair of shoes and had to kid myself that walking around barefoot or in a broken pair of sandals was trendy.'

But when times were hard, Billy took his lead from the Galabunzie man, and busked wherever his travels took him, from Glasgow to Denmark. 'Eventually, when I wasn't getting any work, I wrote thirteen letters to folk club organizers, saying that I would play for just my expenses, provided they would book me if they liked me. I got four replies and that was really a crucial time for me, because after that I never looked back.' For the first twelve weeks, in which he got no work at all, London managers and agents avoided him because they had never seen anything like him, a hybrid folk music and comedy act presented by an incomprehensible man who looked like Rasputin. But the letter-writing campaign began to pay off. He got a solo booking in Musselburgh, just outside Edinburgh – a bit closer to home than he had in mind, but he was pleased enough, even though the gig was not hugely successful. (He returned to the town in 1977, as a big-time star, and enjoyed the honour of being picketed by the fundamentalist preacher, Pastor Jack Glass. Glass, head of the Protestant Twentieth Century Reformation Movement, has been a sort of good luck symbol for Billy over the years, his ranting opposition to the act increasing in direct proportion to its success.)

Billy's extraordinary self-belief was sustaining him. Something had to: in bald terms, he was a few months off his thirtieth birthday, had effectively thrown away a reasonable career (two, if you include the welding, as Connolly's father did) and was now unknown outside Scotland, and barely well known inside. Every prospective gig meant laboriously talking – or failing to talk – a manager into taking a risk. The sort of people and places Billy was dealing with seemed to be more poor man's Vaudeville than Vegas: and, even though folk music always seems to conjure up the ambience of a late-night lounge wherever it is played, these spots were prime examples of small-town mentality, even when located in major cities. Just when he was coming to a punchline, and a few people in the audience were talking a bit, the MCs would interrupt loudly with a confidence-inducing line like, 'Now come on, give the man a chance.' Before a gig, the management would take great pride in their facilities, and not just the PA but the toilets too, taking time to tell Billy and fellow performers the exact economic value of said venue's attributes. When first playing at the Manchester Free Trade Hall, Billy was intrigued by the coming attraction of David Webster from Oban with his fascinating act – a slide show about the Falls of Muchart – and the even more fascinating fact that the act would attract quite a crowd.

After Musselburgh, which was his first trial solo comedy concert, Connolly quickly went to hone his skill in front of the sharpest of audiences with a short tour of the Northern (English) clubs where, he says, 'I grew up, entertainment-wise.' ('In the early days,' says Danny Kyle, Scottish radio personality and childhood friend, 'Billy was very, very nervous. He kept breaking strings and to fill in he used to talk. They say there are a million Billy Connollys down the shipyards. But

there aren't. The man is a genius, the world's first verbal cartoonist.')
The show was now called 'Connolly's Glasgow Flourish', and was also
well received in Scotland. After a show in Glasgow, he met the poet
Tom Buchan.

'I asked him how one writes a play. I invited him to collaborate with
me, which he did, and the result was *The Great Northern Welly Boot Show.*
The basic ideas were mine. Tom Buchan did most of the script, all the
dialogue. I invented the situations and did all the songs and the music. It
was a huge success everywhere, even in London, but died in Glasgow
because it was very bad in Glasgow.' This rock musical was inspired by
the upper Clyde shipbuilders, had a political edge that made the char-
ismatic left-wing shipyard hero Jimmy Reid a friend of Connolly, won
over middle-class audiences at the 1972 Edinburgh Fringe Festival and
the Young Vic in London – and led to a recording contract with Polydor.

Billy Connolly was growing out of the cosy folk scene. 'I jokingly say
it was the first time he got as much money as I did and it was the last
time I got as much as he did,' says Hamish Imlach. The *Welly Boot Show*
was to be the lynchpin of a 1971 Clyde Festival, designed by various
Glasgow personalities as a rival to the Edinburgh Festival. If Edinburgh
got the Bolshoi, Glasgow would respond in kind, by getting two or three
ballerinas performing at a miners' Welfare. 'It was an over-ambitious
fiasco from beginning to end,' says Imlach, 'with glossy posters going
up in New York and Los Angeles and Tokyo at the airports, which was
ridiculous. I mean nobody was coming to Glasgow for a totally unknown
festival, and basically the whole thing was a shambles. But it was very
good for Billy.'

Other exciting developments were crowding in on Connolly, although
one, an American tour, led to one of those soul-destroying, life-defining
moments that, in a perverse way, can give a performer the inner impetus
to drive his career on. In 1970, Hamish Imlach got an offer from Boston,
to play the Irish clubs there. His agent, who also worked for Connolly,
tried to sell Imlach plus Connolly and another Scottish performer as a
package; the Americans responded by booking all three for a month
each.

Imlach went first. 'The places,' he recollects, 'were full of awful
middle-class, middle-aged Irish-Americans, jacket and tie to get in,

Mickey Mouse sort of people, not even liking real music. There was a group there from Cork who would do a sort of Butlins programme: "Hold your arms up and let's see the perspiration, missus." And they'd fall about. There was a very clever song-writer that Billy met there for the first time called Shay [Seamus] Healey, and Shay had written some very funny songs and Billy recorded a couple of them. Shay already had a TV programme in Ireland before he went out there in the Sixties, but was really struggling to get across at this place, The Harp and Bard.

'Billy went out and obviously they couldn't understand him. Even if you speak BBC English they find it difficult to understand in the United States. To stop yourself repeating everything you say time and time again, you adopt an American accent. Billy had a very hard time. He wasn't going down at all well. But there was one time he was playing a small place and there were some guys who were really rowdy. Billy came off and one of them said to him: "I think it's really good." And Billy said, "Thank you." And the guy said, "That you're off." Billy's very quick-tempered. I could see him smacking a guy for that. Well, he didn't, and it must have gnawed at him because years later he told me that. Me, I can laugh things off like that, but with Billy I know it would rankle and rankle and rankle, which for me would explain why he was so determined later on to make it in the States.'

Back in Scotland, however, things were going well. It was when the Big Yin was first seen, in his comic capacity, on the small screen that the kind of success Connolly dreamt about as a child, as a teenager and as a Clydebank welder, started to gel. He was invited onto a local TV chat show called 'Dateline Scotland', presented by Bill Tennant. A guest failed to show up. Amidst the panic, Reggie Bosanquet, the oddly cult newsreader of the time, who was also appearing on the show, reported from backstage that Billy Connolly's storytelling was so good that he should be booked as a talker in his own right. As Tennant recalled, 'It was early afternoon, and rather difficult to pick someone else out of the air at ten minutes' notice. We were left with Billy Connolly or nothing. But it was a forty-minute show, and that's a lot of programme to fill by yourself. I could feel the sweat running down my face as the red light went on. And Connolly talked. He filled it with these funny and fresh stories of shipyards and Glasgow life. I think that show made him.'

CHAPTER 5

Diced Carrots

'A Billy Connolly album will automatically enter the charts and do as well, if not better than the latest release of many of Britain's supergroups. He is the first comedian to represent the rock generation.'
Michael Parkinson on Billy Connolly

What Billy Connolly *was* in the early 1970s is open to debate. Although he was credited with having invented alternative comedy, which he acknowledges he 'probably did' he felt at the time, and continues to feel in retrospect, like a rock star. Alternative or not, what he was unquestionably was the first comedian of the rock era, a comic who was a loudmouth, who stayed out all night and thumped people.

It was in 1973 that Billy decided to devote himself almost solely to comedy. 'I got a wee bit frightened, the only thing left was to do it all again. I've got a wife and two kids and various things that crawl and walk and I'd hate to end up a forty-year-old folk singer and somebody's father,' he told the *Guardian* a year into his time as a comedian.

After the *Welly Boot Show* proved to be more than a one-night wonder, folk had gradually become less essential to Connolly's success – Humblebums records being demoted to a rereleased cashing-in attempt on his comic prowess. Connolly had, according to the *Guardian*, 'a fast-growing word-of-mouth reputation'. Early in that year had come a watershed show at the Glasgow Pavilion, the paper continued, 'after which everything fell into place for Connolly, and he proceeded to pack out every theatre in every city in Scotland'. The line between what he saw himself as was increasingly blurred.

'When I used to tour the folk clubs in the Sixties my humour was always there, but I tried to keep it under control. I would say to an audience, "I know I'm funny, but I want you to listen to this song." In the end I decided that being funny was what I was best at and I had to stop kidding myself. I didn't know where G-minor was on the guitar and cared even less,' he said in 1978.

When he saw himself referred to in newspapers as 'a comedian', he would do a double take, because he still thought he was a funny folk singer, 'too hairy for cabaret, and far too scruffy and wild for variety theatre'. Even when he became a fully fledged comedian, he still sang songs as part of his set, though he was to end up not playing down but mocking his past: 'Songs about dead life-boatmen, how did people put up with that?' he asked on stage at Hammersmith Odeon in 1991. Connolly's tendency to disparage periods of his life he once held dear seems worthy of being described as a 'trait' when it is remembered that the shipyards have also been singled out for, if not actual maligning, a marked lack of reverence. There were some that saw this as his potential nemesis.

The folkies began to resent their superstar a little, a little that they articulated amply in the media, particularly in the late 1970s. In his book, Duncan Campbell identified them as 'perhaps the most critical of all', their view of Connolly centring on wanting Billy to 'come home' to the Scottish folk scene. Contact on both Connolly's and the folkies' side was reduced to soundbites fired via the media. Billy himself turned virtually vitriolic in Duncan Campbell's book, so much so that his most fervent protestations seemed only to confirm the degree to which he cared about the issue. In the book, Connolly referred to 'The stuff I get from the folkies who think I've sold out, all the "Come back home, Billy, we still love you" rubbish that they keep giving you.

'What folkies think about me having a great big orchestra behind me is not a matter of the greatest importance to me. As far as they're concerned, you can have fiddles playing with you, but not violins. I do a show to please myself, not to please the folkies. And if they think that having strings and bass is schmaltzy, I don't care. If I want a big bloody orchestra, I'll have one,' he fulminated.

79

The 'sellout' question never quite left Connolly. As late as 1990, Alan Franks wrote in *The Times* that 'his early days in the folk clubs, full of smoke and democracy' to some extent remain 'his spiritual locus, a fact easily overlooked by the vast majority of his international audience who only knew him once the monologues between the songs – he was never much of a singer – had expanded into an act in their own right. He still reveres the work of Pete Seeger, the American banjo-player, Hamish Imlach, the Scottish folk-singer, and Jake Thackray, the Yorkshire-born songwriter, whom he regards as a genius.'

The people in Scotland in the 1970s who were determined to make their apocalyptically bearded hero a Scottish prophet put him in an impossible position. They reckoned, as do all followers of a cult person when he unexpectedly hits the big time, that they had made him, so he belonged to them. He refused to see it that way. As he grew in stature, so too did the cries of 'too big for his roots'. And if circumstances were placing Connolly further and further away from his Scotland, so too were those compatriots who made him feel uncertain of the welcome he might receive on his return there.

For another past that Connolly was leaving behind as fast as he could was the idea of being a devout Scot. By 1974, Billy Connolly was so popular in Scotland that a fan gained fame for five minutes or so by having Billy's autograph tattooed onto his arm. Connolly's celebrity at home knew no bounds. Willing party or not, he had become the flagbearer of all things Scottish. Connolly was hailed as an emissary for his compatriots, with his ventures across the border treated less as ambassadorial missions than raiding parties. The Scottish view was that Connolly wasn't knocking at England's door, he was barging in.

The problem came when he began to realize that he really liked England. His attitude to England at the time was very much like his (and that of other very different performers, notably John Cleese) later attitude to America. England then represented a new, open-minded world, un-fuddled by pointless theological debate over whether he had or had not sold out the Scottish folk scene, the shipyards, or whatever. The English also seemed to understand his accent (or politely pretended to), as he had discovered from his first attempts to perform down south, when an attempt to Anglicize merely confused and disappointed English audiences.

Billy the conqueror's second coming in Britain in the mid-1970s coincided with a new influx 'abroad' of raw Scottish talent. The Bay City Rollers (described by Billy as 'smashing wee blokes and a smashing wee band') were causing a generation of tartan-clad teenies to swoon; Pilot topped the British charts with 'January' (albeit belatedly) in February 1975; the Average White Band from Dundee stormed America with a number one single and double album. In the *Daily Mail*, Anne Nightingale gushed about 'Scotland the rave!'

But from the outset, he was uneasy about being cast in too nationalistic a light. At the end of 1977, he told the *News of the World*: 'I've never worn a kilt seriously in my life. I'm a great patriot, but I think something like sporran rot set in. The trouble is that most comedians from Scotland never tried to appeal to anyone else outside the country. They'd come on with their kilts and sing Scottish songs. That's not me.' (A few years later, he confessed to having gone down the professional Scotsman route, if only mildly: 'I must admit, I prostitute it a little, because not only am I the hairy comedian who used to wear the bananas, I'm the Scottish one, and everybody remembers me, because there's not that many of them, Scottish comedians travelling round the world.)

As his confidence grew, so did Connolly's irritation at the claims to ownership laid upon his person. He was determined not to become a cause celebrity, and would bristle at the very mention of the Scottish Nationalist Party, which had been courting him assiduously for years. He treated their overtures with suspicion, and this suspicion soon turned to loathing when he realized that they viewed his success in England, which they could not turn to their advantage, as a betrayal. Throughout his career he has had nothing but contempt for them, calling them 'hairies in kilts' and 'fascists'.

The point was, his driving ambition would prove irreconcilable with too political a stance. (In his latter years, he has conveniently become a self-styled anarchist, a non-philosophy which has proved a safe haven for many a confused ex-socialist). Around the age of eighteen, Connolly gave up his Catholic faith for ever, and took up left-wing causes instead. In 1974, he was proud and happy to promote the Labour Party and was often pictured accompanying Harold Wilson and Willie Ross during their election campaigns. He also turned out in Ross and Cromarty for

Brian Wilson. But the need to stand up and be counted soon sat down again. Only a year later, he was much more cautious about becoming a spokesman for the trendy Left.

His politics would remain strictly non partisan, his nationalism, a love of his country, but not tinged with a sense of Scotland being superior to anywhere else. 'On stage I was the first of Scottish professional entertainers to say anything political, to make a fool of religious bigotry. I did a thing about my private parts and it wasnae dirty. I bet I get a bigger cross section in my audience than Victor Borge. I use the same words, I'm the same person as that wee bloke in the street. I took that language to the London Palladium and there was a new surge of pride in Glaswegians.'

Even if he was moving his epicentre remorselessly south, he could never be accused of hypocrisy. Will Fyfe, a Harry Lauder-type entertainer of previous decades, earnt transatlantic fame for the song 'Glasgow Belongs To Me'. The problem was, it didn't at all – he was from Dundee. Connolly, a Partick man to the core, did the reverse and started to feel, to his sadness, no longer quite part of Glasgow once he was starting to enjoy success in England. When, much later, success in America came his way, he felt free to go the whole hog and announce in Chicago, 'I'm Scottish and it was a complete mistake. I would be delighted to be a Bosnian.'

Connolly laid his ideas on Scottish patriotism on the line on BBC1's 'Checkpoint' in August 1978, arguing that Scots needed to shed their insularity in order to make their mark: ' "Scottishness", in my honest opinion, has been growing for a while. Scotsmen used to look upon themselves as the perennial outsiders, but, in the last ten years, there has grown a new awareness of being Scottish – not quite the same thing as the black people feel about black pride, and black power, and "black is beautiful", but almost. But this new awareness of being Scottish is not a nationalist or a patriotic thing; it is a refusal to stay a perennial outsider, to want to be involved in the big league ... Speaking personally as a Scot, I do not have any nationalist, patriotic feelings about Scotland. Indeed, I have much more in common with someone from Liverpool or Newcastle than I have with someone from, say, Inverness, Skye or Fort William, because I am, basically, a city-dwelling British person.'

But when the expansion into England was beginning in the 1970s, the Scottish *Guardian* writer Lindsay Mackie had been concerned that Connolly's humour would not travel outside his own corner of Britain. 'Part of the wild success of his act now,' she wrote, 'is that Connolly takes his audience on a guided tour of their communal past, and sometimes their present. He chronicles the devastation of the Scottish urban childhood, sadistic primary school teachers, and most members of his audiences have had one of those, the odd names kids have had to bear – "Tyr-o-n-e!" – the strange clothes they've worn, the agonies of teenage sex – "kissing for THREE HOURS!" – the fragile virility of boys in a society which demands men to be ostentatiously tough, hard and which fosters gang culture.

'It is disconcerting,' Mackie concluded, 'to play his latest LP to Londoners and Americans and be incapable with laughter, only to hear them say that they understand about one word in fifteen. To give an example, Billy Connolly does one sketch about a minister – the Scots love religious jokes – and his sermon. "I often think that life is like an ashtray – full of wee dowts (dogends)." Hands up all those who didn't get it. But that joke almost stopped the show in Edinburgh.' He had already played such unlikely venues as the Tivoli Gardens in Copenhagen, she wrote, but would he be able to fill the Palladium? We would soon see.

But, although Connolly was strictly a cult phenomenon in the south, the English seemed to lap up this perplexing material, much the same as they would devour American comedy – Woody Allen, for example – without necessarily understanding it all. It drove Connolly to become a self-confessed Anglophile. He had been reading P.G. Wodehouse, Bunter, Biggles and The Famous Five since childhood; the fact that the England portrayed in such works did not really exist hardly bothered him; he still thinks he can discern it in individuals he meets. In an interview with Jeremy Isaacs in 1994, he mentioned John Mortimer in this respect; Isaacs as a fellow Scot was too polite to ask if this Anglophilia perhaps explained his love of the royal family, a characteristic which attracts and repels Scots in equal measure. In 1993, meeting privately at the House of Commons with Brian Wilson, formerly a radical Scottish journalist, now a Labour MP, Connolly astonished his friend by asking out of the blue, 'Have you met Charles?' Wilson wondered who Connolly was referring to, until the sovereign dropped. 'No I haven't, Billy,' he replied. 'Oh, that's such a shame,' Connolly replied, 'You'd *love* him, you'd absolutely *love* him.' Wilson was left wondering if, as a left-wing Scottish Labour MP, he truly would.

His Anglophilia was enhanced by the rough reception he was still provoking on occasion in Scotland from even non-folkie, comedy audiences. Hecklers were always so much a part of the Connolly experience that they sometimes seemed to have been planted (he developed a neat way with them: 'You should get an agent, pal. Why sit there in the dark handlin' yersel' ', was a favourite). Hugh Jordan recalls, however, what a really bad night for Billy would be like. 'This would have been in '73 just as he was knocking on the door of the Big Time. We went down to a place called the Victoria Hall in Helensburgh as part of a thing organized by Radio Clyde. Billy was the top of the bill, and he and I had travelled down. But it was hick town, not used to concerts or anything like that, and Billy went on and he was dying a death. There were hecklers in the audience, but they weren't normal hecklers. Billy would say, "What was that?", and they wouldn't say anything so he couldn't react to it.

'So he walked off and the guy that was running it came to me and said, "Would you ask him to go back on?" And I went, "Billy, come on," and eventually I had to explain to him, "Billy, your fucking dad is in the audience." His father had got the train down from Glasgow twenty miles away, went into a wee pub on his own, had a couple of drinks, walked up and paid to get in to hear Billy, just because that was the type of guy he was. He wouldn't have troubled Billy. So he went back on the stage and he said – I'll never forget his first line to the audience – "I'm back on because the guy asked me to come back on. When you are down here in Helensburgh, it's not as if you can fuck off to your casino." He was treating the audience with contempt, but he went through with it. Billy, his father and myself went for a couple of pints after the show and then we drove home. The only reason he went back on the stage was that I told him that his dad was in the audience.'

But it would be incorrect to suggest that Connolly was, because of a surprisingly good debut in England, becoming one of those products that every country exports, but never touches at home. He owed allegiance to

Scotland and it to him. In a telling 1974 article in the magazine *Glasgow News*, Connolly told Alex Fraser: 'I need an audience. I need to see the people there.' And, Fraser commented, 'There can be no more satisfying feeling to an audience than the knowledge that they are, in a sense, contributing to the success of the entertainer they have paid to see ... One of his most valuable assets is his instantly identifiable mode of speech; here is a voice that hasn't been laundered by elocution lessons; here is an entertainer who, one feels, will always manage to resist the sham personality grafting operations of the showbusiness manipulators. There is no "Me star, you pay" attitude from Billy. Quite the opposite. More like (voice tinged with incredulity) "Me, star?" '

Scotland, as we would say now but not then, knew where he was coming from. Charles Gillies of the Glasgow *Evening Times*, wrote of his 1974 show in Glasgow, 'He has learnt his art in clubs – and in the past two years has accumulated a veritable army of followers. In his debut as principal at the Pavilion Theatre, Glasgow, for this week and next the "sold out" notices have already been put up. Billy Connolly is not in the traditional mould of the Scots comic. It is true that he sings, accompanying himself on both banjo and guitar – but his songs are parodies of well-known tunes to which he has put his own words. Each one, from "Last Train to Glasgow Central" to "Saltcoats at the Ferr", and "Nine-and-a-half Guitars" is greeted by the audience with rapture. He does not rely on "front cloth" jokes – rather he tends to tell stories, the punch line of which is often lost through the inability of the audience to restrain themselves from squeals of laughter at the build-up. Those who think of him as a successor to Lex McLean or Glen Daly might be disappointed. However, he is fresh and he is undoubtedly talented. He is also astute in that he has gathered around him a talented cast of musicians, singers, and attractive dancers for his first real theatrical adventure.'

In the summer of that year, we see some indication of how integral a part of Scottish culture Billy Connolly had become, almost whether he liked it or not. The Scottish football team manager, Willie Ormond, sent a telegram from Munich to Connolly's terraced house in Glasgow asking him to come to Germany, all expenses paid, as soon as possible to try to cheer up the Scottish World Cup squad, whose results and morale were sagging. This was not some daft new-man management wheeze – the players had requested Connolly's presence to make them laugh at a time when their own soccer performances were not doing so. Billy came, and tickled them sufficiently for Scotland to get through the first qualifying round.

For his English fans, when it came to the nationalism of football, his rampant Anglophilia would be suspended. In a BBC interview transcribed in the *Listener*, he explained, 'There are many reasons for the bigoted Scottish football supporter. There is bigotry in the club sense. You have Rangers who will never employ a Catholic, or who say they will, and then do not; and you have Celtic, who have a history of Catholicism and lots of wee priests in the stand. But when it comes to the Scottish international team, I hope that its supporters stay bigoted. I hope that, even if we lost the national championships [the now defunct Home Internationals] ten years in a row, we would still believe Scotland to be the best team. Scottish football brings out a lot of strength in Scottish people, and a lot of aggression and humour. Sometimes, though, this aggression can look humorous to a Scotsman and desperately dangerous to an Englishman. My manager once told me that he witnessed an incident outside a chip shop in Glasgow where three totally innocent English were coming along singing, "England, England!", and there was a big drunk with a fish supper in his hand, glowering at them, with his eyebrows down to about the nostril area. He waited until they got exactly level with him, dipped into his fish and chips and rammed a chip into the ear of one of the guys, stopping the song. Now, to an Englishman, that might seem desperately aggressive, but every time I think of it I get hysterics.'

Connolly's growing cross-border success in 1974 said much for the hype-ing skills of his manager, a famous Glasgow entrepreneur called Frank Lynch. Lynch's father had run Irish dance halls and bookies' shops in Glasgow and given him a pub. He made a roaring success of the pub, then sold it, and started buying up old dance halls and bingo halls and making them into theatre clubs, which he ran along with a fruit shop and a hairdressing salon. Lynch is widely acknowledged as the man who brought Billy from the folk clubs to the big time, the first to say, 'If you want to book Billy Connolly it will cost you £100; it's not £15 any more.' As one of his activities, Lynch had promoted a comedian called

Lex McLean, who was not known outside the west of Scotland. McLean's material would appear tame now, and it never worked on TV, but for two or three months every year he could fill the Glasgow Pavilion. Yet, working only Glasgow, he could walk away with a couple of hundred thousand a year. McLean had died, Lynch was looking for the perfect replacement – and Billy Connolly fitted the bill.

Lynch did all the big things – notably getting Connolly into the London Palladium in January 1975 by filling the house with every Scot in London – but he was also the prime mover in the detailed business of building Connolly's image in Scotland. He created the Billy hysteria, whereby if you picked up any newspaper, you could be sure of finding Billy detailing his favourite recipe, and, if it was the tabloid *Sunday Mail*, you would run into a Big Yin cartoon strip. Billy actually wrote this at first, with illustrations by an old friend from the folk scene, Malcolm (Malky) McCormick. Later in the strip's two and a half year life it was written, too, by McCormick. The strip came to a sticky end and a fallout between Billy and his friend; Connolly, who held the copyright, told his lawyers to get The Big Yin cartoon killed off within a month. Frank Lynch issued a statement saying, 'Billy thought his caricature had become the vehicle for certain views that he doesn't necessarily share.'

What had happened was that the early, folkie Billy, as represented by McCormick, crashed head-on with the superstar, take-me-more-seriously, new-model Connolly. The strip was lumpen and crude, not very funny and quite surplus to Connolly's needs, as he finally realized when he was in Edinburgh for rehearsals of his play, *When Hair Was Long and Time Was Short*, for the Festival. He had been shown a book compilation of the strip called *Bring on the Big Yin*, the cover of which had incensed him.

On it, 'The Big Yin' had a tattoo on his arm reading 'Scotland For Ever' and 'Doon Wirra English'. *Bring on The Big Yin* also poked fun at royalty. The Queen, on her first appearance, says, 'Ahm knackered wi' a' this rulin'.' Prince Charles bemoans the fact he can't find a bride, and the Duke of Edinburgh (aka Chooky Embra) called his wife 'Hen'. Princess Anne recites a poem which concludes: 'It upset my mum, when ah hurtit ma bum, an' shouted BLOODY HELL.' Although 40,000 copies had been printed, Connolly's lawyers asked William Collins publishers not to release the book.

'I don't hate the English and I want that off the cover,' he demanded. Collins reminded him that he'd seen proofs earlier and hadn't objected then. Connolly admitted that he had not got round to reading them. And when the publishers pointed out that the cartoon had already appeared in the *Sunday Mail*, he said that it had been in context then, on the way to the Scotland–England rugby international at Twickenham. 'It is all right to say I hate the English when I am going to Wembley or Murrayfield,' he explained, 'but, out of context, it makes me out to be some kind of racialist and a Scottish nationalist. I am neither.' When Collins suggested that they 'put a purple patch' over the offending tattoo for a cost of about £1,000, Connolly offered to pay for it. On the Sunday after the tattoo row, one of the *Sunday Mail* drawings showed the Big Yin with a tattoo reading: 'I luv masel [myself].'

It was ironic that it was the *Sunday Mail* which was later to be the target of Connolly's fullest loathing when it published a famous interview with his estranged mother. At the time, the Big Yin strip was a major weapon in the circulation battle between the *Mail* and its rival, the *Sunday Post*; in its day, the hapless Big Yin cartoon helped the *Mail* climb within an unprecedented 300,000 of the *Post*'s million sales.

In the meanwhile, Billy, the *Sunday Mail* and its esteemed readers were all one happy spiritual family. McCormick recalled in the *Sunday Mail* in 1988 just how revered Billy was by working-class Scots at his carousing height. The two had gone to London for a Home International match. 'The night before the game, we were in an east-end pub when the Motherwell coach-load arrived. It was like they'd encountered God when they saw Billy. He was engulfed and signed autographs, bought drinks and had them falling about with laughter. They adored him. I remember great bevvies with the man, because he was terrific company. Once, we weaved our way from the whisky pleasures of Dick's Bar in Broomielaw, then lay face up on a summer's night and serenaded the offices.'

On another occasion, when they were being driven up Byres Road, 'Billy suddenly jumped out at Tennant's Bar and began to direct the traffic. I watched helpless as the traffic chaos mounted. Then the cops arrived ready to huckle away the culprit, but when they saw Billy – by then a crumpled heap in the road – they asked him for his autograph!'

Billy was rarely out of the news now; 1974, when he was thirty-two, was his heyday, as well as being the year his second child, daughter Cara, was born. In June, at the same time as his call up for the World Cup, his debut double album, 'Solo Concert' came out, its release delayed because the album sleeve was green, and Connolly, as the *Evening Times* commented, made 'almost a fetish of being non-sectarian'. The album included the controversial Crucifixion routine, and Billy found, not unexpectedly, that he had some explaining to do.

The sketch was based on the premise that the Last Supper took place in Gallowgate Glasgow, and that Jesus and the Disciples were all Glaswegians. This challenged what everybody, especially Scottish Presbyterians, knew for certain – that the Last Supper took place in Galli*lee* and that the Lord and his followers all spoke English like Derek Nimmo. Whether the quarter-hour sketch was blasphemous or not depends on your theological viewpoint; to be fair to the devout, it is unlikely that the Crucifixion story was ever supposed to include drunken Apostles, be funny and arouse raucous laughter and cheering. On the other hand, Connolly's Crucifixion at no time suggests that Jesus is not the son of God. It is not exactly reverential, but there is a powerful sense throughout it that Connolly knows his biblical onions, and then some. Any good parodist (like Les Dawson playing the piano) needs to know what he is mocking, and it is clear that Connolly did. The most curious aspect of the sketch is probably that throughout it, Billy referred to Jesus Christ as The Big Yin (the cult Glasgow name for Connolly – literally the Big One), which some may take to indicate that he was beginning to feel a little more self-confident than he used to.

Although a large number of Catholics were not best pleased by the Crucifixion routine, it fell to the extreme anti-Catholic Pastor Jack Glass to lead religious opinion against the sketch. 'In this cassette recording,' Glass complained, 'Connolly depicts Christ as wearing a jaggy bunnet and entering a pub, steamin' drunk. Christ is further depicted as urinating on a Roman soldier who pierced him with a spear on the Cross. We call upon every Christian who loves his Lord and Saviour Jesus Christ to organize a protest outside the halls in Scotland where Connolly – the blasphemous buffoon – will be performing.'

'There is no intention to be blasphemous,' our one-time Child of Mary explained innocently to the *Evening Times*. 'I have merely taken a situation in history and given it a Glasgow setting which I think is humorous. Certainly it is outrageous – but comedy is a rather outrageous thing. People, I suppose, are outrageous too, and that's why I draw on them for my humour. When I worked in the Clydeside shipyards I couldn't wait to get back to work to hear the patter and listen to some of the things that had actually happened to my mates. That's what it's all about. The things that actually happen to people are much funnier than anything invented.'

If the album was offensive, there were a lot of Scots crying out to be offended. 'Solo Concert' started selling at a rate of 75,000 copies a month, and won a silver disc within weeks. By the end of July, it was the biggest seller in Scotland since The Beatles' 'Sergeant Pepper', qualifying it for a gold disc. An *Observer* reviewer wrote, 'Sadly we couldn't understand many of the jokes, which were about yins, hinnues, jaggy bonnets and coming out of Glasgow pubs with a fish supper in one hand and a bottle of Irn Bru in the other', but the album still rose to number eighteen in the national charts, based almost entirely on Scottish sales. The Beatles' publicist Derek Taylor was in the vanguard of Englishmen subscribing to the Connolly cult down south. 'I heard the album and I just couldn't believe it. The man is another Lenny Bruce,' he told the *Sun*.

Billy's 'dazzling success' as the *Sunday Times* was now calling it, did not stop him touring the remotest locations in Scotland. At the height of the album's triumph and fresh from the World Cup, he was away on a two-week Highlands and Islands tour, playing in tiny church halls, community centres, and village huts. Such venues made no money, but, he said, were 'good for the brain'. (This insistence on travelling out to obscure venues continues undiluted today; on his 1994 Scottish tour, he was still taking in such places as the Assembly Rooms in Wick, the Phoenix Cinema in Orkney and the Garrison Theatre in Lerwick.) The queues in the big cities, meanwhile, were growing ever longer. The *Evening Times*' man Gillies, who championed Connolly early on, wrote

Billy's mother, Mary Adams, discovered by the *Daily Record* living in Dunoon *(Daily Record)*.

The young Billy, already wearing the trademark wellies *(Daily Record)*.

Billy the rock'n'roll tearaway *(Daily Record)*.

Jimmy Lucas (left) and Bobby Dalgleish, Connolly's comic tutors in the shipyard (George Munro/*Greenock Telegraph*).

Connolly as a young folkie in the Scotia Bar, Glasgow in 1962 (Alan Cherry).

Billy and Iris after tying the knot at Glasgow's Martha Street registry office on 27 June 1969 (*Daily Record*).

Billy and Iris celebrate Christmas 1980 with Cara (7) and Jamie (11)
(Eunice Gavin).

The Big Yin, complete with Big Banana Feet at
London's New Victoria Theatre in October 1975
(Mike Putland).

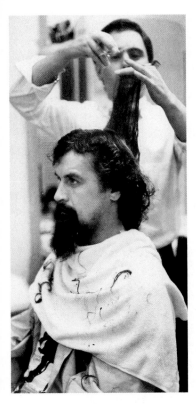

Connolly confronted by an angry audience during a disastrous performance at Brisbane's City Hall in 1977 (Bettmann Newsphotos).

The famous unruly mop is shorn for Connolly's appearance in 'The Beastly Beatitudes of Balthazar B.' (Nikki English/*Daily Mail*).

A smartly-suited Connolly at Edinburgh's Court of Session to get custody of Cara and Jamie (Wilson, Edinburgh).

An angry Connolly about to tackle waiting journalists at Heathrow after flying in with Pamela Stephenson (David Parker).

Connolly takes on freelance photographer Stuart Bell outside the Theatre Royal, Drury Lane (Alan Davidson).

Billy and Pamela leaving Harry's Bar (David Koppel).

Connolly posing in Rome for BBC 2's 'The Bigger Picture' (BBC copyright).

'The Head of the Class' surrounded by his pupils (ABCTV).

An attempt to win over American audiences saw Connolly appearing on a wonderfully varied bill.

that when booking opened for his King's Theatre, Glasgow, gigs, 'the queues resembled those of the great vaudeville days when Johnnie Ray, Frankie Laine and Roy Rogers drew huge audiences to the Glasgow Empire – or later when The Beatles or Rolling Stones were in town.' Two decades on, when Connolly again played the King's (a grand theatre just 400 yards from his birthplace), the scene was identical, with unadvertised shows sold out instantly.

Another tradition Connolly was assiduously keeping up, despite his awesome new success, was doing shows in prisons, especially before the psychopaths and murderers in the 'Nutcracker Suite' – the notorious Special Wing at Her Majesty's Prison, Barlinnie. It would be fanciful to suggest that he identified with prisoners after his experience of one night banged up by the police in his late teens (although you never know), but he steadfastly maintained that he liked the Barlinnie audience. 'These guys are jumping with character,' he told the *Sunday Times*. 'If they want to make a noise, they'll go ahead and do it. They'll not sit and listen to anybody that's duff. Look, these guys are condemned. They're there for an awful long time, if not for ever. They've come through bad times – maybe the worst times – and they're standing upright. They know exactly who they are and what they are. Which is a great thing. Giving a guy like that a laugh is a big thing to be doing with yourself.'

In 1974, Connolly was highly political. He was photographed with Harold Wilson and Willie Ross during the year's two election campaigns, and he spent time on the stump in Ross and Cromarty for Brian Wilson, who was the (unsuccessful) Labour candidate. He had been courted by the Scottish Nationalist Party, but did not approve of it, apart from its having 'brought the arguments right into the pub'.

At the same time as he was wearing his politics on his sleeve, the inevitable question of all the money he must be making was causing interest. 'I havnae had time tae spend it, I was in the red six months ago,' he explained to a journalist who asked about his growing bank balance. The summer of 1974 found Billy and Iris living in 'a nice house' in Redlands Road, in Glasgow's West End. 'But people kept coming to the door all the time and when they passed the dining room window they would cheer ... I had to leave the city. I was turning into a Bay

City Roller. Every time I went out of the front door a wee crowd would shout "hooray". It was no good for the kids.'

Within a few months of this flattering torture, they bought a grand house with an acre of garden and two acres of remote woodland between them and the road in the village of Drymen, near Loch Lomond, Stirlingshire. 'Towards the end, living in the house in Glasgow was terrible, the phone calls, the loonies,' he told Linda Lee Potter of the *Daily Mail*. 'Now we've found a new peace, and Iris defends it like a lioness.'

Peace included the chance for Billy to indulge his taste for expensive cars, with a Mercedes and a Jeep appearing in the drive, for boats, including a small cabin cruiser, and to have a full-time gardener – 'The man who came to build hutches for the rabbits stayed on and turned into our gardener. He comes from May to September. My garden's his, really. I just say let's make it windswept and interesting, and he decides what to do.' Connolly was putting money into forestry and, as the house had a river running through its grounds, spending a lot of time fishing.

By the end of 1974, Billy had a new recording contract with Polydor, and had released three comedy albums, with sales passing 400,000. 'Cop Yer Whack For This' qualified for a gold disc, selling as well as Slade, and by October 1975, had outsold The Who's 'Tommy'. Pop paper editors thus found Connolly's unfamiliar name and material in their LP charts for seventeen weeks, at one point in third place. In 1975, he also had a number one hit with the single 'D.I.V.O.R.C.E.', which he had the luck to have banned by some radio stations because it had the word 'bum' in it.

Connolly's tendency to feel inside himself like a rock star was becoming something near to an external reality, although by now he had decided he was less than happy about rock status. He hated supporting big rock tours, and felt passionately that what he did was harder. 'It's quite a pleasant feeling, but as far as records are concerned, I still feel a bit of a freak. I know I am credible as a live act, but records are a strange field,' he told the *Evening Times* in 1975. 'His caution,' the *Times* added, 'is prompted by the knowledge that the last British funny-man to sell records in any quantity was Tony Hancock – a decade ago. Connolly's album sales now outstrip Hancock's by 500% and he reckons he is the only comic in Europe who is on contract to a record company on the same basis as rock performers.'

As crucial as 1974 had been to his career in Scotland, 1975 was the year the rest of the kingdom discovered Billy Connolly – with a vengeance. Michael Parkinson, then the foremost TV chat show host, was instrumental in Connolly's conquering of the English. Eamon Andrews, presenting Connolly on 'This Is Your Life' in 1980, described what happened: 'In 1975 in Glasgow a taxi driver pulls up outside a record shop and insists his famous passenger buys your LP.' Parkinson then took over the story: 'I thought, well, I'll do it – anything to get to the airport and back home. He gave me a very, very heavy sell. He said, "You must have this man on the show. He's the funniest man I've ever heard." And I actually got the record just to get to the airport. But the nice thing was that not only eventually did I get Billy on the show, I met a mate as well.' It was Parky's son Andrew, Parkinson explained, who told his dad to listen to the record a fortnight later. Andrew was on hand in the 'This Is Your Life' studio to claim that his father had said: 'I'm not listening to any long-haired hippy layabout.'

The first laugh Connolly raised on British TV was on the resulting Parkinson appearance. Looking markedly nervous in a quite revolting tan leather jacket, Billy told the following joke: 'This guy was going out to meet his friend in the pub, and he went down, he said: "Oh, hallo, how's it going?" He said, "Fine, fine." "How's the wife?" He said, "Oh, she's dead. I murdered her this morning. Dead." He said, "You're kidding me." He said, "No, I'm not." He said, "I'm not talking to you if you keep talking like that." He said, "Please yourself. I'll show you if you like." He said, "Show me." So they went up to his tenement building through the close (that's the entrance to the tenement) into the back green into the wash house, and sure enough there's a big mound of earth. There was a bum sticking out. He says: "Is that her?" He said, "Aye." He says, "What did you leave her bum sticking out for?" He says, "I need somewhere to park my bike." '

'I think of all the people we've had on the show,' Parkinson told the 'This Is Your Life' audience, 'and there have been four or five hundred – we never had a bigger single reaction than we had to Billy the first time round. It is quite obvious that he's a huge star.' Connolly unequivocally acknowledges that the Parkinson appearance, and especially that joke – unusual, because he did not normally tell jokes in the traditional form – made him truly famous. It was not until 1994, however, that he admitted (in his TV interview with Jeremy Isaacs) that he was given the joke by an unnamed Scottish football fan before a match in Spain.

He had been in Valencia with his former shipyard mate (and now scriptwriter) Peter McDougall and another pal to see Scotland play Spain. The three were 'a bit drunk' on Spanish brandy, and a Scot ran over, told Connolly the joke, and ran back to his friends. Telling a comedian a joke is a perilous occupation, but this one left Connolly 'leaning against a wall roaring with laughter'. He later told Frank Lynch that he was thinking of telling the joke on Parkinson. 'For God's sake, don't,' the manager responded. 'This is the biggest chance you've ever had. Don't blow it.' Lynch had staved off an offer from Russell Harty in favour of Parkinson, and felt a prime-time joke about wife murder and bums would undo all his good work.

Billy's first appearance at the London Palladium, on which he had set such store, was on 12 January 1975, immediately after another big show at the Free Trade Hall, Manchester. Such was his and Frank Lynch's faith in the still dodgy venture of establishing Billy in England, that Billy put up £1,500 of his own cash to hire the place for his London comedy debut. It was neither a small amount for him, nor an enormously large one, but the possibility of humiliation loomed. (Why the Palladium, he was asked? 'Cos I'm ready for it. There's nowhere more prestigious to play. I want to prove to London that I exist,' he replied. And what if it doesn't work out? 'I'll go home, have a few pints, write new material, come back – and try again.') But embarrassment was not an option for long; all 2,500 tickets for the gig were sold out weeks in advance with no advertising or pre-publicity. There was a thriving black market in tickets, and on the night, Billy received a five-minute standing ovation at the end of the show.

Connolly told the English papers, who were very much taken with the story of the ambitious unknown lunatic from Glasgow who had hired the Palladium for himself, that he wanted to get rid of the stereotyped Scots image: 'All that stuff about a Scot with bow legs, a kilt, red beard, a bottle of whisky in one hand and an Andy Stewart LP in the other is rubbish. Apart perhaps for the whisky.'

Billy's extravagant arrival in London, staged brilliantly by Lynch, was commented upon by the Glasgow *Evening Times*, not least the cheeky and ironic appendage of a sporran (an ironic sporran, but a sporran all the same) to his outfit: 'Booking a suite in the Dorchester was bit of Glaswegian bravado, but walking through its exalted portals dressed in a chamois jacket, faded jeans with a hole in the knee, and an outsize sporran verged on the outrageous, so far as the staff were concerned.'

'Apart from the sporran, it is the way I usually dress. I didn't see any purpose in changing my gear because I was in London,' was Connolly's comment.

At the Palladium, the Sunday night gig began with an esoteric flourish – Connolly first appearing with his head above a giant model of Sir Harry Lauder in kilt, sporran, socks and shoes and singing, 'Keep right on to the end of the road'. The audience roared their delight. For the next hour and a half, he went through his repertoire, with songs, some backed (just to irritate the folkies, one suspects) by a fifteen-piece orchestra. Alan Hamilton, reviewing the show for *The Times*, called Connolly, 'the first of the cultural shock troops, a one man raiding party determined to make Sir Harry Lauder turn in his grave'. Hamilton said he plays guitar and banjo 'with studied badness'.

'He appears on stage,' the review continued, 'looking like an Old Testament prophet in blue polka-dot pyjamas, hiding behind a cardboard cutout of his anti-hero Lauder. His act is an unashamed wallow in sandpaper nostalgia for those fortunate enough to have been brought up in the back streets of Glasgow, or wish they had been. For him the Scottish national dress is not the kilt, but a pair of Wellingtons, and the mark of class distinction is a childhood spent wearing "wellies" in summertime. Connolly, known to the cognoscenti as "the big in [sic]", is something of a private joke to anyone not born within shouting distance of Glasgow Cross. Luckily his full house Palladium audience last night was at least 99 per cent expatriate.'

At the end of the show, the Glasgow *Evening Times*' man reported, 'The audience, mainly Scots, stood, cheered, and sang, "We shall not be moved" and for 10 minutes at the end of the show they refused to leave the theatre, demanding his return. But Billy Connolly did not return. He sat with his head in his hands in the dressing room and said: "What a reception. It was fantastic, unbelievable." ' After the show Connolly invited over one hundred guests – politicians, entertainers and friends – back to his Dorchester suite for a party.

His confidence was soaring, and the tour ploughed on to Newcastle, Corby and Liverpool, a gig that he saw as another eminently sur- mountable challenge: 'I really want to crack them. They know what the patter is all about. I want to get to the people who know about street humour,' he said. With further shows in Aberdeen, Dublin and Belfast (where he said he hoped to be in good form because the people were so depressed), he played before 180,000 people within a few weeks. The Irish part of the tour was made into the film *Big Banana Feet*, which premièred at the Edinburgh Film Festival in September 1976. One not so hot spot, which he can only, surely, have taken on for a dare, was Torquay: 'Died on my arse,' he commented a couple of years later. 'It was a convention of Rotarians in a huge tent and they gave me a bingo caller's mike.'

Another form of adulation and acceptance that predictably came his way was an avalanche of offers to extend beyond comedy and into TV drama. In 1975, he appeared in a supporting role as a Glaswegian hard man in the prize-winning *Just Another Saturday*, by Peter McDougall. McDougall had worked as a brass-finisher in Glasgow when Billy was a welder, and the two became friends in the early 1970s. They would later collaborate on a sitcom (which never happened), 'The Highland Queen', and a film script called *Travelling Man*; Connolly appeared in McDougall's *The Elephant's Graveyard* in 1976 and in *Down Among the Big Boys* in 1993.

In October, he was back on Parkinson for the second time, and in the mood for fun, so he attacked Pastor Jack Glass, as 'a watered-down Ian Paisley'. (Glass later demanded the right to reply: 'Almost ten million viewers will have got the wrong impression of me,' he moaned. Connolly had meanwhile developed a routine where he sang to the tune of the Stones' 'Jumping Jack Flash', 'Pastor Jack Glass is an ass, ass, ass!') This time, Connolly, one of the TV critics wrote, 'had his host falling around helpless in his swivel chair and the audience hanging on his every fractured vowel.' Billy Connolly on the Parkinson show, which was simultaneously at its brilliant zenith, became for a couple of years almost the definition of high quality late-night TV, the golden age of both men, that millions of people look back on with a quite possessive affection. 'The day after the first one I was at Heathrow on my way home to Glasgow, and a Chinese guy came up to me and asked for my autograph. I've cracked it, I thought,' Billy told the *Sunday Express.*

The two Parkinson appearances ensured that when he took the show to the New Victorian Theatre in London in October, this time there were thousands of English in the audiences. His stage outfit was now either a leotard and tights or purple polka-dot suit. 'I don't set out to shock people, but many are shocked at some of my material,' he told the *Daily Mirror.* 'I believe in being honest and giving people a good belly laugh. I think there is room for a new-style comedian, and I'm the guy who is coming up.' He pointed out that he would not talk about sex on stage: 'Och, it's been hammered to death. Anyway, people aren't yet prepared for straight talk on sex.'

It was as if Connolly was now officially a phenomenon, and everything about him, from simple details of his home life to relatively intellectual analysis of his humour, was up for grabs. The *Sunday Times,* for example, suggested interestingly that a major explanation of his success was 'his obvious relish for the language that he uses, broad Lowland Scots (a much discouraged tongue). At the same time his audiences delight in the savage way he puts down the white-heather style packages, with their troupes of mincing dancers and cardboard mountains. (To the tune of Scotland The Brave: "Land of polluted river/Bloodshot eyes and sodden liver/Land of my heart forever/Scotland the Brave.")'

Startling, fresh Billy Connolly observations were insinuating themselves into everyday use at a quite alarming speed, as if they had always been part of the culture, needing only to be awoken by the cult Scotsman. Bums, for example, were suddenly a subject that was discussed and positively relished throughout the country; the bum/bike joke would be told and retold in a million not-quite-right Scottish accents – it simply did not sound right recounted any other way. And, as far as anyone at the time could remember, no comedian had ever extracted comic mileage from the ticklish subject of vomit. Yet here was this harlequin character airing his famous monologue on drunk's vomit: 'It's no' the eighteen Guinnesses that does it, it's the diced carrots.' ('Connolly's drunks do not just have problems articulating; they also have vomit down their jackets and their trouser legs are soaked in urine,' the *Sunday Times* observed.)

Roderick Gilchrist, the *Daily Mail*'s showbiz man, would not have been allowed to think of – let alone write – words like bum, wee and vomit, but alerted sensitive *Mail* readers to what he saw as universal truths in Billy's act. 'Connolly's humour is straight from the terraces of Hampden Park, the tenements of the Gorbals and the shipyards of the Clyde ... A Scot, whose opening music is a parody of Scotland the Brave and who ridicules Harry Lauder, Connolly has mined the rich vein of humour peculiar to Glasgow street life and yet has touched base instincts that exist in all communities,' he wrote.

The London hack pack was, if it is possible, in even fuller enthusiastic cry over Connolly than it was in January, and Billy reacted by becoming ever more garrulous – and boastful – in response. John Blake, in the London *Evening News*, hailed the birth of a superstar. Billy told the paper, 'The way I see it, the days of the one-line, stand-up comic in a mohair suit are over. They committed suicide in that series The Comedians, one joke after the other, bang, bang, bang. They used up all their material ... People want more out of their comedy than that. I think the time is right for the story teller. I just come on there and talk to them like I was in their house. I say hello when I come on, not "good evening." Who ever says "good evening" for God's sake? I don't tell jokes either. I've never told a joke in my life.' (This was arguable; he had just become famous almost as a result of one joke – the bum and the bike. It is not clear what made this a story rather than a joke.)

'I'm just steamin' along and these two Cockneys come up and shake my hand and tell me I'm magic,' he continued. 'It was great. I couldn't understand half of what they were saying, but it seemed they couldn't get tickets. The problem was all these Scots buying the place up. I thought of going through the English Embassy to smuggle tickets to Londoners.'

For the *Sunday Express* (whose predominantly elderly southern English readers were hardly obvious Connolly territory), he explained why it took eight years to become a success: 'I was too scruffy for the theatre and too folksy for cabaret. The truth of the matter is, I didn't fit in. People just didn't know what to make of me – or my sense of humour. And can you blame them? I mean, look at me. Do I look like someone who's currently the toast of London? Because that's what I am, you know. I didn't want to boast about this, but one has to be truthful. And as my entire act is based on telling the truth, no matter who it offends, I may as well tell you that I'm probably the most exciting performer to have hit this city for a long time.' (And he had not finished with the *Express* man yet: 'You don't have to take my word for it either. Just ask any of the thousands of people who have seen the show this week. At my hotel they've had to hire a special bird to sit at the switchboard and handle all the calls I get each day.')

When the New Victoria show opened, Alan Hamilton of *The Times* was given space to write another Connolly review. 'Since his last appearance in London [at the Palladium], Connolly's timing and delivery have improved greatly with his growing confidence before an audience which was at least partly English ... Glaswegians revel in language and make colourful and brilliant use of it in a way which can make the broadest Cockney sound dull and pedestrian.'

The question of whether or not Billy was now modulating his accent for English audiences was hotly debated. 'A friend' was quoted in the London *Evening News* as saying, 'I know when he works for Scottish audiences his accent is guttural, but he modifies that for non-Scots. So Londoners will have no difficulty understanding his patter.'

Connolly would have none of this. In a two-hour show, he translated only twice 'for the benefit of the English who've sneaked under the barriers'. 'I don't give an inch. I watered it down a bit in Liverpool and a girl came backstage and told me I was daft. Do that and you weaken the act. They soon pick up the words.'

The Glasgow *Evening Times*, still keeping a proprietorial eye on the city's prodigy (and biggest export) noted that 'the exile element in most of his audiences is bound to remain an important factor for a long time to come. Reaction to esoterically Glasgow cracks like: "After this it's back to the Ashfield Club," serve as a reminder that Scots may now be sharing their superstar, but they are not giving him up.'

He also refuted that if he got a TV series he'd lost his rough edges: 'There's nae chance of that. I'll never get slick. I'm not professional or anything like that. I just sing my songs and tell my stories and hope people will like them.' Connolly was, of course, being disingenuous. Whether he quite realized it or not, his British act was highly tuned to southern ears; it is only necessary to listen to an early recording of Connolly, especially when he parodied drunken Glaswegians (as he did in the Crucifixion) to realize that a large proportion of his words were truly (and, you have to feel rightly) incomprehensible outside Scotland. As with Guinness, there is a home version and a subtly different export recipe.

It was not only the press that was falling over itself to acclaim the new comedic Messiah. Celebrities and political figures were desperately keen to associate with him. When he had his self-sponsored night of glory at the Palladium, it was Billy who threw the parties; now distinguished homage-bearers were queuing outside his dressing-room door. One night after the show, David Essex hosted a party at the Kensington Hilton, and there was no doubt that the star of the evening was Connolly. He showed every sign (and still does) of being thrilled to be welcomed into celebrity circles, but while he had been delighted to help out the Labour Party a year before, he was rapidly going into reverse as regards politicians, or at least the trendier metropolitan type of lefty.

A persistent phone caller was the Workers' Revolutionary Party's own Vanessa Redgrave, but Connolly was as wary of her as a rabbit of a ferret. His instruction to Billy Johnston was pragmatic, sensible and ultimately unheeded: 'Gie her a ticket,' he asked Johnston, 'but keep her out of my road.' Redgrave's eventual appearance at the theatre was no more invigorating than Connolly expected it to be: 'She had a great big bag of mussels,' he complained. 'The place stank.'

CHAPTER 6

Touring

'When you're touring for three months you get in a strange mental state. You might say: "When is my next day off?" They say: "Sunday." You say: "What day is it today?" You count up the days to Sunday and when it comes you just sit and look at your hands.'
Billy Connolly in 1976

With two Top Twenty albums, two theatre tours, three trips to the USA and Canada and TV appearances, Billy Connolly was rarely home in 1975, and back in Drymen, Iris was beginning to pay the price of her husband's unexpected fame. An unfortunate image has arisen of Iris Connolly as a result of the couple's eventual divorce settlement, under which Billy and his lover Pamela Stephenson were awarded custody of Jamie and Cara, and Iris was prevented from ever speaking publicly about the marriage. Nobody, least of all the couple's friends, many of whom continue to keep up contact with Iris at her home in Spain, disputes that Iris was hitting the bottle in grand style. But she was, by general admission, also a very likeable woman.

The family's home life was not a conventionally unhappy business, and there were moments of great fun. 'Iris was a very funny person. When Billy was thirty-five Iris organized a surprise party in The Salmon Leap pub in Drymen. Frank Lynch was there with his second wife at that time, who looked like something out of "Charlie's Angels", but wasn't one of the world's great conversationalists, you might say. Iris was a great one for a practical joke and just causing madness out of nothing, so there was this girl looking just as though she had stepped off a film set, her hair was perfection and her beautiful blouse and suit on and everybody was quite drunk and the whole place is in full swing and Iris cuts a big slice of this birthday cake of Billy's and just shoves it in this woman's face and rubs it all in. The girl was horrified. Frank Lynch was furious but couldn't say anything because Billy was the goose that was laying the golden egg.' (Cake-based antics had become very much the theme of the party by 3 a.m., when Billy threw a piece of birthday cake which hit a friend, and the friend hit another guest when he returned the throw. A full-scale cake fight ensued. 'It was good fun for them, but I had to clean up the mess; I wasn't too happy,' said a miserable pub manager the next morning.)

'I went to see Iris once when Billy was away', relates Hamish Imlach, 'and she'd had a little Golf which she'd written off, and Billy had a Mercedes, and she'd taken that out to do the shopping in, and she'd caused 4,800 quid damages to the Mercedes. She never hurt anybody. It was only lamp posts and trees on Loch Lomond side, there's not many people there. Then the only vehicle she had left – the Golf was a write-off, the Mercedes was being fixed – was his pride and joy, this Panther De Ville thing with exhaust things coming out of the side, and all gleaming. You couldn't park it anywhere because people would take bits off it. It was a ridiculous car. But Iris put a big scrape along it, from the front wing to the back wing, and decided she'd call for a taxi belatedly. So it was three cars while he was away on one tour, in the space of five or six weeks.'

The couple's general waywardness was renowned locally. On New Year's Day 1976, Billy did a six-hour show on Radio Clyde with Tom Ferrie, and started by complaining with mock sadness, 'I insulted all my neighbours last night. I don't know how I'm gonna go home. I'm gonna disguise my car, black out all the windows, I'm feart to go up the street. I do it every year. Every year I make a New Year's resolution I'm going to be nice to people and quarter of an hour later I insult a neighbour. I shout at all their houses and things, and go round asking them if they've had a good time the following day. I'm getting really fed up with it. I think it's a rotten time, New Year. I always think it's going to be a gas and end up getting shuffled out of doors in embarrassed silences.'

Far from it; the Connollys, with Billy at the apogee of his popularity, were revered neighbours. Their random acts of kindness were also legendary. 'There was a guy at school with me called Hugh Niven,' Connolly's friend Hugh Jordan recalls. 'And Hugh is a fine guitar and banjo player. This guy Hugh Niven was known as Hugo Niven and he would have known Billy because the two of them were banjo players. There's a pub in Drymen – the oldest one – and Hugo was in there when Billy came in. They were chatting away, and he says, "I bought myself a Gibson Mastertone banjo", which at that time in the early Eighties was £1,500. It was a lot of money – we're talking nearly three thousand now – and Billy said, "Oh, great banjo. What kind of guitar have you got?" And Hugo said, "Well I actually had to sell my guitar to get the money for the banjo." And Billy said, "You've not got a guitar? Listen, I've got a Gibson that I'll sell you for fifty quid."

'How Billy got the Gibson was that Gibson in America had given it to him providing he played it on stage. The following Saturday, Hugo was desperate to get his hands on the guitar for fifty quid and he arrives back in the pub at Saturday teatime, which wasn't really his way, and Billy arrives and says, "Oh fuck, is that you who was looking for that guitar?" And Hugo says, "Oh no, Billy, I was just passing." Anyway Billy says, "Hold on," and he went and got the guitar and he brought it to him, so Hugo said, "Billy how much do I owe you?" And Billy said, "Give me a fiver." So he gave him a fiver and Billy bought a round of drinks. So he gave him the guitar for nothing.'

The year that followed Billy's six-hour confessional New Year's Day stint on local radio contained his two biggest foreign tours yet; and along with the highs these marathons inevitably brought, came some of the most depressing lows of his career, movements that were to reduce him to tears more than once. It would all have been so much easier had Connolly not been so fiercely intent on his goal of making it in America.

As Britain sweltered and ran out of water in the drought summer of 1976, and Iris was on holiday in Malta with the children, Billy was touring the USA with Elton John, or more correctly as the singer's support act. As Elton was to put it diplomatically on Billy's 'This Is Your Life' show: 'We played in amazing places. In Texas this incredible Scotsman would walk out in banana skin boots and generally amaze the crowd. And he did incredibly well. And sometimes he did incredibly not so well.'

Until he got to New York, where hordes of expatriate Scots (and Americans who wanted to be thought of as such) rescued him, Connolly's reception was often brutal, even by his own upbeat assessment. There were standing ovations in Milwaukee, but as Connolly later recounted, 'I would go on first, and they would all throw bottles at me for a while. Then when they're knackered the band comes on. It's one of those situations. So you're a victim of their audience all the time. And with Elton, it was the strangest thing, when we got to nice places the audience treated me really badly and then when we got to horrible places, like Cleveland, they treated me really well. And in New York where we finished it was amazing, just extraordinary. They loved me.'

The crowd would be so stoned, he went on, that 'they didn't know whether it's New York or New Year. So they go, "Ladies and gentlemen ... [crowd roar] ... Elton's ... friend ..." and the atmosphere changes, "Billy Connolly." And then there's this resounding, "Who?" And that's what I go on to. And sometimes when I go, "Hi everybody, how you doing?" "Booo". And one day I lifted the banjo, and they all started to "Boo." I said, "You want to boo my banjo?" And they went "Booooo." I said, "Well, would you like to boo the back of it?" And I turned it round, and they went, "Boooo." So I said, "Would you like to boo it lying down? I'll put it on the floor, here watch." And I stood back and they went "Boo." So I said, "Hang on, I'm going to boo it for a while myself." And I was booing at it and they started to laugh, and the whole thing started to get better. But, God, what an experience.'

The tour had started on a chaotic note, as George Miller, Billy's roadie at the time, recalled: 'At 7 a.m. on the day I had to drive him from Drymen to go to the airport, neither he nor Iris answered the door when I arrived with the Merc. In desperation I broke in and there was Billy, fully dressed and snoring on the living-room floor. He had been blitzed the night before. I tossed a bucket of water over him and told him to move – *fast*! He grabbed his banjo and guitar and stumbled to the car. We just made the flight ... I lost count of the times I threw a blanket over him because he couldn't make it to bed.'

Even though the gigs were a struggle – 'It scared me shitless. Every night before I went on I'd vomit into the fire bucket,' he says – Connolly motored on with the tour, missing home and his children the more as he travelled on. 'I miss home food, too. I could murder a plate of good old Scottish curry,' he told the *Sun* reporter on the trip. Towards the end of the tour, he formed a publishing company called Sleepy Dumpling Music. Sleepy Dumpling was his pet name for his daughter Cara, given to her because he decided her face looked like a sleepy dumpling when she was asleep. He made his father, Billy senior, a director of Sleepy Dumpling Music and invited the old man out to the States to see the workings of Billy's new life.

'Old Billy was a very conservative, Catholic Glasgow man, a very formal nice man but very shy in a lot of ways,' says Hugh Jordan, who was in Malta, at his brother's house, with Iris, Jamie and Cara, and receiving regular reports on the tour from his friend Connolly and the lead guitarist in Elton's band, an old pal from Billy's folk club days called Davy Johnson. 'Also on the tour was Kiki Dee and the big encore they did was Elton John's 'Saturday'. The arrangement was that Elton would introduce people and they would come on and one by one sing the chorus "Saturday, Saturday, Saturday!", with the band all rocking away, and it would get to "... and, now ... Billy ... Connolly!" and Billy came on ... "Saturday, Saturday!" ... and Billy would be standing singing in the same microphone as Kiki Dee. And then the next thing a guy, another friend of theirs, runs on dressed as a banana, and then John Reid, who was Elton's manager and is now Billy's too, would come on dressed up as a strawberry and they would all be singing "Saturday Saturday". And out of the corner of his eye, Billy spots his father at the end of the stage just looking at all this, and he hadn't a fucking clue what all this was about. He's looking at guys dressed up as strawberries and bananas and his son, who had been a welder in a shipyard, was in the middle of all this. If you knew old Billy, you'd know the look he would have given to Billy – it just would have been bewilderment. He wouldn't have understood what any of this was about.'

The tour culminated in seven nights at Madison Square Garden with an instant sell-out of 175,000 tickets. 'Connolly is not the centre of attention, and there will be precious few Scots in the audience,' commented Brian Wilson, writing in the Glasgow *Evening Times*. 'But his mere presence is a remarkable achievement. It is unheard of for a comedian to provide the support on a rock tour which has played to over a million people in stadiums with capacities up to 80,000.

'It is difficult to exaggerate the sheer scale of stadia like this, and that guitar and banjo have never looked more lonely than when they were borne on to stage, followed by Billy – himself something of a Lilliputian figure in the middle of the vast arena, which last month housed the Democratic Convention ... He appeared duly clad in the famous black leotard and banana wellies. This he announced was the new national dress, because the Scots were fed up with Americans asking what was worn under the old one.'

Billy adapted his style to win over the American audience, but over all, they were not massively interested in a comedian from Scotland, however hysterical he might be. When the Madison Square crowd bayed for Elton, Connolly joked, 'You'll get him in a minute. They're walking him round the building trying to sober him up.' He later played the Carnegie Hall, where a large number of expatriate Scots, from communities such as Kearney, New Jersey, attended. Jane Gaskell, a *Daily Mail* correspondent in New York, wrote: ' "I love New York," he says later backstage, where Eric Idle of Monty Python is sweet enough to look amazed as my daughter asks for his autograph, a drunken pop-group manager is throwing ice-cubes up ladies' dresses and Connolly is roaring with relief at having got through the show. "It's been super playing for you at Carnegie Hall," he told the audience, adding, "though I must say it's been the best laxative I ever had in my life." '

It was on the Elton John tour that Billy first began to attract the attention of the American press, albeit it in a minuscule way. He played a small joint in a town outside Boston, near the scene of the humiliation a few years earlier (when he was told by two Americans the show was great – when he came off), and the New York *Daily News* was on hand to observe, 'His clothes reeked hippie and he had hair dyed blue and blond, so he was a surprise to the local Irish who wanted to hear songs of the old country where everything was remembered with a halo. He tried humour. "They didn't like my comedy. They wanted 'My Wild Irish Rose' and all that pish." '

The 1976 American tour gave Connolly a permanent taste for mass audiences, despite his initial nerves. 'The smallest audience was 18,000 people,' he said in a Glasgow arts magazine interview when he got home. 'We had about 35,000 in Washington ... I do occasional forays into folk song clubs but I don't like it. I think it's easier, not more difficult, to get over to a big audience. Everything I do now is written with a big audience in mind. Och, a wee audience is like singing to your aunties. My gestures are huge now. They don't work in a wee room. I attack everything in a big way.'

Much later, when he was doing infinitely smaller scale – but solo – tours in America, his tune had changed subtly: 'I've always come over before as the opening act for a rock band. I've been booed longer and louder than Hitler, you know. I used to go on and do three quarters of an hour of well-thought-out material and die the death of one thousand cuts, then be followed by these spotty youths singing a load of rubbish who would get a standing ovation. It was incredibly frustrating,' he said.

There was other evidence of this slight disillusion with pop welling up inside Connolly as a result of the 1976 tour. When he got back, he was regaling his friend Hamish Imlach with stories of all the stars he had hobnobbed with in the States. It happened that Imlach had been in the US himself during the same summer, albeit in a more low-key manner. As Imlach says: 'The first group Billy played with were called the Skillet-Lickers after a semi-legendary 20s group from Tennessee. I went to work out of curiosity for two weeks in Nashville and to my utter amazement, I discovered that some of these old guys were still alive. I'd met two surviving people from the Skillet-Lickers, both in their eighties, and both still playing, and I'd taken their photographs. Billy was all excited when he came back. He'd been in Led Zeppelin's private plane, and I was waiting to show him these photographs of these old chaps, but he was still going on about Los Angeles. So I told him, very briefly, about meeting the surviving Skillet-Lickers in Nashville, and showed him the photographs. He said, "You swine, I thought they were all dead. I'd rather have met them than Led Zeppelin." '

In the autumn of 1977, he ran into massively publicized trouble on a three-week Australian tour. Really, there was only one disastrous evening on the trip, in Brisbane, and the press's quite understandable concentration on that débâcle was to start the progressive and puzzling souring of Connolly's relationship with newspaper journalists. It was on a Monday night in the City Hall of the ultra-conservative Queensland capital that Billy was booed before an audience of 1,500, and then chased off stage by drunken angry fellow Scotsmen who demanded their money back, one shouting into his mike.

One 6' 6" Scotsman grabbed Connolly's £850 guitar and threatened to smash it unless he got his £5 refund. Another, a giant believed to be a prison warder, picked up the tour manager, Ian Smith from Melbourne, and tried to throw him against a wall, before landing a blow on the side of his head which left him stunned. Billy left the stage after forty minutes, but later returned to finish his act in front of the 'less than rapturous applause', according to one report, of the rest of the audience, who had refused to leave after about a third of their number – the Scots – had been cleared out by the police. Then many of the audience, some descended from expatriate Scots, queued at the empty box office to demand their £5 admission back. 'I was bloody scared and flabbergasted,' Billy told reporters. 'It's never happened before. All of a sudden I feel bloody homesick. Home seems a long way away.'

The *Daily Mirror* correspondent got the measure of it, reporting, 'The MacAussies *expected* someone like fresh-faced Andy Stewart, with kilt, sporran, "clean" jokes and tear-jerking Highland ballads. They *got* Billy, in leopard-skin leotard and banana skin wellies with his own brand of street corner jokes and bawdy songs.' To make its view self-fulfilling, the *Mirror* mischievously contacted Mr Stewart back in Scotland. 'Billy's humour is very obviously not the same as mine,' he philosophized. 'I play Brisbane every two years and the audience know exactly what they're going to see. Billy's comedy contains a social commentary and reflects Glasgow's dire poverty. I just tell gags.'

Billy went on to play in the Canberra Theatre the following night, and made an 1,100-strong audience laugh at Brisbane 'hick town' jokes. He went on to a reception at the local Burns Club, where he kept the expat Scots happy into the small hours reciting poetry and singing songs.

The Australian experience had a profound effect on Connolly, and he continues even today to refer to it in interviews, musing on the idea of returning to Brisbane in a Lancaster bomber loaded with horse manure, and describing Australians as 'a well-balanced people. They have a chip on both shoulders.'

Connolly's attitude to Australia remains almost as ambiguous as that he has to Scotland. The Brisbane experience has never quite left him, yet he was back in Australia to great acclaim within a year, and remains extremely popular there. He also, of course, has married Pamela Stephenson, born a New Zealander, but brought up in Sydney and to all intents and purposes an Aussie. In his fifties, he has now said that he would like to settle in Australia 'one day'. It seems to be a characteristic of Billy to give uncritical love to countries he likes, but has no real connection with (England, the USA) but have a stormy, love-hate relationship with places he takes more seriously.

'Before I tell you about Brisbane,' he told Radio Clyde when he got back, 'may I state that I was a bit hurt at the press coverage because Australia was an outstanding tour, and one of the happiest tours I've ever been lucky enough to have been involved in. For instance, Melbourne was one concert, and it became four concerts. Sydney became three instead of one, Perth became two, Adelaide was two. And they were all great except for Brisbane. Now I'm not terribly sure what happened, maybe I was rotten, maybe I had an off night, but it didn't feel that way, but all these lunatics came charging up, shouting and bawling and just giving me a bad time, and they were all chanting about Rangers and chanting about Celtic, and shouting in the middle of my jokes, and at the punch line they would shout out things and people didn't get the point at all, and the whole thing began to fall apart, and it was just a rotten gig.

'But I kind of enjoyed it,' he went on. 'I went off twice, and the third time when I came on I was in my street clothes by this time, and there was a guy on the stage, and he had my guitar. And the police came and threw them all out, all the loonies, and there was a big fight. And it was funny because I was singing on stage, and all the punters who were left were loving it, but directly in front of me I could see up the centre aisle and the doors of the hall were open. Now Brisbane Town Hall is in the town square and it has a fountain in the square and it's all lit up. And there was this fountain, squishing away there, all lights, and a big fight in front of it. They were all battering each other to this lovely backdrop.

And I was on stage killing myself. The audience couldnae see it, they were facing me. And I did about half an hour longer in Brisbane than I did at any other gig. It ended up a success. But I'll never understand it as long as I live, and I wanted to like it too.'

The mid to late 1970s Billy Connolly boom (unequalled until his unexpected revival in 1994) showed no sign of abating in 1977, when he launched into a mammoth, April to July British tour, during which privileged journalists were exposed to many of the backstage secrets of his performance skill. The fifty-three-night 'Billy Connolly's Extravaganza' was said to be the largest ever British concert tour undertaken by an entertainer.

Just before it started, there was some other business to transact. His management contacted Fyffes Bananas to ask if the company was interested in using Connolly (who was still in his giant banana boots phase) for commercials. Fyffes decided, in an immortal expression, that they 'did not want a family fruit associated with Mr Connolly'. (If a banana was a family fruit, the question begged itself, precisely what did a non-family or adult fruit resemble?)

Then he turned down an offer to appear in a Royal Silver Jubilee Command Performance before the Queen. 'I did it for the best of reasons. Can you imagine me on stage doing a heavy number and looking up at the Royal Box to see if she gives the royal approval for everyone to laugh. It's not on.' He also pointed out to the organizing committee that he could not submit a script because he improvises. At the same time, he received a minor wrist slap from a court in Edinburgh, before reaching an out of court settlement with the owners of a shop called The Big Yins. Connolly claimed Seymour Gordon and Sydney Rose were trying to cash in on his good name; Judge Lord Stewart, well aware that the expression was a common Scottish one, snapped, 'You can't go around interdicting everyone calling themselves the Big Yin.'

The Extravaganza tour opened in Oban, went on to, among other spots, Largs, Rothesay, Arran, Ayr, Whitley Bay, Clacton, Skegness, Paignton, Bournemouth, Hastings, the Rainbow Theatre in London and the Glasgow Apollo, where it ended. It looked as if Connolly had contrived to take in seaside resorts, back-of-beyond towns and mining communities. Michael Parkinson, in the *Sunday Times*, maintained that

'Connolly planned the tour by spreading out a map of the British Isles and sticking pins in the names that appealed to him around the coastline.' Parkinson wrote: 'Stretched out in the back seat of the presidential-size black limmo, Billy Connolly surveyed the passing towns of Southern England. "The last time I did this trip was by public transport. In those days I could tell you where every Woolies, pub and public toilet was in any town in Britain."'

Before each performance, he would drink large numbers of cups of tea, made by the tour manager, Kenny MacPherson, and talk to anyone around about anything and everything. MacPherson would, at the same time as brewing up constantly, be dealing with endless requests for interviews, photo calls, spare tickets – and the dreaded invitations to parties after the show. 'I'll tell you about those parties,' Connolly told one reporter. 'They come round and say, "Back to my place after the show, you'll have a lovely relaxing time." So back you go and when you get in the room there's eighty people sitting in a semicircle facing a chair. Then you realize you are not a guest – you're the bloody act.'

After each performance, in the dressing room, he would have his first drink of the day; he was rigid about not drinking before a show. On the road, he demonstrated a penchant for the catatonic trance, happy to sit for hours in hotel rooms with a roadie or a driver eating crisps and biscuits. 'I like the nothing of it. Every ten minutes through the day I get the faint stirring of fear in my gut and I begin to anticipate the night,' he said. 'There's a lack of responsibility in touring. I mean, supposing we blow Torquay, tomorrow they can't boo you in the streets because you've moved away. And, in any case, you can blame them.' Sometimes he would suddenly be inspired to write something on the road; he felt he did his best material on the spur of the moment, in a pub or restaurant.

He later confessed that he hit a trough of depression during those moments of 'nothing' on the 1977 tour, although it was hard for those around Connolly to know this. As Hamish Imlach says, 'It's very, very seldom that he confides his innermost thoughts to anybody. Billy will lapse into trivialities on top of generalities or exercise his opinion on some particular thing that enrages him.'

'It started when a friend of mine, Matt McGinn, died,' Billy said of this depression. 'I began to think a lot about death. I wondered what would happen if I died, what kind of flurry of activity there would be. It suddenly occurred to me that I had three accountants. For Chrissake what does anyone need three accountants for? I felt like a circus freak ... It became so bad that I thought about suicide. I don't mean that I drew up plans to throw myself under a train or something. I just pondered the possibility of it as a way out of it all. I envy religious people. They get a lot of solace from it. I envy their peace of mind. What do I believe in? Was it Behan who said, "I'm a Communist during the day and a Catholic as soon as it gets dark"? Well, I'm something like that. Would you believe I sleep with the light on? Sometimes I do. It's bloody incredible, really.'

There was no sign of these dark feelings in his ebullient stage persona, naturally. Hecklers, who could get you down if you were already that way, continued to be meat and drink to him. In Bournemouth, of all places, a man demanded the Crucifixion story. 'Give us three nails and I'll show you,' said Connolly. He was keen to try out new material, as the record company was demanding a new album, but the heckler persisted and got aggressive. 'Be careful friend, you're playing with the big boys now,' Connolly warned; the man continued almost as if he was paid by Connolly to interrupt. 'When they put teeth in your mouth they ruined a perfectly good bum,' he sparkled; it was precisely what the crowd had paid for. At the close of the show, the cheering was deafening. Billy gave an almost embarrassed raised fist salute, and walked off. He never returned for encores. Even Torquay was a triumph on this tour, and Billy's liking of England and the English increased. 'It proves what I always liked about the English – their curious quality. I mean, any nation that invents train spotting and the Royal Pavilion at Brighton has got to be a bit special,' he said. He became perversely fond of Torquay, once his bête noir, and opened a 1992 English tour there, to another blinding reception.

Connolly was pursued for part of the tour by his old sparring partner Pastor Jack Glass and his banners ('Godless Connolly' and 'Connolly the blasphemer'). On 18 April, they caused uproar at the Brunton Halls in Musselburgh, where Billy made his solo debut in 1971. Billy had to be secreted in his dressing room after being pursued into the foyer by Glass and a dozen followers. They threw copies of Glass's newspaper, *Scottish*

Protestant View, at Billy, and screamed, 'Blasphemer!' and 'Man of the Devil!' at him as he arrived at the venue in a black Mercedes. It was, if the fundamentalists would pardon the expression, a godsend to Connolly, who blew kisses to Glass and waved and smiled to the demonstrators. After Connolly had left the foyer, 950 angry fans queuing for tickets shouted abuse at Glass and his supporters.

He said mockingly after the show that Glass had got excited about the demonstration because he was not used to crowds as big as Connolly's. Billy was asked if he had deliberately come through the front door, to provoke the demonstrators. He replied, 'I didn't know where the back door was. If the Forth was lava I would throw him in,' he continued on the subject of Pastor Glass. 'He gave me a big smile when I arrived – and I found that most upsetting ... He looks a bit more satanic than I do.' Connolly admitted that he had given Pastor Glass the V-sign the previous week, at Oban. Pastor Glass and his followers announced that they planned to travel more than 1,000 miles picketing Connolly's venues on the tour. He said that the money for this was coming from a protest fund, which his church, the Zion Baptist Church, in Glasgow, operated. He had a regular congregation of about seventy people who contributed an average of about £100 each week, he claimed.

In London Connolly performed for three nights. Ned Chaillet in *The Times* described the act, for which Connolly now wore banana boots, rainbow braces and a leotard. 'He transcends the label of Glaswegian comedian from the beginning. Glasgow sparks many of the stories he tells, from bouts with the police to tales of Rangers and Celtic. Some of the stories even happen to be old ones, but in his peculiarly graphic and lavatorial speech, his hilarious enactments of his stories' characters, he conveys more than regional wit and something more special than any ' other contemporary comedian.

'His songs, with their folk virtues of rhythm and blues, tackle everything from a list of Britain's financial scandals to policemen lying in court,' *The Times* continued, 'but they cannot contain the wit and rising zaniness of his monologues. They, bringing in such characters as God and Allah, drift in uncharted directions to the limits of scatology ... It will not interest everyone to hear his graphic report on the after-effects of eating curry, nor will everyone know how to answer the question: "Have you ever thought of being a pervert?" Connolly has answers, confessions, lies and jokes and the most unfettered imagination on the British stage. He is a brilliant performer.'

But there were signs that the thrill of touring was wearing off, that, having stretched the comedy experience about as far as it went, Connolly was in need of a new challenge. In a telling *Daily Mail* interview with Thomson Prentice, he said he would like to make more of his talent as a writer, and would henceforth spend more time writing. 'I have to move on. I'm doing well, there's no problem about that, but if you take a look around this business, you see a lot of failures. People who were good for a wee while, a couple of years maybe. But they got cocky, they stood still. I don't fancy that happening to me.'

'Later, after a long night of making people laugh,' Prentice observed, 'he returned to his ninth-floor hotel suite and wandered around, opening and closing doors. "This is what being a star means," he grinned wearily. "They give you hotel rooms that big that you can't find the toilet."' (At this stage in his life, he still felt distinctly uncomfortable in five-star surroundings. An actor friend recalls standing next to Connolly at a urinal in a posh London hotel; Connolly turned to him and said: 'It kind of makes your dick feel shabby, doesn't it?'

The years 1976 and 1977 were the start of Connolly's serious acting and play-writing period. Peter McDougall's *Just Another Saturday* had been his television actorial debut in 1975 (he played a supporting role as a Glaswegian hard man for this BBC production), but now he was getting into his stride. In his Tom Ferrie interview on New Year's Day 1976, he spoke with great excitement about *The Elephant's Graveyard*, a Peter McDougall Play For Today, which was then in the planning stage. 'It's the most serious thing I've done in my life, I think. There's just two of us for ninety minutes, and I'm really looking forward to it. The dialogue's just between two people, two men. And I've seen the script, I've had a wee look at it and it's quite astonishing. So I'm really looking forward to that. Because I'd like to move in that kind of direction, the drama side of things ... As far as I can see, it's the direction I should be moving in if I'm going to broaden as a performing artist.'

A few days later, in an interview in a Glasgow arts magazine, he was asked what his ambitions were: 'He would like to write another play. A serious one, a big yin. *And* more acting. *And* films. *And* directing. *And* metal sculpture. *And* ... "In ten years' time I don't want to be on stages. There are no more Tommy Morgans or Harry Gordons [old-time Scottish comedians]. Those days are over for everybody." '

Getting serious was to be a frustrating time for Connolly, but, a little perversely, he seemed to refuse to be frustrated by it. The critics often appreciated his acting, even if to do so seemed to stick in their throat a little, but they simply were not set alight by Billy's writing. His first play, *An' Me Wi' A Bad Leg, Tae*, was performed at the Edinburgh Festival Fringe ('I think I'm banned from there for dipping my willy in a gin and tonic') in 1976 to a less than rapturous welcome, and the response did not improve subsequently. Even three years later, when he was commissioned to write a play, *The Red Runner*, for the Festival proper, the *Daily Telegraph* critic, John Barber, leapt on it as 'as feeble an offering as anything I have seen in all my years of Edinburgh theatre-going'.

An' Me Wi' A Bad Leg, Tae, was put on by the seven actors of Borderline, an Ayrshire travelling group, and opened at the Harbour Arts Centre, Irvine. 'A play bearing the Connolly imprimateur,' said the *Guardian*, 'could fill any theatre in Scotland and many beyond. It is a measure of the man's cautious good sense that he handed it over to the very talented, but relatively obscure, Borderline Company.' The newspaper called the play a milestone in Connolly's career, although David Lambie, the local Labour MP, complained: 'There's not enough politics in it.' ('You learn to play the banjo and I'll become a politician,' snarled Connolly, before delivering an extremely political assault on the Callaghan Government's right-wing deficiencies.)

The *Guardian* called Connolly's first effort, 'a slice of real life, Glasgow's working class actuality, which never puts a foot wrong in terms of authenticity', but the *Stage* and *Television Today* took more what would later be the *Telegraph*'s damning view, reporting, 'It scarcely merits the description of a play. Rather it is an extended music hall sketch larded with a succession of soliloquies as Connolly unsuccessfully attempts to be the philosopher. However, in delineating the humour and pathos of the Glasgow tenement Billy Connolly scores a brilliant success, and one forgives the jejune ramblings for this creation.'

The play was the story of a boy, Peter, coming home from the army to the Maryhill tenements and what his mum calls 'a toilet with an outside hoose'. In his boots and tartan trews he feels smart, but to his brother, a bitter Clydeside militant, he's just daft. His mother is the one who's got quite enough to bear with her bad leg too. 'Her cross is her belted bedroom-slippered old man (Bill Paterson)' said the *Daily Mail*. '. . . Sparks fly – capitalism, Ireland, the Army – aided by the arrival of an Auntie who looks like Maryhill's answer to Dolly Parton, and her husband, a Partick Thistle supporter. The big Yin himself has filled the spaces between the laughs with a talent for dialogue and building characters on deep and solid bases.'

Connolly got back from the Elton John tour of the US in time to see the play performed at the Edinburgh Festival, at the Old Chaplaincy Centre. In October, it transferred to the Theatre Upstairs at London's Royal Court. On the first night Billy, wearing a strawberry-coloured jacket, chuckled all the way through it. 'Connolly, sipping whisky donated by the distiller whose product is the central feature of the action, said he had two other plays in mind [*Groan Up*, and *When Hair Was Long And Time Was Short*, which opened at the 1977 Edinburgh Fringe] and was growing tired of performing the comedy act which made his name,' said *The Times* Diary. The *Observer* reviewer was not impressed: 'Mr Connolly as playwright is the nakedest emperor to ride into London for some time . . . sub-O'Casey rowing, philosophising, boozing and singing, leading to a mighty mawkish ending and punctuated by spotlit monologues as a guarantee of seriousness.'

Groan Up, Billy's second play, was about a teenager thrown out of home, who is a woman from the waist up. 'I was out of the house when I was eighteen and this is what gave me the idea. The half-man, half-woman character is not so much a sex problem, but a split personality,' he explained. The play was first staged by Borderline at the same time as he was making a pilot of 'The Highland Queen', a sitcom about oil rig workers in northeast Scotland; Billy playing a foreman welder, and the series was to be produced by Ian MacNaughton (of Monty Python fame) and scripted again by McDougall. The show did not succeed beyond spawning seven scripts and a pilot. McDougall said: 'It has taken a year out of our lives. Of course we are disappointed. We really thought it would take off. Part of the problem was that the BBC would not allow us to film it. It had to be made in the studio, and you can imagine the problem trying to pretend that the TV Centre is the middle of the North Sea and attempting to crowd thirty big-assed welders into a tiny studio.'

Before 'The Highland Queen's' pilot came the October 1976 showing of *The Elephant's Graveyard*, which went out as a Play for Today. It was about unemployment in Glasgow. There were only two parts in the play, and Billy was on screen for its entire hour and a half length. The film was made secretively, because, at the height of his popularity, there could have been a riot had it been known that Billy was out and about. The play was about two men meeting on a hill in a Glasgow park and sharing a bottle of cheap wine. Both men are out of work and on the dole, but neither has managed to tell his wife. The possibility is that the two are the same person at different stages of existence – one is young and confident, the other older, yet still living in hope. 'Billy Connolly was miraculously restrained for a stand-up comedian, and full of assurance,' commented the *Daily Mail*.

'It's a mammoth part. Nothing like anything I've ever done before,' Connolly said. 'It's about a man frustrated with poverty and life on the dole. I accepted the role because that man could have been me. I was a shipyard worker, and probably now I would be out of a job. But he is not me. The difference is that I would have got out of that place. I wouldn't have stayed poor in Glasgow. I'm a fully qualified survivor.' Connolly would later collaborate with Peter McDougall again: 'We started writing this film, called *Travelling Man*, but we found we couldn't work together. Put me in a room and I'm like a lion in a cage, whereas Peter is a loner by nature, a tortured writer who should never be let out of a room. A brilliant, brilliant man. So I went off on my bike and he just got on and finished it.'

In the midst of all this new dramatic activity, in September 1976, came the Edinburgh Film Festival launch of *Big Banana Feet*, the seventy-seven-minute documentary of Connolly's 1975 Irish tour. Produced by Murray Grigor and Patrick Higson, directed by Grigor, the film attracted reasonable reviews, which, even if their favourable comments were for the filmmakers, reflected well on Billy. 'A longish sequence when the camera studies Connolly, on his own, apparently rehearsing mentally, prior to going on stage, while unconsciously sucking at a cigarette and absentmindedly uncapping a bottle of beer, is masterful,' wrote *Variety*.

Billy was aware that its success was gained with the minimum of effort by him. 'The film came about in a most bizarre fashion. Somebody said to me, "Why don't you make a film?"' Despite having toyed with plays, and being privately in the course of writing a novel (an imaginary autobiography of a non-existent but non-violent Glaswegian, that has yet to be published), he had no ideas at all for a film, so they just filmed him. 'I thought it would be useful for a promotional thing. But it was shown at the Edinburgh Festival, and when I was asked if I would like it to go on general release, I said yes.'

The film was welcomed partly because it demonstrated so clearly why Connolly had been such a unifying force in Ireland, where he came across as a natural, non-political bridge between Ulster and Eire. In Belfast he says: 'I'm no' feart, but I drop the orange and green stuff because I thought they were having an evening out to get away from it.' When someone from the Dublin audience shouts, 'Up the IRA', Connolly countered: 'That's really brave. I'd love to hear you say that at Ibrox.'

Molly Plowright of the Glasgow *Evening Times* wrote: 'When someone had said wasn't he afraid of going there and being blown up he answered he didn't think of it. Anyway it was a duty to go because a lot of his records were sold up there. One passage I did find regrettable, though – his cracks at the British Army while he was in Dublin. "Soldiers are not completely bad, they're completely conned," he said and the Dubliners loved it. I thought of this again when he was in Ulster, signing autographs for those smiling young soldiers with Scottish accents. But then I had another thought – maybe they're the ones who buy his records.'

CHAPTER 7

Breaking Up

'The years between 20 and 40 were the best part of my life ...
before then things were difficult for me.'
*Billy Connolly speaking at fifty. He set up home with Pamela Stephenson
aged thirty-nine*

Then again, perhaps he was not that intent on being a serious actor and
dramatist; in 1978, Billy Connolly, like any soul-searching actor, just
didn't know. 'I'd rather be a comedian than an actor. Well, with my
accent I think I'd be severely limited as an actor, but this is a lovely
diversion,' he explained, speaking in a field in Buckinghamshire,
about his first serious film acting role to Scarth Flett of the *Sunday
Express*.

The film was *Absolution*, written by Anthony Shaffer of *Sleuth* fame,
and Connolly was cast as Blakey, 'a sinister hippy', who comes into
confrontation with a conservative Jesuit priest, Father Goddard (played
by Richard Burton) at a Catholic boys' school. When the film came
out, in America the following year, in Britain, as late as 1981, it won an
award at the Miami Film Festival, and his performance was highly
acclaimed at the Oxford Film Festival.

Connolly's description of his role had a certain familiarity; it was as a
banjo-playing 'wild travelling man of the woods', exactly, he still maintained, what he always wanted to be in real life. 'That film gave me a
magic moment. Having been brought up as a Catholic, I was able to
demonstrate to Burton how to sit in the confessional box.' (The magic
moment was not a lot in terms of exorcizing, or whatever it was he

wanted to do to it, his own Catholicism, but in terms of career progress, it is easy to see Billy's point here.)

'The first day I met him, he said, "Right, let's rehearse." It was a real baptism of fire. I felt really shaky. I thought I was going to faint. He has this magnificent presence. I've only done three films, two for television and one that was just about me, and I thought, he'll laugh at me, he'll chase me off the set. But he has been very helpful.'

The *Absolution* venture, which slightly dented his burgeoning confidence, made Billy reassess his comedian's life; perhaps he had merely become jaded in 1977? The year 1978 had started pleasantly enough on the comedic front, with a fourth appearance on 'Parkinson' – a record – and, in February, a vastly less traumatic American tour, a series of one-night stands, the Glasgow accent ironed out a little, no lunatic drunken expat Scots and no bad publicity back home. When he got back to Scotland, BBC1 was showing a rerun of his 'Parkinson' interviews, the sort of acclaim that, flattering though it is, would make anyone begin to wonder if he had run out of steam.

There was another American and Australian tour – still very quiet – until in August, Connolly found himself causing controversy in Scotland again. He presented a BBC1 'Checkpoint' programme on Glasgow, one of a series of six programmes on Scotland, and infuriated councillors by savagely attacking them for creating 'reservations' such as Drumchapel. The programme opened with Billy wandering through Partick, 'the big bad lands of Glasgow', as drunks staggered past on the pavement. He praised green-belt estates such as Knightswood; 'Maybe it was costly, for whatever reasons they abandoned that type of housing project and started to build the Drumchapels, the Castlemilks, and the Easterhouses. Desperate, just a modern slum ... We called it a graveyard with fairy lights, or sometimes a forest of wardrobes.' Sitting outside Glasgow City Chamber, he continued, 'Millions of pounds have been spent on this town by a London Government, and squandered in my opinion, by this party political squabbling that goes on in there.'

In November, he was in the soup in a more serious sense when he assaulted a *Sunday People* reporter, Hugh Farmer, at the Connolly home in Drymen. Farmer ended up with a black eye and bruised ribs after going to investigate a story about Connolly being involved in a dispute with a neighbour. Iris had invited him in, then called her husband at the pub; he stormed home in his red Jaguar, rabbit-punched Farmer in the neck and kicked him with pointed-toe cowboy boots as the reporter ran to his car for protection. Farmer said Iris hung on Connolly's shoulders saying, 'Stop it Billy.' He denied being rude to Iris, or refusing to leave. 'He called me a bastard,' Farmer related. Connolly also was said to have thrown something at Farmer's windscreen. 'I was terrified of what Connolly would end up doing to me if I did not get away,' he said. Farmer claimed £2,000 damages in a civil action at Stirling Sheriff Court nearly two and a half years later, where Connolly's counsel, Kevin Drummon, said damages, if any, should be no more than £200. Connolly was eventually forced to pay £400 damages plus interest to Farmer. He did not attend the hearing. (Farmer, a rather correct man − not an untypical characteristic for a skilled toe-in-the-door hack, as he was − had previously successfully sued *Private Eye* for suggesting that he had procured the services of a prostitute for the anarchist Stuart Christie, whom he was 'minding' on the *Sunday People*'s behalf. He is today the editor of the Scottish Catholic *Observer*.)

In the same period as setting about Farmer, Connolly was playing the jailer Frosch at a gala Scottish Opera Christmas performance of *Die Fledermaus* at the Theatre Royal, Glasgow, conducted by Sir Alexander Gibson. David Pountney, the director, explained in rehearsals, 'The role requires a brilliant comic with loads of acting ability and invention and Billy will be ideal. We haven't restricted his material in any way and have virtually given him *carte blanche*. His script is up to himself.'

Doing opera was not as great a contrast to the everyday business of joking on stage about jobbies and dealing with inquisitive tabloid hacks as it seemed. As Billy reassured his fans, 'I've never ever been to an opera before. The only time I've been connected with one was when I drew a lottery winner and that was a Mrs Macbeth. But I'm not terrified of taking part. Audiences are much the same throughout the world. I want to diversify as much as possible and you can't get a much bigger change for me than this.'

As Billy's frenetic 1970s drew to a close, it was hard to discern any great change or development in his basic model stage show, or indeed any public desire for him to do anything other than what he was perceived as doing best. The delicately named Big Wee Tour of Britain's smaller towns – the likes of Workington, Barrow, Canterbury and Preston – was a sixty-two-gig sellout, culminating in six nights at the Theatre Royal, Drury Lane. At the end of the 1979 tour, Connolly was presented, bizarrely enough, with a plaque by Lloyds for having the longest-ever tour without an insurance claim.

John Heilpern caught up with the show in Preston, his vivid description adding to the impression that Connolly had become, despite his frequent, and frequently earnest, diversifications, a little fossilized. He was, to put things in perspective, not far off forty, about to become a panellist on 'Juke Box Jury' and only a few months off his 'This Is Your Life' appearance. More disturbingly, although he was hardly to know this at the time, the election of Margaret Thatcher on 5 May was, within a short time, to unleash a new generation of highly political alternative comedians, as much as fifteen years younger than Connolly, whose opportunistic ranting against 'Fatcher' was to make Billy's comedy appear oddly staid and out of date. It was nice to be acknowledged as the father of alternative comedy as he soon was, but the *Zeitgeist* dictated that it was preferable to be the son of the genre, not its aging parent.

'To a roar from the audience,' Heilpern observed, ' "The Big Yin" came on stage dressed like a hipster wizard, apparently without preparation or nerves, to sing a song, an adaptation of a punk rock hit: "Hit me with your greasy chip! HIT ME!" … Appealingly, "The Big Yin" laughs as much at his own jokes and wild stories as his audience does. His show is a kind of party; a rave-up. "I do laugh on stage," he says. "I enjoy myself. What you see is what I am. It's also what you get. It's the real thing!" There then followed about two hours of near-manic improvisation, during which "The Big Yin" mixed it with hecklers and talked, as he does off-stage, about almost anything which happens to come to mind: the lethal effects of curry; the man dying to pee; two Glaswegians sightseeing in the Sistine Chapel ("Very nice. Who does the wallpaper?"); the lion-tamer whose gimmick is that he puts his willy in the lion's mouth; the popularity of mechanical sex aids: "Darling, come to bed." "Won't be a second, dear. I'm just changing your batteries…" '

Alasdair Buchan of the *Mirror* had his turn at trying to redefine

Connolly in the tea lounge of the Grosvenor Hotel, Chester. Buchan dwelt on how incongruous his faded jeans and straggly hair looked in a genteel setting. 'We've come across some pretty whacko hotels,' Billy said. 'They're not used to someone who gets up after lunch and wants breakfast.' Buchan wrote: 'One man who objected was brusquely told a new place to store his roast beef.' On tour, Connolly spent his days reading, going for walks and sometimes listening to tapes of his show to see if any of his ad lib stuff was worth keeping.

At the theatre, Buchan noted, there were wet paint signs back stage. 'It makes you feel like the Queen . . . she thinks the whole world smells of new paint too,' Billy told him. During the show, he got the standard hecklers: 'The last time I saw a mouth that big Lester Piggott was sitting behind it', and 'With a voice like yours I'd teach my bum to sing,' were Connolly's lines to rile them this evening. Who these hapless Billy Connolly hecklers were, and why, in the face of irrefutable evidence that they could never win, they did it, was to remain, as ever, one of life's mysteries.

In April 1979, just as half the British expats around the world were thinking of coming home to take advantage of the end of the Labour Government, Frank Lynch decided to emigrate to Florida. 'Frank wants to escape the British press and Spain is too handy. He will be settling in Miami,' Connolly announced. The possibility that he wanted to escape him apparently did not occur to Billy.

In May, Connolly was interviewed by Melvyn Bragg on 'The South Bank Show' – another stage on the road to establishment acceptance – the interview interspersed with chunks of the Big Wee Tour, which was in mid-stream at this point. Prompted by Bragg, Connolly remembered the first time he told a story about farting. 'The audience exploded . . . It was a different laugh to any I'd ever experienced,' he said, shaking his head in wonder. It had hit Connolly like a dam breaking, 'a sudden release of suppressed guilt'. Now he tells his audience, 'Don't be embarrassed or offended, it's nature . . . it's not dirty.

'I talk about the things that hurt and embarrass me. I'm getting rid of my own taboos. I'm chasing the witch. . . I dwell on absurdity and isolation – the feeling of being lonely in the crowd. . . I feel I'm exposing an area where no man has gone before, touching the untouchable.'

The slick, glossy allure of 'The South Bank Show' may have had some part in provoking a surprising statement by Connolly in July; he announced in the Glasgow *Evening Times* that he was thinking of moving to London: 'I've been thinking about it for some time and I suppose it's almost inevitable. London is where the action is – I mean, what's here? The Apollo? Down there they have got all the facilities for an actor.'

'An actor?' queried the writer. 'Yeah, well, that's my future,' replied Connolly. 'I don't want to be known as Billy Connolly the comedian. Acting is my game. So I've been thinking about moving. I'm spending a lot of time in London and I'm getting sick at the sight of the Shuttle.' He had seen it reported here and there that he was moving to all sorts of places, even to America. 'So I suppose London is on. There's only one thing frightens me – have you seen the prices of the hooses there?'

In August, Billy was burning the cultural candle at both ends. He released a record of 'In the Brownies', a parody of the Village People's 'In the Navy', making a TV film to accompany the song, dressed as a Brownie. As this was climbing the charts, his comedy *The Red Runner*, about three men in prison, opened at the official Edinburgh Festival, which had commissioned it. 'I've never before been in the official Festival,' he said. 'I feel a bit strange about it. I'm a hairy. I don't belong. This success is giving me the confidence to announce that it is time some of my plays were produced in the West End.' *The Red Runner* was panned and there were reportedly rows of empty seats, although the official biographical details sent out by Connolly's management at the time said, '*The Red Runner* played to packed houses, with an extended run after the Festival.' ('A crowing fringe partisan', meanwhile, told a London *Evening Standard* critic, 'They say he only started writing it three weeks before the Festival was due to begin, and I can believe it.')

'This static "Little Yin" is a low-key report of the misery of three men confined in a Scottish prison cell,' reported the *Telegraph* critic, John Barber. 'The excruciating boredom of the men lying on their beds communicates itself to the audience. They bicker among themselves, exchange puerile stories, receive disappointing visits from their dispirited womenfolk, or pretend the cell is haunted by a ghost. Mr Connolly raised some laughter with the coarse language of his trio: an old lag of a housebreaker (James Kennedy), a boy caught pushing marijuana

(Alexander Morton) and an unfeeling ruffian worried about his constipation (Tony Roger). But before the end, the first two have been reduced to tears of self-pity for their plight. Psychologically the play is too superficial ... And although it has compassion, it is too meretricious to be taken as an implicit argument against the penal system.' Barber wondered how the Festival organizer John Drummond 'could have initiated the drama in his first festival by accepting and promoting so inconsiderable a script.'

In the autumn, Billy returned to familiar territory with, incredibly, another 'Parkinson' appearance, alongside Warren Mitchell. (The journalist Stephen Pile wrote in December 1980 that it occurred to him that 'Michael Parkinson is killing off the art of profile writing. Would Boswell have bothered if Dr Johnson had walked down Parkinson's staircase seventeen times in a year?') Also at this time, Connolly went through a curious football phase, going to a few matches in Glasgow, having not been to a local match in years, and having steered well clear of football in his comedy. He had been to a game at Wembley, and this had served to increase his dislike of the game, or more accurately, of the football ethos. 'I never saw people behaving so amazingly badly in my life. A guy shouted at me, "I hope you die soon," and I thought, oh God, what a rotten thing to say to somebody.'

'I like talking about the crowd better than the game,' he explained on local radio. 'I've never done anything about the actual game apart from a thing about Martians and I don't think I recorded that. About Martians coming down and having a look at football and going back to report. And they'd come to the conclusion that there was twenty-two guys running about, and two sides of eleven men. And the object was to hit the goalkeeper with the ball, and if you missed and the ball went into the net, your mates all kissed you and you felt a right eejit. Apart from that I haven't touched it at all.'

One night, he went to a game with Hugh Jordan, who at the time (he is now a broadcaster in Northern Ireland) was a publican, and had been Billy's barber – a job that sounds a little like being the costume manager for Radio 4, but the flowing Connolly locks did need frequent maintenance. 'I met Billy in town one day because he was a great Celtic supporter like myself and Celtic were playing that night – Kenny Dalglish would have been playing at that time – and he said to me, "Do you fancy going to the game tonight?" And I said, "Aye." So he came down and picked me up at my mother's house and we went to the game. At half time Billy was talking away to people and younger guys were asking him for his autograph and older guys were saying, "Leave that boy alone. Fucking give him a break," and that type of thing, and he kind of liked that. Then the next minute an announcement comes over the microphone, "Would Mr Billy Connolly come to the main gate." The older guys were saying, "Maybe they want you to play, Billy." And he's saying, "Aye, I hope so. I'd like to go on for the second half," and all that. So we went down and there was Billy and another older man who was obviously called Billy Connolly as well. The steward said, "Billy, I think it's you," and pointed to Billy and said, "You've got to go home right away. Your sister-in-law has died," and this was Iris's sister who had died of cancer. She had been a dentist. So I drove him back down and we went to the funeral a couple of days later up in the crematorium near where I live. He spoke at the funeral. He was reading from Oscar Wilde and he started crying as he spoke about Iris's sister. This was a year before things started going wrong between Billy and Iris.'

The definition of when a new relationship starts to develop is always problematic. Did it start when they met? Or earlier, when each was first aware of the other's presence? When they first talked a little longer than necessary? In 1979, at the time Billy made his emotional and very touching speech at his sister-in-law's funeral, the most popular and outrageous comedy show on TV was the BBC's 'Not The Nine O'Clock News'. He was invited to appear on the show, in a pub sketch, playing a hard man who bursts in and asks: '[gruffly] Has Jimmy Chainsaw McPhee been in here lately? What about Jock the Kneecruncher ... [limply] Can I have a Campari and soda please.' The four mainstays of the NTNOC News team appeared on film on Connolly's 'This Is Your Life'; Pamela was, of course, included, although she did not speak. But for posterity's sake, it is worth noting that on this occasion, Iris Connolly, embarrassed to the quick by the show anyway, was there in the Thames TV studio looking at her rival.

Just as the world carries on uninterrupted the day after you die, life and work did not stop to accommodate the growing relationship between

Billy Connolly and Pamela Stephenson. In June 1980, Connolly was on the verge of his first British TV series for LWT with producer Tony Cash, who had produced LWT's Connolly 'South Bank Show'. Each week, it was proposed, Connolly would look at a different institution (such as religion and the army), accompanying his monologues with songs, banjo and guitar. In a pilot show, he looked at the world of advertising. 'One day I came across one of them rules laid down by the Independent Broadcasting Authority on the subject of TV commercials,' Cash explained. 'It said you could show the inside of a lavatory, but not the inside of a lavatory pan. I thought to myself, what would Billy Connolly do with that? It sparked off the idea of the series.'

Connolly was as studiedly ambivalent as ever about the prospect; he would call the familiar attitude fear. 'I must confess I don't go around the streets on my hands and knees screaming, "I want a series on television." You can tell from my career that it's not my favourite medium. It's a very strange feeling, because most comedians are willing to crawl over miles of broken glass to get on TV. But my sort of act is ad libbed and anarchic, and I've never felt really settled with it on TV. If you asked me honestly I'd say that I don't really want a TV series.'

On the other hand, he went on, 'Working with people like Tony Cash is amazing. He usually does highbrow stuff. He likes my fun and it's a lovely way to work because I'd hate to work with a red-nosed producer.' Of his suspicion of TV, he said, 'It's not a medium I like because I don't really know how to use it. I'm not a professional or anything like that. I just sing my songs and tell my stories and hope people will like them. That's all.' Billy's uncertainty about the project gained its due result: London Weekend scrapped plans for the series.

He knew his touring days *ought* to be fading away, yet it remained his strongest suit bar none. 'I want to write more. I'm thirty-seven now and I certainly don't want to be still doing the stage thing at forty-seven. It's not the sort of life you relish as you get older. There's nothing so uncomfortable as an old hippy, an aging rebel,' he said in a 1980 interview. 'But for the moment I enjoy doing the tours. I was speaking to Graham Lyle [of the pop singing duo Gallaher and Lyle] the other day and he said he was bursting to get back on the road and tour again. I said I felt the same. I suppose we are all tarmac junkies hooked on the M1 and exhaust fumes and waiting to mainline on Forte's motorway meat pasties again.'

His 1980 dramatic experiences amplified the point for him. In June, the Pavilion Theatre, Glasgow, put on a three-week season of three Connolly plays, 'based on leaving home. It's made that part of my life stay alive.' A month later, he decided not to appear in his own pantomime, *The Sleeping Dumpling*, which was scheduled for a three-month run from 4 December at the same theatre. *Variety* put this down to the 'troubled three-week run of his own plays and personal appearances recently at the Pavilion. The shows were poorly attended, received unfavourable reviews and had some performances cancelled.' In the end, the £250,000 panto was cancelled altogether. ('I've done everything except ballet and pantomime, and I don't intend doing pantomime,' he said three years later. I hate the way people edge their acts into it. Glenn Daley, who's a wonderful Scottish singer and comedian, had the all-time great panto line. He was King of Siam and he had to come off the throne and say, "I may be the King of Siam, but I'll never forget that old Scottish mother of mine ..." Cue to strike up the orchestra.')

It was during the three plays' second week that Connolly, frustrated by their lack of success (and very possibly other developments on the domestic front) declared in the local paper, 'I'm finished with Glasgow. I'll never appear on stage again in the city. I've nothing against the people of the city. It's the press. They just won't leave me alone. Perhaps if I had gone to London like so many others, things would have been different. But I really don't want to move. I like living here. Sure, the people have their faults. And there are some things that really annoy me about them too. I mean, they demand to have my autograph when I'm right in the middle of a meal. They don't have the manners to wait until I'm finished. It's different in London. Down there, at least they wait until the meal is over. But I'm being continually criticized for bringing the city down. For painting a bad picture of the violence and the drunks. But that's the way I see it. I don't try to gloss over it. But it is a friendly place and that's why I'm reluctant to move.'

Connolly was not particularly in the habit of sticking to his views – who is? – and he was under severe strain. He partly refuted the story, interviewed on Radio Clyde two years later, and has oscillated ever since on the matter of whether or not he has 'abandoned' Glasgow. 'I said something like that,' Connolly told Sheila Duffy on the station. 'I was under severe attack. I'd brought my plays to town, and I was putting on a play a week. And the play would be the first half and I'd go on and be the second half, and it was very, very good, but I got the most astoundingly bad publicity, incredibly bad crits, grossly unfair. People who in my honest opinion couldn't write home for money, they gave me such a bad time.

'I'll give you an instance. There was one day, the sets were on a sort of rotunda, like the London Palladium thing, and they started to warp, so doors wouldn't close, but the scene was prison and it made it funny because a door kept opening, and in prison that's not supposed to happen. This door kept flying open, and the prisoners had to go up and shut it, which doesn't really figure in real life. It started to get funny and people started to giggle. At one point Tony Roper the actor had to go over to Jimmy Kennedy the actor and say, "I'm sick of you," and the door opened. And he said, "I'm sick of that effing door as well." And at that point, half the audience were on the floor – as I was, I couldn't breathe for laughing – so were the cast. I lifted the paper the next day: "The audience were infuriated by this door that kept opening." It also told a blatant black lie, that the place was half empty, which was a total and absolute lie, so I was under all that attack at the time.

'Then, in the middle of it all, the Pavilion Theatre started to have a matinée that they didn't tell me about. So at six in the evening these people all turned up and there was nothing there but the doors. And we all arrived around eight at the normal time. So we were trying to sort all this out, and we'd sort it all out so there is no matinée, and the next week some more of them turned up, I don't know why, but they did. And they were saying, "Billy, what is this, is it because you couldn't sell it?" They was never on sale. There was no such beast. So on the third non-matinée this eejit turned up from the papers and said: "What's going to happen tonight?" I said, "What do you mean, what's going to happen tonight?" "About the matinée." I said, "There's no such thing. There's no matinée." And the following day it says, "New storm breaks out."

'I don't know what they're thinking about. So in the middle of all that I was supposed to do a pantomime for the Pavilion. So I told them, "I'm not coming to Glasgow to do the pantomime. I cannot put myself up for grabs like this. I'm not coming here to stand against a wall and be fired at by hacks, overfed and underworked hacks. That's not my gig. I'd rather go where somebody likes me." And that's where a thing got about that I wasn't going to play in Glasgow again, which is absolute nonsense. I always intended to come back in concert, but not to sit for three weeks and be sniped at by people who have got nothing better to do with their time. That's all.'

In 1980, meanwhile, he seemed to be backing up his threat not to play Glasgow with deeds; his fifty-venue On Yer Bike Tour of Britain (he travelled on a 750cc Kawasaki motorcycle) with a total of eighty-six concerts, began with two Saturday midnight preview shows at the Edinburgh Festival, then started properly at Stroud Leisure Centre, and ended in Belfast, taking in not a single Scottish venue. At the Danny McGrain memorial dinner in September, he said to an *Evening Times* journalist, 'If you want to learn about what I am doing read the English newspapers. Nothing personal, but I am finished with the Scottish press.'

Time was running out on the marriage, and it is arguable that the strains and problems of 1981 were more due to trouble at home than truly professional reasons. Not performing in Scotland kept Billy away in England and abroad for increasingly long periods. On 'This Is Your Life' in December 1980, Iris and the children were first shown on tape in Drymen, she highly embarrassed, the children sitting in front of the fire with three labradors. Jamie said, 'We miss you when you're on tour and we know you miss us.' Cara added a hallo from all the animals, and a puppy was seen eating out of Billy's banana boots. 'You're very much a family man,' said Eamon Andrews. Then Connolly's father, sister Florence and husband Ian, brother Michael (a Woody Allen lookalike) with wife Helen trailed on. (Connolly was said to have gone to work at 'John Brown's Shipyard', rather than Stephen's, the yard he actually worked at. He was then reunited with a man he did not know; Tam Harvey appeared on the programme, and he and Billy played 'Dixie Darling' together; no mention was made of Gerry Rafferty, only that Harvey and Connolly had been together in the Humblebums for three years.)

In May of the next year, 1981, he was featured in 'A Life in the Day Of' in the *Sunday Times*, and appeared to be paradigm of domesticity; had *Hello!* magazine existed in its English form then, you could have bet that the happily married Connollys would have featured across several pages at this sensitive point. 'I don't intend being a writer, but I have another play in mind, which I must write, about a guy who finds God,' Billy was quoted as saying in the 'Life In The Day' piece. Ominous thoughts indeed.

His 1981 Bite Your Bum World Tour took in the Middle East, Hong Kong, Australia and New Zealand. In Egypt, he played a St Andrew's Night dinner for the 200-strong Cairo Highland Dance And Song Society. Wherever he went, the local Scottish community would turn out in force. And wherever he went, too, or so it seemed to Iris reading the tabloids at home by Loch Lomond, Pamela Stephenson turned out in force. In Hong Kong in July, she met him, and was spotted by a reporter, on her way to New Zealand and Australia, and the *Daily Express* was writing about the 'well-publicised, strictly-platonic friendship' of Connolly and Pamela, whose names had been linked by those in the know for more than a year.

In February, the William Hickey column in the *Daily Express* ran a photo of Connolly and Pamela 'at a lively gathering in Chelsea'. 'The clever couple, who have become firm establishment favourites, are, I hear, working on a joint project. It would be an intriguing combination. The irrepressibly [sic] Connolly is one of the most outrageous Scotsmen to ever have vaulted Hadrian's Wall. And Pamela is without doubt the funniest lady on television. I think that teamed together they would give us a particularly rare treat on the usually appalling magic lantern.'

Connolly denied stories that he was having an affair with Stephenson. 'They're all absolute nonsense, wild rumours' said Billy, who was said to clock up great phone bills on tour, calling Iris and the children. Paradoxical it may seem, but, quite truthfully, he was a home-loving man. Long after the affair with Stephenson became the status quo, he was seriously thinking of returning to Iris. 'My family is where the joking stops,' he had said not long before. 'I'll never involve them in my work. Home is home. My family is mine and I won't share them with anyone.' He would tell a quite touchingly dull story that illustrates his strong protective feelings towards Iris: 'Our attitudes haven't changed, but people's attitudes towards us have. Some have had to be shown the door. There was this time when Iris was discussing clothes with some women at a sale in one of the clothes shops in the nearest town. One of the women turned to Iris and said something like: "Yes, it's terrific value. A real bargain. But then you won't be interested in bargains now, will you?" Now, I don't care if you're Jackie Onassis or a queen. A woman is a woman and they still like bargains the world over. To say that to my wife is an offence to her housekeeping standards. It's probably just jealousy, but that kind of thing hurts because it makes us think twice about certain people.'

He was, however, alongside those big, guilty phone bills, also clocking up considerable restaurant bills in his alternative world with Pamela. 'I know the lady, we are managed by the same people,' he told another tabloid. 'We have written a play together. I suppose that's where the gossip started. So sure we had dinner. Why not? Most of the time I think the gossip is funny and so does she.'

Billy was also being erroneously gossiped about apropos a twenty-five-year-old commercials actress, Victoria Burgoyne, who greeted him at a charity screening for his new video. Connolly walked away from Victoria as she was being photographed joking 'Tell them about the love child.' He said he, too, had read about his affair with Ms Burgoyne, but 'I have not even shaken her hand. Maybe she wants to be famous. She said in the article that we were going to be seeing a lot more of each other. Then she said she was going to Philadelphia for two weeks – and I left the following day for Australia. I don't know how we were supposed to manage it. The whole thing is cuckoo. But that's life.'

In May, with Billy's 'Life In The Day Of' barely cold, he and Stephenson attended a charity party in the West End. Pamela described Billy as 'one of the top three comedians in the world, along with Richard Pryor and Robin Williams'. 'She rates me that low does she?' joked Billy, adding, 'At last Britain has a comedienne. When she arrived, the sigh of relief was audible in Jersey.' He dismissed reports that they were together as 'garbage and nonsense ... but it's fun'. Connolly was dressed as a waiter with his hair tied back in a rubber band, Pam was in a mini-version of Lady Di's engagement outfit, wearing badges reading 'Gay

Whales Against Racism' and 'Clean Up London – Eat a Tourist'.

Back in Drymen, Iris commented to the local newspaper, before heading off for a hairdressing appointment to celebrate Billy's imminent return from London, 'Billy and Pamela now have the same manager, Pete Brown, who also looks after the group Earth, Wind and Fire. They are often seen together because of Pete. There is nothing more to it than that. Quite honestly I am more concerned about Billy being on tour away from home than being with Pamela Stephenson. He is going away soon to America and then to Dubai.'

Pamela Stephenson was a New Zealander, thirty years old to Billy's thirty-nine as this drama developed. She grew up and went to university in Australia. She played a lot of straight acting roles in Sydney, was a non-smoking vegetarian, came to England in 1976, and was in the process of separating from the actor Nicholas Ball (famous for playing the TV detective Hazell). Lesley Stephenson, her opera singing sister, gets Pamela about right, describing her as '... always a very theatrical person on and off stage and [she] would always observe people closely and be able to capture their mannerisms ... Pamela was into entertainment long before I was, and I think even as children it was easy to see that she was going to do very well.'

Their parents lived in Epsom, Surrey, 'in a house they have kept there because their academic and medical work often brings them here from Australia'. The Stephenson home life, as outlined by Lesley, was happy and prosperous, in stark contrast to Billy Connolly's upbringing. 'After a long day rehearsing it's comforting to come back here, and I can sing while my father plays the piano, and he doesn't care how loud I am. I like that,' Lesley said.

Billy first met Pamela at a flat he was renting in London. When the 'Not the Nine O'Clock News' team said they wanted him to appear on the show, he was petrified, felt out of his depth, and, as he often does, felt he wanted to say no. One evening, John Lloyd, the producer, came round to the flat with all of them: Gryff Rhys Jones, Mel Smith, Rowan Atkinson and Pamela. In 1979 terms, this was the most fashionable group of young comics trying to join forces with a veteran comedian: it was not quite a meeting of minds. Billy was not keen on her, even though she was clearly rather struck by him. It was decided that the six would have lunch together, and this time he liked Pamela, but said something that hurt her feelings about Australia, which she took personally: there was clearly more than a little attraction between the two.

When they did the show, he thought she was wonderful. In the first sketch they did together, she was Janet Street-Porter interviewing Billy Connolly (there has been a consistent, puzzling, trend for Billy to be cast as himself: it was still happening in 1993, when he played a cameo as Billy Connolly in *Indecent Proposal*). 'They were all smashing to me and I was really delighted to have done it. And that was the last I saw of her. And a year later on, I was on tour – and I'd never thought about any of them – and I was in Brighton, I was doing a concert at the Dôme – that place that looks like a big Indian restaurant – and Pamela and the rest of them were down at a greyhound track, doing a sketch where Pamela was a nurse and they were all doctors, sort of postgraduate types. It was about laxatives. They were testing laxatives and they gave it to all the doctors – they had white coats and no trousers and they were in greyhound traps – and they gave them all a different laxative, and then they put a toilet seat where the rabbit would be, and the toilet seat shot away and the doors would open and they'd come careering after it.

'Well they were down doing that sketch. And I didn't know they were at Hove or one of those places near Brighton. But anyway, a wee boy came up and asked for my autograph at the hotel, and I signed it. And the same wee boy knew they were in town – he must have read it in the paper – and he went along to them and got their autographs. And the guy who owned the greyhound track had said to Pamela and all of them, would you like to stay tonight and see the greyhound racing? And the boys said, well that might be interesting. And Pamela thought, oh God. She was rapidly losing the will to live. But the wee boy came along, asked for the autographs, and he said, "Are you going to the Dôme tonight?", to Pamela. And she said, "What's the Dôme?" And he said, "In the Brighton Dôme, Billy Connolly's on." And she thought, great I'll get away from this greyhound track. So she came to see me.'

The split came nearly a year after that, in August 1981. Iris, now thirty-six, announced to the *Sunday Mirror* that she thought her marriage was over. 'I blame the breakdown on show-business. We have been living in different worlds recently. When Billy comes home from his world tours all he wants to talk about are the exciting places he's been to and the interesting people he's met. He doesn't want to know about the washing machine that has broken down. I must admit that he has been seeing Pamela. But I don't blame him altogether for what has happened. Perhaps if I had moved to London, or even America, things might have been different. If Billy is to stay at the top it is necessary for him to make long world tours. This has put a strain on our marriage. We are still very fond of each other – even though we are no longer in love. We have talked for hours about separating and I am only announcing it now after a great deal of thought and many tears. Billy is very fond of the children Cara and Jamie, and in an odd sort of way I expect to see more of him in the future than I have in the past.'

In London, Billy and Pamela found themselves under siege. Meanwhile the tabloid comings and goings at Drymen, where, in the hot sun, a crowd of reporters had gathered, were described by the *Daily Mail*. 'Wearing dark glasses and driving a gold Ford Granada, dark-haired Mrs Connolly continually passed through the village, sometimes alone, sometimes with the children, Jamie eleven and seven-year-old Cara. For nearly two years she had dismissed talk that their marriage was on the rocks. But at the weekend she broke her silence to admit that it was "all over". Later in the local pub, her father, Bill, said, "She's been instructed to say nothing. She spoke to Billy today but I'm not prepared to say what was said . . ." '

The real drama, however, had taken place more than three weeks previously, and was witnessed from the inside by Billy's friend Hugh Jordan: 'It was the day Princess Diana married Prince Charles,' Jordan recalls. 'Iris had invited me out to the house and I brought a girlfriend with me called Margaret Peebles, who Billy knew. I had arranged to go out to Iris's that night. Billy was away on tour, and we went out for a drink and to a wee disco. The idea was that we were going to go out on Billy's boat on Loch Lomond.

'The next morning, we were all up and getting washed and I was getting shaved and I remember it was good fun. We were getting ready to head out and there's a knock at the door, so I answered the door and a journalist said, "Is Mrs Connolly there?" So I said, "Yeah, hold on," and got Iris. Iris went to the door and the guy had a small cutting from a newspaper in his hand and it said something like, "Mr Billy Connolly is off on his travels again. He was spotted last night in a restaurant in Singapore. Also in Singapore was a zany Australian actress Pamela Stephenson. Could this be a chance meeting?"

'Iris slammed the door shut, bang, and it was only at that moment that I realized that something was wrong. Iris started drinking Remy Martin, and she said, "That bastard told me there was nothing in that." She was very upset and next thing was that other people started to arrive and so our day trip on the boat was cancelled and I realized there was something seriously wrong here. She wanted to phone him but she couldn't because she had pulled the phone out from the wall because journalists were ringing.'

Iris was friendly with a schoolteacher called Mrs Callan, who lived down the road. Jordan went down to Mrs Callan's house and asked if he could bring Iris to use the phone, because hers was not working and there was an emergency. He went back to fetch Iris, and she drove herself in Billy's Mercedes, which she crashed on the short drive. 'We got the car off the road, and I took her down and she got on the phone to Los Angeles. Jamie Wark, who was a roadie who came after Billy Johnston – both of them had been welders together – answered the phone. Jamie was a good guy and a good friend of mine as well.

'Iris rang through to the hotel. Now when Billy was drinking you've never seen anybody like it – especially when he was playing on stage. He was just wound up so much that when he came off he would drink alcohol for hours and be unaffected by it. So Jamie Wark had this problem. He was working with him and when Billy wound down and would go to bed Jamie was wanting to get him up to travel on to the next gig and he said he was afraid to go and wake him because he would punch you. So anyway Iris gets through to the hotel and gets through to Jamie and says, "Get Billy for me." And Jamie says, "He's not here Iris."

'And Iris starts shouting and yelling. "Yes, he fucking is there and you're protecting him and I want to talk to him." So then I spoke to Jamie and he said, "Hughie, Billy's not here, he's fucking out drinking. I wish he was here because I have to get him up." So I said, "Will you get him to ring because there's something fucking seriously wrong here

Jamie." So a while later, Billy rang and they spoke and they spoke and the phone got put down and they were ringing back and different things, and then I spoke to Billy and I said, "Look, Billy. I'm here, you're there, there's a load of journalists and photographers wanting to talk to Iris. Do you want me to do anything? If you want me to do something I'll do it. If you don't want me to do anything, I will also do nothing, but just tell me what you want me to do because there are thousands of miles between us.' "

Connolly asked Jordan to try to stop Iris speaking to the press. 'Then after that I put Iris back on the phone and I heard her saying to him, "Are you coming home to us," and he must have said, "No", because when she came off the phone she said, "He told me that he's not coming home." That was the actual break-up of the marriage. Mrs Callan knew what was going on – she wasn't a fool. She would have been in her late fifties, she was mature, and she knew that Iris had a drink problem and she knew obviously there were marriage problems – much more so than I did.'

Once the cat came publicly out of the bag in August, the action shifted to several locations. Nicholas Ball, who was appearing at the Royal Court Theatre, told the press, 'It's none of your god-damned business where my wife is ... She has agents and managers to handle these sorts of things.' On the subject of her husband, Pamela told journalists, 'We have always dated other people and there's nobody special for either of us. We are splitting up for six or eight months to see how it goes.'

The day after the *Sunday Mirror* story, Billy confirmed publicly that his twelve-year marriage was over, but denied Pamela's involvement. He issued a seventy-word statement through his Glasgow lawyer: 'The root cause of the difficulty did not involve any other party ... Both Iris and I have been unhappy for some time, due mainly to the pressures on me. I understand Iris intends divorce proceedings. I will not contest the action since it would obviously be the best solution.'

As the statement went out, Pamela was away from her house all day, but 'returned by taxi last night looking close to tears.' When the dam broke, Billy had been in Dallas, Texas, four days into filming a BBC documentary on the city – 'Dallas Through The Looking Glass' – which he was doing in a break from his world tour. The documentary, which was being directed by Nicholas Roeg, had to be scrapped in its present form, costing the BBC around £20,000. A corporation spokesman said: 'There was absolutely no point in trying to keep a man out there whose whole world was collapsing back home. The parting from us was very amicable.' Connolly's promoter, Harvey Goldsmith, happened to be in Dallas with Billy, and said, 'I was with him and the pressures on him were becoming unbearable. I just had to get him out of there. He was in touch with his wife every day and he just had to get back to see her and the kids. I wasn't involved, but I'll tell you that I felt it for myself and for him. There was no way he could have stayed and completed the film with everything that was going on.'

Connolly arrived home on Monday, organized the statement with his solicitor and effectively went into hiding at Pamela's terraced house in Knightsbridge where, the *Sun* man learnt, many of Connolly's belongings were. From there, he went straight to the Edinburgh Festival. The *Sun* carried a front-page headline: 'TOP COMIC BILLY FLIES TO SECRET LOVE PAM', and said Connolly was furious to be discovered at Pam's. 'How the hell did you find me? Only two people knew I was here,' he said, as if it had been a detective masterstroke by the reporter. Connolly then reportedly went to nearby pub with Pete Brown, where he 'played darts alone and drank a pint of bitter'.

In Edinburgh, he embarked on a pub crawl more worthy of the name with another Scottish comedian, Bill Barclay, who said afterwards: 'What a night. Billy was really determined to get steaming. He has been like a bear with ten sore heads this morning. We were in all sorts of pubs, drinking pints, meeting old friends and chatting about old times. But Billy was on the lookout all the time for reporters. He doesn't want to talk about the marriage break-up at all.' Outside the Festival Fringe Club, where Connolly was not allowed in until he had coughed up £10 membership, Barclay had to restrain his friend from having a go at a Scottish newspaperman.

Back in London, Pamela was in Hyde Park to present prizes for a sponsored cycle ride for the British Heart Foundation. 'She smiled bravely as she posed for pictures but she constantly bit her lip to stop the tears. She even splashed water at the cameramen and told them: "I enjoyed that," ' reported the *Daily Mirror*. When a reporter gave her an orchid, she said: 'I suppose this is off expenses.' A similar remark had been made by the Princess of Wales the previous week, and Pamela said: 'I feel I have something in common with Lady Di.' Then she slipped and fell in the Serpentine, and was shaking later as she told reporters, 'It is very tasteless to bring up my private life.'

Pamela's banal later explanation of events had a distinctly royal touch; the bitter un-love affair between Connolly/Stephenson and the press was on, the couple, battered, emotionally stretched and lacking the sophistication to play the press to their own best advantage, the reporters pressurized to produce copy on the biggest showbusiness story of the day, and increasingly irritated by their subjects' exponentially galloping luvviness. 'I fell very sorry for the people whose charity events I was supporting,' Pamela said. 'When I fell into the Serpentine I was there on behalf of cyclists who had ridden from London to Brighton to raise money for the British Heart Foundation. They were the people that it was about, yet they were pushed aside and everything was focussed on my situation. Also last week I judged a painting competition in which 70,000 pictures were sent in by children and I am going to present the prizes. I am very anxious that people should not come along and gloat over me.'

A *News of the World* 'exclusive' at the end of August revealed that Stephenson was 'hopping mad'. 'I'm fed up with it all. I have said again and again that I will not talk about Mr Connolly and I mean it. Anyone who claims to have an interview with me suggesting that I have talked about him is misrepresenting me. It's a sensitive situation. Too many people are involved. Maybe I will come out of it reasonably okay. But my husband is going mad with it and my friends are very unhappy too ... Two weeks ago a journalist did an interview with me about my work. In particular we talked about my part in the new Mel Brooks film, *History of the World*, which comes out in October. Now a Sunday paper is suggesting I talked about Mr Connolly. This is just not true. They have no information at all. The only thing I said which they could have made something out of was when we talked about marriage. I said I didn't want people to think I was mean, and that because my own marriage was rather unusual, I didn't consider that everybody else's marriage should be the same way. I shall be very angry if that has been taken out of context.'

Iris, in the same article, gave the impression of being very generous to her husband and his girlfriend, a characteristic that would continue, even if there is a suspicion that many of her utterances at the time were tinged with alcohol. 'I hope Bill has Pamela because he has no one else. I feel sorry for her because her marriage to Nicholas Ball has finished, but I haven't spoken to her. I've asked Bill about Pamela and he says he's been seeing her. He says it's because he likes her. But when I ask him if he's in love with her he doesn't answer.'

The break-up, she said, had been coming for two years. 'He wanted to talk about showbusiness and I wanted to talk about the dishwasher that needed mending. When he came back from tours we wouldn't speak for two days. He just couldn't sit still. He was never around when we had our crises. I'm happy now just to be with the kids.' There was, she added, a dramatic homecoming when Billy returned from the world tour. 'We cuddled and he cried,' she revealed. 'I didn't cry. I have done all my crying. He was worried about the kids, but we're not getting a divorce yet. We're just splitting up. He will probably see more of them now because when he came back before he was always out.'

Despite the very reasonable things Iris was saying, there was a discernible drift of public opinion in Billy's favour. Sally O'Sullivan (now the editor of *Good Housekeeping*) wrote in the *Sunday Standard* about Iris: 'Desperately trying to sum up what had caused their separation she eventually said that her husband spent a great deal of time away from home yet when he returned he did not want to know that the washing machine had broken. This struck a lot of people, I have since discovered, as utterly reasonable' – though not Ms O'Sullivan, who sympathized with Iris.

The Connollys' friends were on the whole surprised by the marriage break-up. 'Some friends of mine suggested to me at one point he would have gone back with Iris like even after the first baby with Pamela was born,' says Hugh Jordan. 'They said, "I'll put a tenner on with you that he will go back," but it obviously never happened.'

CHAPTER 8

Pamela

'Marriage is a great invention, but then so was the bicycle repair kit.'
A Billy Connolly-ism that entered the Oxford Dictionary of Quotations *in November 1992)*

Pamela Stephenson's influence on Billy Connolly was immediate and profound. While she found the attraction of a rough-diamond Glaswegian caveman enticing, even as the contemporary queen of outrageous behaviour, she was not prepared to put up with Billy's drunkenness. As someone brought up in Australia, she had seen quite enough in the culture of drunken males; it also offended her feminism, her middle-classness, and – a big and – Billy's chances of getting access to his children in the forthcoming divorce case. Although Iris's drinking was legendary, she was still the children's mother. By the autumn Billy had consulted the London Buddhist Centre as a first step to cleaning up his off-stage act.

Pamela had put the idea of Buddhism into Billy's mind, having been involved with it for many years, and it seemed to fit the vacant spiritual part of his mind that had been empty (something he felt) since he gave up on Catholicism twenty years before. He first phoned the Buddhist Centre in Bethnal Green and asked to see Dhammarati, an ex-psychiatric nurse and graphic designer who, as luck would have it, was from Hamilton, near Glasgow.

'I was a bit taken aback at first,' said Dhammarati. 'We sat down and discussed things for about half an hour and it appeared that a mutual friend from Scotland had advised Billy to get in touch with me. He's a very intelligent man and seemed genuinely interested in knowing more about the Buddhist way of life. We had a cup of tea together and I explained the basics of the meditation techniques. Then we took our shoes off and sat together and meditated for about twenty minutes. I taught Billy to meditate and I would say that he made a very good student. I explained that meditation wasn't a magic spell or trick and that it requires a bit of effort on behalf of the individual.' ('From that second I owned up,' Connolly said. 'Now I have twenty minutes to myself every morning and it has saved me from the disaster for which I was heading.' He claimed now to enjoy 'just a pint or two'. He had also vowed not to fight the press any more.)

The rediscovery of his spiritual side was more than a passing phase. 'I don't do it every day,' he said of meditation a few years later. 'All it does is give me peace. And then I go and do my job, and that's it. It's just peace, I don't worship anyone or anything like that. I'm not heavily into the spiritual side of things. Maybe later I'll investigate it deeper. But right now I use the meditation, and it's amazing what it's done for me. Personally it's given me great solace.'

Spirituality was not new to Connolly; in many ways, this was not a surprising diversion. Catholicism had been very important in his child-hood, and a tradition he liked. He had relatives who were priests and nuns, which as he said, 'does imbue your mind and your thoughts'. There were religious pictures at home, and Billy clearly recalls as a child standing outside St Peter's in Partick after confession, 'thinking I was transparent, thinking I was made of crystal, I felt so clean'.

And the religion proved to have more than a skin-deep influence on him, as it has had on many twentieth-century celebrities, from Joyce to Madonna, who use the religion's imagery and indoctrination to fuel their art. In Scotland, he still includes a lot of Catholic references in his act. (He does not let other sects off; he tells of a Jehovah's Witness at the yards who used to take his willy out with a hankie when he was having a pee and look the other way.)

However, you can lead a young Catholic to the altar but you can't make him think all the Church may desire him to. The Catholic initiation process, from First Communion to Confirmation, includes the first lesson of First Confession, when children are called upon to confess their sins. If, at that age (through lack of opportunity perhaps as much as desire), there are no 'sins' for the young Catholic to commit, it is not uncommon for the children waiting in the pews outside the confessional to make them up. Then, after the priest's absolution of these 'sins', they may feel, well, they've been admonished and done penance for something they didn't even do in the first place. Such early introduction to the art of feeling guilty had its effect on young Billy.

Apart from giving his audience something to muse over when realizing the irreverent, hairy glee-master before them was once a 'Child of Mary', religion gave Connolly an opportunity to express himself, as he explains: 'At school itself I didn't get much of a chance to perform but there were all the Gang Shows, when I was in the Cubs and Scouts. And there were other things that Catholics have, like a priest having a Jubilee, just like the Queen, when he's been twenty-five years in the business, sort of thing. They would have a concert in their honour and give them a bung and I would get into that.'

In adulthood, Connolly has retained a fascination with the spiritual, and speaks willingly about his 'relationship with Jesus' being 'in good shape'. Since the late 1980s, he has read widely on Jesus. At Heathrow Airport once, he bought the book *Jesus: the Evidence*, and read it all the way to America. On the long, empty days on an American tour, he not only devoured the book, but went through the bibliography and started searching for the source material. 'I think Jesus was a great guy. I'm not going to tell you my findings because they're really quite radical,' he said mysteriously in 1992, insisting that his reading had not made him religious – but not discounting the possibility that, in its mysterious way, St Peter's Church, Partick had almost got its man. Even now, he still gets a nostalgic reassurance from echoes of a Catholic boyhood. He loves BBC early-morning religious programmes on the radio, cleaving to the traditional hymns, never the new ones. He suspects this is pure nostalgia, but he cannot be quite sure.

But back before the start of his life with Pamela Stephenson, Billy felt he had been travelling down a dark tunnel; he had even considered suicide. 'Before Pamela there was a period in my life that was pretty morbid and dreadful. And I was drinking too much and I was in a terrible mess,' he recalled on Radio Clyde seven years later. 'And it came to a terrible crunch. I'll never forget it. I was so depressed and down that I read a report in the paper of a boy who had committed suicide in Claridges in London, and he was eighteen or something, and they found him dead in the room and they also found some pamphlets from Exit, the euthanasia society. Now normally I would have said, "How awful." But on that occasion when I read it I thought, I wonder where you get those pamphlets. And as soon as it crossed my mind I thought, oh come on, get a grip on yourself. And from then on life got a wee bit better, once I had realized I needed to get a grip.'

His new lifestyle (with plenty of cycling in Richmond Park) also meant a change of diet to vegetarian food, which, again, Pamela had lived on for several years. Billy felt better, and discovered he loved cooking at the couple's home, a flat in Disbrowe Road, Fulham. 'He's got this apron with Vegemite written on it, and he puts it on and gets stuck into cooking,' Pamela said. 'In fact he does all the cooking because he's incredibly talented. But he's a very manly cook. He's always up to his elbows in flour, kneading dough in a strong determined way. Of course, I just lie down and paint my toe nails while all this is going on.'

There was another lifestyle bonus to being with Pamela Stephenson. Eating his new diet led to the virtual demise of drinking. Although Billy did not drink before shows, in the past couple of years he had been making exceptions even to that rule. In December 1980, Stephen Pile met Connolly in a hotel cocktail bar at happy hour. 'Although he does not drink while on tour, he made an exception on this occasion out of politeness,' Pile wrote. 'So polite was he that he ordered two Bloody Marys and then another two after that.' At Christmas 1981, he told a Scottish radio show that he had had a big drink problem: 'I was getting smashed every night because I was wholly unhappy. I always had a hangover. Whenever I had a problem I'd go to the pub and have a few pints. Some people do it with dope – I did it with pints of heavy.'

But now, he could do it with broccoli and mushrooms. 'When I ate the vegetarian food, I couldn't drink as well as I used to. You know I used to be quite good at drinking, but when you're vegetarian you can't hold as much as you did, so I was drunk more often and quicker and I'd get really fed up with it because I was playing darts at the time in this wee pub in Fulham, and I got really worse and they threw me out of the team, and I was seriously fed up. I stopped drinking just after that because I couldn't do it right any more.'

As it does for highly motivated and professional people, work continued unabated – indeed this was a reasonably successful period, even if it was overshadowed by non-professional considerations. In September, Billy starred in *The Secret Policeman's Ball* at the Theatre Royal, Drury Lane. After the last night party, Nicholas Ball left first, then Pamela disappeared into a taxi. Ten minutes later, at 5.15 a.m., Connolly emerged and asked photographers why they were waiting. He chased a freelancer, Stuart Bell, down the street, before Harvey Goldsmith separated them. Billy was driven off in Goldsmith's car.

In November, Connolly did a fortnight of sellout shows – *The Pick of Billy Connolly*, at the Cambridge Theatre. Mick Brown, reviewing the first night for the *Guardian*, wrote, 'If you expected the programme for a show called *The Pick of Billy Connolly* to bear a photograph of the comedian with his finger firmly planted in his nostril then you would be absolutely right. Connolly is never one to miss an opportunity to belabour a joke about nasty habits or bodily functions – the ideal Connolly gag contains both – and this predictability is clearly what his audience cherish most of all. He has only to walk on stage and the air is rent with paroxysms of laughter; the words "willies" or "fart" have people clutching at their sides and toppling uncontrollably off their seats.

'There are actually a lot of willies and farts in Connolly's performance – and vomit and excreta and endless sexual activity. The curious thing is that despite all this he belongs to a distinctly old-fashioned tradition of humour. No attacks on Thatcher or the Social Democrats; instead he recycles the circumstances of his upbringing and the foibles of the Scots with a nudge and a cartoon-like innocuousness. His best moments grow out of an ability simply to characterise the idiosyncrasies of everyday behaviour; he is particularly good on the minutiae of Glasgow drunks on the last bus home.'

Brown may not have been too impressed – alternative comedy was now mushrooming, and he was particularly disappointed that Connolly did not spend more time on the attack, save for a scathing mention of the press – but the public was still lapping up the material. *The Pick of Billy Connolly* album went gold by early in the new year.

Billy threw a party to celebrate his shows at the 'chic' Main Squeeze Club in the King's Road. 'Celebrations were in full swing when [Pete] Townshend and [Steve] Strange swept unsteadily in,' related the *Evening Standard*. 'For reasons best known to himself, the huge Connolly began to insult the gently swaying Townshend. Then, Strange, the *enfant terrible* of the romantique movement, leapt to Townshend's defence – much to Connolly's apparent bewilderment. Guests were taken aback as the three traded insults that would have embarrassed a Panamanian stoker. Fortunately, no blows were struck.'

Not very surprisingly, domestic issues were still dominating the media coverage of Billy Connolly. In September, a 'close family friend' of Billy and Iris was quoted in the *Daily Mirror*: 'Billy wants desperately to go back to Iris and their two children. I also know that she wants Billy back. Everyone is working very hard behind the scenes to bring them back together. It won't be today or tomorrow, but hopefully soon.' Neither was available for comment, but 'the family' said, 'Divorce is now the last thing on anyone's mind.' On the same day, the *Mirror* diarist wrote ironically: 'Billy Connolly arrives at a London theatre raising his jacket to shield himself from the glare of photographers' flashguns. His friend Pamela Stephenson is accompanied by a burly "minder". What few seem to realize, it seems, is that although Billy can tell lavatorial jokes for an hour on TV, and Pamela shows her knickers in restaurants, both are very private people.'

Nobody in the Billy/Iris/Pamela triangle seemed to share the rest of the world's definition of privacy; despite all three repeatedly demanding to be left alone, this was the most public of divorces. Thanks to the garrulousness of all parties, it was, in effect, a kind of four-sided triangle, in which the extra axis was the press and public. In September, Iris broke her silence in a *Daily Star* interview. She still believed showbiz was what had destroyed the marriage, and said she would like to get back together with Billy: 'But I don't see it coming ... If he is having an affair it doesn't really bother me. He hit it off with Pamela – their personalities match. Quite honestly, I don't really think that there is anything in it. We hope to be together for our daughter's birthday and the sooner it can be sorted out the better.' She later phoned Billy to 'find out what is happening.'

On the day this appeared, Connolly beat a photographer, Paul Massey, around the head with a French loaf outside Pamela's flat. 'He told me that if he ever saw me again he would cut my goolies off,' Massey said of Dhammarati's newest pupil. (Buddhism was clearly having its effect; in his welding days, Billy would never have set about an adversary with a baguette.)

Pamela gave an interview to *Woman's World* in the same week, but was still coy about Connolly. 'My name's been linked with several people. Billy and I do have a lot in common, including the same management. My love life is not always easy. Sometimes it can be difficult to find men. I've made some awful mistakes with men. I allow myself these little indulgences. I've been known to lapse from the straight and narrow and wake up next morning discovering I don't even like the guy. But usually I'm very suspicious. Anyone who asks me out will come in for a fair share of the limelight, so I tend to wonder if they are publicity seeking.' A few days after this, Billy and Pamela attended an Alternative Miss World at Olympia, dressed, for discretion's sake, as sheikhs.

A messy estrangement of sorts was also developing between Connolly and elements of the establishment in his home country. Things came to a head in 1980, when Billy was spending less and less time in Drymen. His marriage on the rocks, his new London friends proved more alluring than those in Scotland whose attitude to him was one of embarrassment. In 1980, councillors and churchmen called for a boycott of a Variety Club tribute to Connolly to be held at the Central Hotel, Glasgow, on 28 March. Proceeds from the £20-a-head bash, attended by the likes of Scotland boss Jock Stein, Billy McNeil and Michael Parkinson, were going to charity.

SNP bailie Frank Hannigan grouched: 'Connolly has brought Glasgow and Scotland into disrepute. If the Lord Provost [David Hodge] eulogizes such a person, it will be a gross betrayal, a night of shame for the city.' District councillor and university lecturer Stewart Taylor added: 'Connolly has ridiculed people's religious beliefs and has portrayed Glasgow as a city of drunks and violent hooligans.' The dreaded Jack Glass was on hand, of course, to delight in finding others warming to his theme, and have his say: 'By mocking Jesus Christ and the Crucifixion on cassette and record, Connolly stands condemned as a blasphemous buffoon.' Revd John Brentnall, clerk of the Southern Presbytery of the Free Presbyterian Church of Scotland, said: 'Connolly should be disgraced rather than honoured.'

Even Lord Provost Hodge dithered: 'I do not condone blasphemy if it has been committed and I agree that Billy Connolly might have left a better image of Glasgow. I am not going to eulogize him, but he has provided a lot of entertainment and pleasure for thousands of people. It is his contribution to the city.'

When Connolly finally arrived in Glasgow, the Wee Frees chanted 'Judas' at him. Even so, Connolly had yet to feel the extent to which he was loathed by some quarters at that time in his home city.

In June of the same year, the fiasco over the staging of three Connolly plays at Glasgow's Pavilion Theatre indicated that backlashes were the order of the day, wielded both by Glasgow and Billy. During the second week of a three-week run, it became clear that Connolly's relationship with his home city was on a rough par with that with his wife, Iris, a sweet, lonely woman who knew the game was up, and was drinking herself into luxury oblivion on Loch Lomond-side.

In December, Iris announced she would start divorce proceedings. She spoke, ostensibly to the press, while Jamie and Cara were at school, but something in the quality of what she was saying suggests that it was Billy she was really addressing through the medium of the fourth arm of the triangle: 'Frankly I've had enough. I just want out. I don't care if I divorce Billy or he divorces me. I have had all the showbusiness hassle I can stand,' she said. 'Billy won't be here for Christmas, but the kids will go to London over the festive season to spend a few days with him. Billy adores the kids and they love him. I just want to get it over with. I'd love to take a holiday in Spain to get away from all the pressure. This thing has been looming up for about eighteen months. Bill has hardly been around here for the past eight months, so I've had time to get used to the idea. We want to be as adult as possible about it. I'll be happy looking after my children quietly away from all the headlines and frantic phonecalls.'

Billy, meanwhile, in a Radio Scotland interview, was telling his old

Drumchapel friend Tom Ferrie that it was pressures of showbiz and touring rather than Pamela that caused the marriage bust-up; if he did have regrets, it was getting a little late. At the time he gave the interview, Pamela was pregnant, and the couple were looking for a house together in both the country and London. In July, in the *Sun*, Connolly spoke at length about Pamela and about divorce.

'What attracted me to her at first wasn't her beauty or her mind. It was because she was very nice to me at a time when I felt particularly friendless. It is a friendship that we have and share that I particularly value. Friendship comes first. Love comes later and it would be crazy if it didn't. I understand that ... When people fall out of love it is total hypocrisy to pretend that nothing has changed. For both sides it is a stunning process and it hurts ... Pamela doesn't suggest what I should do. I don't really talk very much about showbusiness with her. That is shop talk and it doesn't belong at home,' Billy said – an indication that, even if he was not quite telling the truth, Iris's point was belatedly getting through to him.

Interestingly, Billy said he could take a joke about Pamela and himself – if it was made in public, on stage: 'Barry Humphries had a go at us when we were in the audience at his show once. That is allowed. That is fair game. I might be embarrassed but not offended because when you are on stage anything that moves in a theatre is fair game.'

The concept that criticism is fair if made by one's showbusiness peers in a suitably public setting was a new and bizarre one, that perfectly reflects the odd way Connolly was leaning at this tempestuous stage of his life. (Much later, in 1993, his analysis of the same period was infinitely more sound, more grounded – and evoked the sympathy he entirely failed to evince a decade previously. 'It really wounded us that we were made a kind of joke, because what we felt was deeply, deeply serious. Pamela was really hurt by it, and her career was deeply hurt by it,' he told the *Daily Telegraph* magazine.)

The new year began with Connolly flying to Los Angeles to discuss a TV film with Marty Feldman, and continued with a huge number of charity performances and events. It was not so much that the pair were getting into charities to improve their image, but that their social attitudes, led by Pamela, were moving ever closer to that dizzy establishment milieu where charity this and that is simply the done thing, with little thought or discussion permitted about the matter. It was unfortunate in a way, because Billy (and Pamela too) was entirely sincere about wanting to support charities. 'He is the most generous guy I know. He does all kinds of charity work,' says Tom Ferrie, who is far enough removed from the glitzy unreality of the society charity world to know what he is talking about. In February Billy and Pamela, at a champagne party (after a charity performance of *Cinderella* at the Prince Edward Theatre) announced a truce in their war with journalists. 'We have decided to stop fighting the press. We now realize we have to accept the situation and not become paranoid every time a photographer turns his lens on us.' Pamela said. The *Sun* reported the following week that Billy now had a minder to keep the press at bay.

(In May, they returned to Heathrow from a Far East holiday – which had followed a charity cycle ride from London to Glasgow – and were indeed friendly to the press, a story which, paradoxically perhaps, made all the papers. By August, it was business as usual, with Billy said to have given hacks a 'foul mouthful' at Heathrow when quizzed about his romance with Pamela. The following January, he was spotted at Heathrow, heading for LA with Pamela; Connolly reportedly shouted 'Fuck you' to the press. When a reporter observed that his language was a little strong, Connolly shouted: 'Then you should leave me alone you fucker'. Pamela kept silent.)

There had been bad news from home a few hours before the *Cinderella* party: Connolly's father, William, had a heart tremor. Billy cut short his role in *Cinderella's Star Night* (Charlie Drake took his part). 'I'm sure the old man's all right,' Billy said. 'He's a hard old man ... I couldn't go on with all they wanted me to do for the show. So I just danced across the stage. My father has always had a touchy heart. I had to stay in close contact with my family up in Glasgow just to see that he was all right.' William died in 1989.

In June, Connolly, his hair cut and beard trimmed for the first time in seventeen years, took over from Simon Callow as Beefy, the womanizing bum-about-town in J.P. Donleavy's play *The Beastly Beatitudes of Balthazar B.* at the Duke of York's Theatre. In rehearsals, he decided his voice sounded 'like a goose farting in the fog' and resolved to give up smoking. He found he never wanted to start again. 'It is very nearly a first-rate performance: diabolical energy and jolly, rogering zest is combined with an essential kindliness of spirit. Whether tearing the knickers off a Dublin whore with his teeth or delighting in his own violent erection, Mr Connolly brings to the role an insane sexual brio,' wrote one critic. 'With his long tapering body, his sober suit and his pre-Raphaelite face, Mr Connolly actually does look like "a man who will one day follow quite closely in the heels of Christ." Yet he also suggests a Savoy Grill satyr, a magnificent masturbator from the pages of *Debrett*, a man with a seven-second itch. It is an inspired piece of casting.'

What grabbed the headlines at the time, of course, was that Billy had to appear naked in the play, or at least wearing just a flying hat, goggles and wellies, and that someone took a photo of him in his (nearly fortieth) birthday suit. 'I thought at first, no way. I couldna do it. And I actually went to the theatre to say no – but I lost my bottle. The first few nights were just a blur, like a blank on my memory. But there's nothing wrong wi' nudity, after all. The thing that spoilt it was the scum that sneaked in and took a photo of me naked. *That* made it dirty. No doubt it'll surface some day in a gay mag as these things always do.'

November the 24th was Billy's fortieth birthday. He celebrated with a surprise party in his dressing room at the Eden Court Theatre, Inverness. Harvey Goldsmith asked for a cake made out of bananas and nuts, decorated with forty candles. Chris Johnson, the Eden Court's Director, said: 'Mr Connolly is now a vegetarian and that would be the reason for such unusual ingredients. I was asked to provide a high degree of privacy for the party. Immediately the show was over, security locks went on the doors leading to the dressing rooms. I was told that Mr Connolly was very touchy, his privacy was important to him. The theatre was packed – all tickets were sold within half an hour of the appearance being announced two months ago – but not one of the audience knew of the little party backstage.' Among those present at the party were Harvey Goldsmith and 'a mystery guest' whose identity, even twelve years later, Goldsmith will not reveal, but presumably, as Pamela was on stage at the Drury Lane Theatre that night, was a royal from nearby Balmoral.

August 1983 saw an unusually horrible and shocking court custody battle in Edinburgh between Billy and Iris, who accused each other of being drunk and unfit to look after the children. Billy wore a light grey double-breasted suit and polka-dot tie and sat just in front of Iris, who wore a light brown floral dress and dark brown suede coat. Two female friends sat with her at the back of the court.

Jamie and Cara had gone to London for a holiday with Billy and Pamela, but had not returned for the new school term. Billy had allegedly phoned Iris on 15 August, according to Iris's counsel. 'He said he had something to tell her which he hated to tell her – she was not getting the kids back.' Billy had refused to let the children talk to his father or his parents-in-law. Iris, who wanted custody of the children at least until the divorce hearing, accused Billy of heavy drinking and assaults before their separation and claimed that he had to go to a monastery to dry out for three weeks in 1982.

Billy muttered, 'No way ... lies,' as this was said. Billy's counsel, Charles Boag-Thomson QC, opposed moving the children on the grounds that Iris was a 'wholly unsuitable person' to have custody. He alleged that Iris was drinking to excess, to the extent of failing to look after the children.

Mr Boag-Thomson quoted from a social work department letter: 'There is some justification for concern over the welfare and development of both the children and a number of indicators that all is not as it should be in the household.' He also claimed that Jamie was afraid to remain with Iris and said she would have to sort herself out. Iris's lawyer denied these allegations, and produced a medical certificate from the family doctor which said she did not drink heavily. She added – correctly, as Billy and Pamela were to announce a few days later – that Pamela was pregnant, and that because they were both entertainers they kept irregular hours. 'Who is going to look after these children?'

Judge Lord Robertson adjourned the case for a week to allow both sides to put their allegations in writing. Meanwhile, the children were to stay in London with Billy and Pamela. When the case came before the Edinburgh Court of Session for the second time, Lord Mayfield said he did not want a 'repeat of the public wrangling' which marked the first appearance. He granted temporary custody of the children – 'a purely technical order' – to Billy. Years later, in his 1994 TV interview with Jeremy Isaacs, Connolly admitted that he had been a 'lousy' father – 'a drunk absentee', as he put it.

By Christmas, Iris was sending out perplexingly odd messages to Billy and Pamela through the usual channels – the Sunday tabloids. She wanted to say how much she liked Pamela: 'My biggest problem now is to know what to get her for Christmas. What do you buy for a woman who has got everything? It may seem strange that I'm going to all this trouble for Pamela. A wife is supposed to hate the other woman, and I admit that I harboured feelings of hatred and vengeance at first. But an uncanny friendship has built up between us amidst the heartbreak that has surrounded the breakdown of my marriage. For this I must thank Pamela and my two children, who are staying with her and Billy in London.'

Iris said the children loved Pam. 'She is a giggly, good-natured woman who finds time to play with them. We speak frequently on the telephone and she keeps me fully informed about their progress. How for instance my son, who will be fourteen later this month, has taken to oil painting. And how my daughter, who is ten, is progressing with ballet. Pamela has become a great mother to both of them.' She was said in a *Sunday Mirror* interview to have knitted a shawl for the baby Pamela was expecting.

Even giving due credit to the tabloid-ese spin on her 'quotes' ('I admit that I harboured feelings of hatred and vengeance . . .'), what Iris was saying seems to be quite remarkable. And it was not to be the last of her good wishes, although there was plenty of what the psychotherapists would call 'bad stuff' to come out. When the baby, Daisy, was born by Caesarian section on New Year's Eve at the expensive Portland Hospital in London, up in Scotland, the *Sun* kindly asked Iris how she felt about photos of the beaming Billy and Pamela and their baby in the newspapers. 'When I saw them I wept. I tore the page and threw it into the fire. It was a spur of the moment thing and I probably regret it now. They seemed so happy and had everything, while I'm struggling to rebuild my life . . . The main thing is I miss our two children, who are living with Billy in London. I phone them two or three times a week and they come to see me at Easter and Christmas. I have reasonable access to them, but I'd be a liar if I said I didn't miss them. I hope when they are older they will return to me . . . I'm told [Billy] has stopped drinking and smoking and eats organic food. He's looking well – but, frankly, he seems to me to be a bit boring now.'

In 1985, when the divorce came through, Iris said of Billy: 'He's the best friend I have in the world. I tell him all my problems,' and added that Pam was a 'smashing person'. 'I have no grudge against Billy. There is no bitterness. He is a great guy and we are closer now than we have been for years. A lot of the aggro has left him. I can forget the sad times and remember the happy times ... I realize now divorce is not the end of the world and I can still see my children. I was with them when I stayed with Billy and Pam in London recently. Pam and I are the greatest of friends and we had some good girl-to-girl talks. She's a great sport and let Billy and I go out for a meal while she looked after the kids. I can still talk to Billy about anything and even when I'm home I phone him with all my problems. It's super.'

Four years later, when the talk was of Billy and Pamela getting married, the story was the same; Iris said she'd rebuilt her life and become friends with Pamela. 'I get on very well with her. We talk regularly and I visit her and Billy at their home.' She said she expected to be at their wedding when it happened. (She was not invited to the Fiji ceremony in the end.) Even Billy's mother was keen to join the enthusiastic chorus. 'I like Pam very much, though I was disappointed when Billy's marriage to his first wife Iris broke up. Iris was like me – not keen on showbiz razzmatazz. I think that's why the marriage ended.'

Life after Billy Connolly did not work out very well for Iris, a black cloud that dogged both her and Billy for many years afterwards. In November 1984, Stirling Sheriff's Court heard how Iris had been assaulted by her boyfriend, Michael Johnston, an unemployed local man. Iris was living in a caravan while the Connolly home was being decorated, and a drunk Johnston 'had ordered another woman out of the caravan because he felt she was interfering in his relationship' with Iris. He punched Iris's face and body and smashed a video cassette. Johnston had broken bail following an earlier breach of the peace charge. Iris and Johnston had since been reconciled, so he was fined £100. They planned to 'get away from individuals taking advantage of Mrs Connolly's situation'. (Iris today lives quietly in Spain, fifteen miles inland from the Costa Brava. She lives on her own, but has several friends over to stay, including Tam Harvey's former wife, who was once a busker, and is now a librarian doing a doctorate as a mature student.)

Seven months later, on Billy and Iris's sixteenth wedding anniversary, Iris was granted a 'quickie' divorce by the Court of Sessions in Edinburgh, due to Billy's adultery with Pamela Stephenson. Billy was granted custody of Jamie and Cara, now fifteen and eleven; the children would see their mother during the Christmas, Easter and summer holidays and for two weekends. The judge advised the couple to 'stop your public wrangling' and reach a quick settlement. 'Iris told me that basically Billy walked away from the house in Drymen, which would have been worth £100,000 at that time, plus a couple of cars, a couple of jeeps, a Mercedes and a couple of boats,' one close female friend says. 'She was given the lot plus ten grand a year. But there was a clause that she didn't speak to the press. We all told her to agree to it, although she was very keen to tell all. But she eventually took the deal. And as time went on things have mellowed inasmuch as the kids, Cara and Jamie, used to go up and see her although they were living with Billy and Pamela.'

The events in Connolly's life during the new dawn year of 1983 were suitably novel and refreshing for a man just turned forty, with a beautiful new wife, a baby on the way and cult status having long since given way to basic wealth and fame. He made his classical drama debut by starring in G.B. Shaw's play *Androcles And The Lion* for BBC Schools television. Mary Kenny, not a typical Connolly fan, reviewed *Androcles*: 'Billy Connolly certainly put in a gentle and whimsical performance as the animal-loving Androcles, condemned to die in a Roman gladitorial circus as a martyred Christian, only to be spared by the lion whose paw he had healed ...' Billy did not attend the press conference to launch the play because of the publicity surrounding his divorce.

In November, he passed his advanced driving test and gained membership of that less than iconoclastic organization, The Institute of Advanced Motorists. He passed driving a Ford Escort XR3. 'I've played the Albert Hall, Carnegie and Madison Square Garden, but I never felt like this. It's absolutely splendid. I wasn't too bad at driving before, but I felt I had fallen into some sloppy habits, and the test has put paid to these. They can't call me a bad driver now can they? I've got proof.' Seven months later, as fate would have it, Billy was charged with careless driving after his convertible Volkswagen Beetle hit a kerb and overturned at 5 a.m. on the M5 at Kingston Seymour, near Clevedon, Avon. He was on his way to Devon for a filming appointment when he crashed, sustaining a badly cut head and a bruised eye. He was kept in Weston-super-Mare General Hospital overnight for observation; Pamela rushed to his side with Daisy. The careless driving charge turned out to be a bum rap – he was cleared, and the accident put down to a split brake drum.

After the divorce from Iris, Billy and Pamela felt free to re-establish the kind of home they were used to. They bought a five-bedroomed house in Mallard's Mead, a 'millionaires' row' in Bray, Windsor, Berkshire. The house cost £500,000, and came with one and a half acres of grounds; the neighbours included Terry Wogan, Rolf Harris and Michael Parkinson. 'Guests are said to be asked to remove their shoes and socks on entering,' reported one of the Scottish papers, perplexed by what had happened to their man with the wellies.

One Bray resident commented to the *Daily Express*, 'Although some people here might not be keen on him as a neighbour, there aren't many on first-name terms with the Royal Family.' Billy made news locally by applying for an allotment. 'It is believed "the Big Yin" wants to work alongside experienced gardeners on the allotments,' it was reported. The couple sold Mallard's Mead for £1 million in 1988 because of the lack of privacy. 'Billy and Pamela like to keep themselves to themselves,' a neighbour said. 'Everyone knew where they lived and they just wanted a new place so they could have some privacy. Day trippers used to stare right into their garden from the boats cruising up and down the Thames. They both got fed up with it.'

In August 1988, they bought a seven-bedroom Victorian mansion in the village of Winkfield Row, near Windsor, for £1.8 million. The house was close to the then home of Fergie and Prince Andrew, and was set in four acres and screened by high brick walls. They changed the name of the house from Westfield House to Grunt Futtock Hall as soon as they moved in. (Grunt Futtock was one of Kenneth Williams' names in 'Round the Horne'.) Neighbouring villagers were not pleased about the name change: 'It used to have such a simple, elegant name. Grunt Futtock Hall just doesn't have the same ring. It sounds so awful – especially if you try saying it on your way back from the pub!' said one.

Billy and Pamela spent an estimated £300,000 turning their home into 'a space-age palace,' as the *Daily Mail* would have it. 'Old beams and woodwork art being ripped out of the £1.8 million country mansion to make way for a futuristic interior. Said one visitor to the house, which the pair bought three months ago: "It is like something out of a science fiction film set. They have had a top London designer in and it's costing the earth, what to most folks would be a pools win. It's all white walls, huge stripes and mirrors with ultra-modern furniture and the latest electronic gadgetry." '

'Someone who should probably remain nameless recalls attending a recent dinner party at the new home of Billy Connolly and Pamela Stephenson,' reported one of the broadsheet Sundays. 'It was a sumptuous affair, apparently. And while the couple mulled over the problems of the Third World, deprivation and so forth with the likes of Neil and Glenys Kinnock, the hosts' domestic staff moved, like a silent demonstration of heavy irony, among the diners.'

Before Christmas 1983, with Pamela about to give birth, Billy embarked on a brief British tour. When the show came to London, Arliss Rhind writing in the *Mail* had especially perceptive observations to make.

'It's an unusual talent that can make Scottish footballer Charlie Nicholas — with all his goal-scoring problems at Arsenal — double up with laughter at the flick of a knowing eyebrow,' she wrote. 'Or reduce a stern-faced 007 Sean Connery to tears with a memory . . . Billy Connolly . . . is that strange amalgam of the companion with whom I have spent hours swopping risqué stories in a peeling Glasgow barn, an embarrassing uncle at the family wedding, the archetypal reveller on the top deck of the last bus home and an angry young man with a conscience.'

The short season was called 'a triumphant milestone in the Connolly career'. 'His changed life in the "Soft South" has brought no respite or sophistication to the roaring fusillade of bad taste, lavatorial jokes and dissertations on the bodily functions (expletives *not* deleted).'

May 1984 brought another new direction; Connolly went on location with an eighty-strong crew in St Lucia for three weeks filming *Water*, a film written by Dick Clement and Ian La Frenais, and made by Handmade Films, George Harrison's company. The £5 million film was a box office flop. Billy was the revolutionary Delgado Fitzhugh, who has sworn not to speak until his people are liberated from the British colonial rule. 'As a Scot I kind of identify with it. I know how it feels to be the perennial outsider. Rightly or wrongly, we've always felt we've been overpowered by the big cousin, England,' he said in a very rare nationalistic statement.

Billy co-starred with Michael Caine, and in one scene sang with a band that included Eric Clapton and Ringo Starr. Caine and Connolly reportedly hit it off from the start. The director, Dick Clement, had known both socially for some years, and said, 'This is Michael's fifty-something film and Billy's third but they got on like a house on fire. We had the funniest dinners ever on location. Everyone knows Billy is a brilliant raconteur but Michael matched him joke for joke and anecdote for anecdote.'

Press coverage on-set was wall to wall; the *News of the World* was on hand to describe Connolly and Caine spending six hours in the Plantation Bar eating and making each other laugh. 'Caine: "Did you hear the one about the policeman who came home to find his wife in bed with three men?' ' 'Ullo-'ullo-'ullo,' he says. And his wife says: 'Aren't you going to say hullo to me?'" Connolly guffaws, then he says: "Hey, d'you know the difference between Bing Crosby and Walt Disney? Bing sings and Walt disna!"' A film executive said: 'It's genius casting. On paper, you'd never think it could work. They're the most unlikely combination you could imagine. But on screen, it's magic. And the secret is that they're both genuine comedians.'

Caine was euphoric – and perceptive – about Billy; 'It's very hard to make me laugh, I promise you, but Billy does. It's the way he tells 'em – the honesty of it. With Billy you know it's going to be funny, even before he starts. What's more, I can understand his voice, too! Billy doesn't have the eyes of a comedian – he has very dramatic eyes, they're almost savage. It's not only his humour that people identify with – it's his anger too. I wouldn't want to get on the wrong side of him ... Billy's got an almost barbaric humour which goes straight for the jugular. Me, I'm laid back. So we can play off each other all the time.'

The press were all given generous slices of Billy, except for Baz Bamigboye, of the *Daily Mail*, who approached him for an interview, having had a pally chat with Caine. Connolly shouted, 'You are lower than a snake's navel. Get away from me. And stay away!' Bamigboye wrote: 'It appears he had not liked a story I had written about him when he was having his clandestine affair with Pamela Stephenson. "But that was over three years ago," I protested to the aide who reported this to me. "Billy Connolly is not a man to forget," he said. "You'd better stay away."'

Connolly chose the *News of the World* to get his own back on Bamigboye, who is a Nigerian prince. 'I've a lot to protect – I'll defend my family to the death. If it means punching someone on the mouth or breaking cameras – I'll do it and pay for it later ... Listen, I'm not a wimp, okay? I'm not a violent man by nature, but I'm not a wimp. If you were a joiner or builder, and the same kind of harassment happened to you that I've been through, you'd fire up too. I don't want to be eternally praised, and I don't mind being criticized, although I don't enjoy it. But I hated being lied about.'

'Man I'd love to be a movie star,' he said in a more expansive moment. 'I want to break into America. Over there, they don't even know I've been born. I'd like to do more films. I'd even shave my beard off if I had to. Actually I have this overwhelming desire to see what's living there underneath it! I've had the thing now for over twenty years, but I'd be prepared to do away with it for the right role.'

Later in the year, Billy found himself doing an unusual regular spot 35,000 feet up on a Virgin Atlantic aircraft. Pamela was working on 'Saturday Night Live' in New York, so Billy would fly over to see her every ten days. He did a deal with Richard Branson to get a free eight-hour first-class trip in return for giving a one-man show in-flight. 'It seems a good way of stopping people getting bored during the flight,' Branson said.

In December, Connolly caused uproar nearer to the earth's crust, in the Hampshire village of Nether Wallop, by saying fuck all the way through a two-hour show recorded there as part of the village arts festival, with Rik Mayall, Wayne Sleep, Peter Cook, Rowan Atkinson, Mel Smith and Bill Wyman. He also told masturbation stories, and discussed willies and dog turds. The local audience of 250 included children; the vicar, Revd Guy Chapman, said, 'Some people found it very offensive'; and the philosopher A.J. Ayer, who captained a quiz team during the three-day festival, added, 'I thought his act was a disgrace.' For the pre-New Year's Eve broadcast of the show, LWT cut out two minutes, including a joke about a cripple in a wheelchair, and a scattering of fucks. Four fucks survived.

Weeks later, he was outraging his home city, or some of its more pompous prominent citizens. A dinner was held at the Glasgow Albany Hotel to mark the golden jubilee of the comedian Hector Nicol, one of the few Scottish comics Connolly admired. Connolly, there with Pamela, was one of the speakers and top table guests. He opened by saying that since he had gone to live in London he was supposed to have become more cultured – 'Ah read it in the fucking *Daily Record*,' he explained. A few people walked out, and it was noticed that the Lord Provost of Glasgow, Mr Robert Gray, also at the top table, notably failed to smile, even though most of the audience was roaring with laughter. Nicol himself said that Connolly had done such a great job making people laugh at Chic Murray's funeral, at the beginning of 1985, that he had immediately booked him for his own. Sadly, Nicol died soon after the dinner, and Connolly honoured the engagement. Connolly's admiration of Murray led to him acting *in loco parentis,* and giving away the veteran comedian's daughter Annabelle at her wedding in a Cardiff Methodist church; he wore a blue, green and yellow tartan suit with a lime green shirt and matching socks for added solemnity.

Taken as a duo, Billy and Pamela were cornering the market in outrage; what had started as a clever, cultish thing, was in grave danger of becoming boring. Pamela once appeared on Radio 4's 'Start the Week' (hosted by Richard Baker) and poured a glass of water down the neck of Kenneth Robinson, the 'resident pundit', having asked him if he was feeling hot. Robinson said, 'I shrugged it off because I had met her before and wasn't too surprised.' Pamela then sabotaged his regular 'funny piece' by reading out the script (which he had worked on for twelve hours) along with him. On air, Robinson exploded: 'It's imposs-ible to work in these circumstances.' He later said: 'She is a vulgar little person – such an unprofessional nut.' 'Before going off-air,' the *Daily Mirror* reported, 'Miss Stephenson uttered an old Anglo-Saxon expletive. She then bid Robinson goodbye with an expression that I could not possibly print in this paper of good taste.'

A consensus grew up – among all kinds of groups, from tabloid journalists to Billy Connolly fans to students – that the couple were becoming a bit dull in their apparently strident efforts to be scandalous at all costs. Their studied riotousness appeared to be almost an offshoot of the gung ho-ho pranks of young aristocrats and royals – not a coincidence, since the royals were on the point of 'discovering' Billy Connolly and finding him very much their cup of tea. The taste left by their 1980s joint persona persists today in many people's mouths. The received wisdom about Billy Connolly and Pamela Stephenson today remains that he is still funny and always was, whereas Pamela was always the unfunny supernumerary on the 'Not The Nine O'Clock News' ship. Much of this anti-Pamela feeling, there is no question, was anti-woman, much was anti-Australasian, but much came about because the British simply did not find her as funny as she had hoped they would. Even Pamela's feminist and Australasian friend, Germaine Greer, said, as quoted by the *Mirror*, 'I think she is completely professional – she's making a little talent go a very long way.'

In April, Connolly replaced his agent, Harvey Goldsmith, with John Reid, the Paisley-born entrepreneur who managed Elton John. 'I feel a change is going to do me a lot of good,' Billy said. 'And I know that John Reid is happy at the idea. I've felt for some time that I needed a manager rather than a manager-promoter, which Harvey was. John is going to concentrate on another crack at the United States. I've had some success there in the past, but obviously I want to get right into the market there.'

In October, Billy did a rare late-night Channel 4 TV show, 'An Audience With Billy Connolly'. A roll-call of the audience at the recording gives both a useful list of 'in' personalities in the mid-1980s and an idea of the mind-boggling progress Connolly had made in terms of public acceptance. It included Bill Wyman, Ringo Starr, Barry McGuigan, Bob Geldof, Michael Parkinson, Jimmy Tarbuck, Julie Walters, Twiggy, Eric Clapton, Michael Caine, George Michael and Elton John. Apart from occasional cameo roles on Kenny Everett's series, Billy steered clear of TV because he felt it 'cut out the bite'. Even 'An Audience' had an hour cut from the original two-hour recording. 'Connolly was at his funniest talking about his Catholic childhood ("I took my A levels in guilt"),' wrote the *Mail*, 'and decrying the dirge-like melody of God Save the Queen. He suggested that the signature tune of The Archers would make a far jollier national anthem.' 'The Archers'' theme was later played at Connolly's wedding in Fiji.

Another Channel 4 appearance went less well. On New Year's Eve, Connolly and Robbie Coltrane fronted a much-hyped Alternative Hogmanay. It was a failure. Andy Cameron, who appeared on the rival Scottish TV show, said: 'I accept praise or criticism as it falls, one man's meat is another man's poison and so on. However, what bugs me is the way the Alternative Hogmanay Show was described as hilarious and a refreshing change from the haggis and porridge shows. And that was before it was shown ... It was crap.'

Billy escaped the country days afterwards, taking his show (Not so Much a Comedian, More a) Wreck on Tour to thirty-five dates in Australia and New Zealand. On his way to Australia, Connolly stopped off at Nepal, where, as you do, he played elephant polo, with Ringo Starr and his wife Barbara Bach among the members of his team. 'Now there's a game,' Billy enthused on local radio in Glasgow. 'Ted Rogers plays it (you know Ted, "3–2–1"), Ginger Baker used to play it very well – he's the drummer with Cream. Aye, there's a few people getting into it, a few rock stars, people with a lot of money, you know. But you don't actually need all that much dough. You don't need to be like a squillionaire. But you need some dough, because even the clothes are dear. But the game itself is just brilliant ... you don't go so fast, but you're up awful high. But you know, that kind of thing is fraught with snobbery and inverted snobbery. I went to a polo match because I was invited. It's a once a year thing that Cartier the jewellers run. And because I'm managed by John Reid who also manages Elton John who has spent a few bob with Cartier, I get invited. And it was nice. I didn't go this year because I'm fed up with all that photography stuff and the press. I just can't smile anymore. There comes a point when your face is sore and you just can't do it anymore. And you just end up in those Sunday supplements with jokes about you.'

If it was not already obvious, Billy Connolly and Pamela Stephenson in 1986 were a very establishment couple indeed. In June, just before the 4 July birth of their second daughter, Amy Hira Stephenson Connolly, they attended a party held by Jackie Stewart in Chester. Pamela was talking to Fergie, who was wearing a green-and-white spotted dress flapping in the breeze, when Sean Connery interrupted them: 'If I did that with my trousers I'd be arrested for indecency.' Fergie was not particularly amused. Billy Connolly, the former welder, wearing a red jumpsuit smattered with teddy bears, diplomatically changed the subject.

They were by now great friends with Prince Andrew and his fiancée Sarah Ferguson (even though, ever the colonials, they always addressed Diana and Fergie by their proper titles − 'I try to do what is accepted protocol,' said Pamela) and were guests at their royal wedding on 23 July 1986, where Billy danced all night. The friendship with the royals unquestionably irked Billy Connolly's public, and turned him into a virtual scratching post for catty journalists. In retrospect, it was probably one of those situations where both protagonists and critics were right up to a point. It *was* an unpleasant prospect in theory, the (apparently) toadying court jesters and the (seemingly) patronizing royals, but, as Connolly has continually argued − what *was* he supposed to do? Had he turned down Andrew and Fergie's friendly advances, he would have been regarded as 'chippy'; had he accepted their friendship, but without gusto, he would have been churlish and hypocritical. As often turns out to be the case, Andrew and Fergie were doubtless more sympathetic characters than their image suggested. And anyway, which of Connolly and Stephenson's critics would not have done precisely the same as they did, given the opportunity? Social climbing is something ninety-nine per cent of the population would do if offered a social ladder.

'I was very proud to have been invited,' he explained to the New York *Daily News*. If the British press were interested in Billy's royal connection, it was quite an informed interest, as a new angle on the class struggle, even. For the American press, it was the sole thing of any interest about this wild and unknown Scottish comedian who kept on turning up in their country. 'But a lot of people disagreed with me because of my standing,' he continued. 'I've always been for the working class and they saw it as changing sides. I'm incapable of doing that. I'm not a monarchist. I feel very much like Mark Twain, who said if there was a country without a monarch and they had a vote, only lunatics would vote for one.'

Billy attended a celebrity clay-pigeon shoot (for charity, of course) at the Gleneagles Hotel. 'The one-time denizen of Drumchapel mingled with Prince Edward, the Princess Royal, Mark Phillips, Michael Parkinson and others in the shooting butts, attempting to hit "clays" flighted to resemble moving grouse or pheasant,' the *Sunday Mail* commented a mite sniffily.

At the clay pigeon shoot: 'I had a passionate conversation with them [Fergie and Anne] about an anti-heroin campaign which we all cared very deeply about. A few days later Pam and I were invited to the big ball before Prince Andrew and Fergie's wedding. That led to a very gentlemanly stag night with Prince Andrew – it wasn't like my stag nights, all drunken lunatics. It was all very nice, they don't drink very much because they're all pilots – while my wife had the time of her life running all over town with these princesses and duchesses.'

Before the wedding, Pamela, a few days after giving birth to Amy, arranged for Fergie, Princess Diana, Elton John's wife Renata and herself to try to crash Andrew's stag night dressed as policewomen. Billy was going to the Duke of York's stag party, and when Pamela saw the Duchess a fortnight before, she asked if she had anything planned for that night, to which the Duchess said no. Pamela, her sense of fun ever closer to the lumpen royal japester idea of a good time, saw Fergie a few days later and said she had had a wild idea. The Duchess asked how wild Pamela was talking, and Pamela said 'seriously wild', which was enough, with its hint of serious cake-throwing to come, to make Fergie roar with laughter. 'We had terrific fun going out in disguise,' Pamela said later. 'Princess Di and the Duchess of York were absolutely hysterical, and once we got under way there was no sense in which I was forcing them along. They really let go and loved every minute. I think the public really liked the idea when they found out. I don't think anyone criticized it.'

The original plan to crash Andrew's stag night fell by the wayside, so the gang all went to Annabel's in their disguises and were ignored by the other customers, who, one imagines, were too embarrassed to do anything other than ignore them.

The friendship continued and grew. Daisy, Amy and Scarlett, Billy and Pamela's third daughter, regularly played with Princesses Beatrice and Eugenie at Sunninghill Park. Fergie turned to the Connollys for comfort and advice after her separation from Andrew. As late as 1992, the families went on holiday together.

It fell to Joan Rivers to ask Billy on TV in America if he talked about sex in front of the royals. 'They kind of talk at me. With the royal family, it's a bit like meeting The Beatles or The Rolling Stones. When I meet Princess Anne, I like her as a person – but she was on my savings stamps when I was a little boy,' he replied.

CHAPTER 9

Beardless in America

'I have no trouble understanding his accent. I watched all the episodes of "Upstairs, Downstairs".'
Dan Frischman, who played nerd Arvid Engen with Billy Connolly in US sitcom 'Head of The Class'

Scarlett Leyla was born at the Portland Hospital, by Caesarian again, on 28 July 1988. Fergie was about to give birth to her first child at the same hospital. As soon as Scarlett was born, Pamela phoned the Duchess.

'I think it must be really pleasant for friends to be pregnant at the same time – particularly if one of them is having her first baby ... I'm not one of those yuppie fathers who like to say, "I was there", but I was, and there have been few moments in my life more dramatic,' Billy told the London *Evening Standard*. He advised Prince Andrew to be sure to be present at the birth of his child.

The press speculated on whether or not the two couples would godparent each others' children, even on whether the Queen would insist that her new granddaughter's godparents must be a married couple, as Billy and Pamela were not yet. 'We're not really God people. We have never had a God person – they have to promise to bring up the child in some sort of religion or other and we don't have any,' Billy said, squashing the notion fairly firmly.

He was moved before long to defend his position angrily (and rather powerfully) *vis-à-vis* the royal family in the left-wing *New Statesman*. 'I'm forty-six years old and if I had the same friends as I had thirty years ago I'd be horrified. I'm not working-class. I'd be living a complete lie if I said I was. I'm a rich man. My wealth and fame brought me into contact with people I used to hate. I went to a charity rifle shoot organized by Jackie Stewart and met Princess Anne. It deeply troubled me. I like her and we got on well, but I kept telling myself I hated her. I felt I had to hate her. That's ridiculous. She's an extremely nice woman, and I'm not going to throw away the hand of friendship to suit a hundred fucking Trotskyists in Glasgow.'

In *The Times*, he continued the argument: 'I still get teased mercilessly about the royal family. "What do you want to go hanging around with the Queen for?" I do know some of that family, and they're very nice people. They make me laugh, and we have dinner; and the kids play together. I look on it as a friendship. Me, with my Scottish upbringing, I could hardly refuse when Andrew and the Duchess asked me to dinner. I couldn't very well say: "I can't come to dinner with you, I'm working class." I'd met the Duchess socially at Jackie Stewart's clay pigeon shoot. She invited us to the ball before the wedding, so I thought, "Let's have a look at this." Actually you're not invited, you're ordered. The invitation says you're ordered by some chamberlain to turn up.'

He explained elsewhere that he is invited to royal dinner tables because he is funny, which is why he invited people to his house. 'I don't invite dullards. I like Stephen Fry to come to dinner because he makes me roar with laughter ... when I'm invited into other people's homes I know it's because I'm funny, and I'm glad, and I wear it like costume jewellery ... I don't think I'm there because they think I'm one of them. God forbid.'

For a man scaling such Olympian social heights, Connolly was making a remarkably good job of cultivating his roots. In another of his wide-ranging interviews back at Radio Clyde, his confessor Sheila Duffy, remarked on the out-of-the-way gigs he was still doing in Scotland. 'I had a meeting with my accountants six months ago,' Billy replied. 'I try to keep it as regular as that, once a year is plenty – and one of them said: "I think we could make some adjustments here, Mr Connolly. For instance, what's the point of going to Shetland? You don't make any money." As if that was the whole point of the exercise. To go and get a big bag of loot and run away. You go to Shetland because some of them will buy your records and they find you funny and nobody ever goes there because their accountants are saying don't go. So eventually you're going to have to say, "Well who's in charge here? Is this what I started out to do? Did I ask accountants who to fall in love with or what bike I should buy?" You must start making decisions. I go to Shetland because I like it. I go to the seaside in the winter because I like the people who live there, and I play in Belfast because I think the people are lovely and the place is nice. And once you get established that way, you can't stop doing it. I would love to have played more, like Milngavie Town Hall. I would love to have played Drumchapel – but there's nowhere to play in Drumchapel.'

Yet even if Connolly had by now reconciled his roots happily with his present social elevation, and pretty well mastered the art of being rich and famous, the pieces were in place for his effective emigration to the USA. He may have become intimate with the highest and mightiest in his own country, but disillusion with Britain, always under the surface in many respects, was now becoming open. Whereas in 1979 he told the Glasgow *Evening Times*, 'I've seen it reported that I'm moving to live in America. I'd sooner live doon a stank in Govan than live there', now, he would come back from the US and complain that everything in Britain looked hangdog and black and white compared with the Technicolor of Los Angeles. Like a lot of creative people, he felt the now ten-year reign of Margaret Thatcher had knocked much of the goodness out of Britain; like a lot of middle-aged people, he found the British version of the Yuppie phenomenon unbearable. He had a foreign wife whose work was much more highly regarded in America than in Britain; and he was sickened and baffled by the adverse press and public reaction to his royal connections. His comedy was as funny as ever, but he needed a new challenge as badly as when he broke out of the folk scene to become a comedian, or as when he decided that he could not be happy until he had established himself in England, and even paid for his own booking at the London Palladium to try to expedite the process.

Above all, even though he had never even approached getting famous in America, the US offered a fresh field, where none of the pre-conceptions and prejudices that dragged him down and bored him in Britain, the Commonwealth, and expat places like Dubai, meant a thing. Above all, Billy Connolly thrives on being a novel, unpredictable, and possibly dangerous talent. He relished being new again, perhaps even born again; the Chicago *Sun Times* entertainment writer rang him up in Dublin to interview him about a forthcoming gig in Chicago, and it was just like when the English papers 'discovered' him in the early 1970s. Not that American journalists were wide-eyed: Ernest Tucker wrote in the *Sun Times*. 'The 46 year-auld long-haired Connolly has attempted to storm America's comedic castle during past tours, yet has not gotten past the front gate. Surrrrrrre, he has been on NBC's Late Night With David Letterman five times, yet despite such exposure, Connolly was so little-known that the producers of HBO's Comic Relief dropped him from the show because they had not heard of him.' Humour, Tucker pointed out, was not something Americans associated with Scotland. 'A quick check of the comedy Rolodex reveals entries only for poet Robert Burns, bagpipes, The Bay City Rollers, and Rod "The Mod" Stewart – and not all of them were intentionally funny.'

A new start was not even a secret longing. Billy was openly thirsting for America. 'I have mushrooms with my breakfast now. I drive a Mercedes. My children go to great schools. I've got all the clothes and I've got the hat, but America is the feather. I've always wanted this one,' he told the New York *Daily News*. *Rave* Magazine pointed out, however, that 'no British stand-up comic has *ever* made it here . . . In the past year two Great Brit Hopes were dashed: Jasper Carrot's album on Rhino went nowhere, and Rowan Atkinson on Broadway was no Jackie Mason. You'd have to go back to Flanders & Swann or Cook & Moore for British success (and they were on Broadway, not playing stand-up gigs), and Harry Lauder for a famous Scot.' Would Billy Connolly, the writer pondered in 1987, be the first?

He never baulked from admitting that he died on stage a few times in America. He soon worked out that an appearance on Johnny Carson could do the trick. 'I wanted to get on there and get famous and they wanted me to audition. And it's physically impossible for me to audition. I can't do it. I don't have a five-minute bit. And I spoke to Robin Williams and Richard Pryor and said, "What am I going to do?" And he [Pryor] said, "You'll have to go and get someone to write you a five-minute bit, and do it, because we had to learn to do it. Because Richard doesn't do little sections and jokes, but he had to go and learn how to do it to be on Johnny Carson. And so not having that I'm totally unknown in America. I have pockets of admirers, little dedicated bands of men and women.'

American reaction to his stand-up comedy was fascinating to Connolly, the audiences often as uncomprehending as the English had been twenty years earlier. In 1990, *Variety* attended a show at the 1,270-seat Wilshire Ebell Theater, in Hollywood. 'It requires such a sympathetic ear to decode Connolly's accent and parochial references,' their critic wrote, even though he used a lot of material about the West Coast, earthquakes and so on. 'Well into the show Connolly mentioned Prime Minister Margaret Thatcher, eliciting a round of boos from the crowd. "You've made an old man very happy," Connolly responded. "I thought you'd never wake up." From then on, the crowd largely was with him through territory that covered politics and childhood memories. Connolly ended with a piece that continued the disturbing practice of insulting Jehova's Witnesses. One wonders why that group and the Hare Krishnas are allowed to be subjected to ridicule that would be intolerable if aimed at anyone else.'

A few days later, he appeared at The Bottom Line in New York, an alternative venue; the city was liberally fly-posted in Billy Connolly posters, which led to the not quite accurate impression that he must be the coming man. The New York *Post* reviewer counted 'at least 127 f-words', all, he hastened to add, seeming entirely appropriate. Connolly introduced himself by saying it was 'lovely to be mentally ill for a living'. 'Those who saw Connolly's hilarious description on a recent HBO special [with Whoopi Goldberg] of a fellow passenger aboard Cathay Airlines with a wind problem might have been disappointed he didn't get quite so raunchy this time ... Connolly will go off at a tangent, digressing several times before coming back to his central theme, which might be Margaret Thatcher's dental work or what freedom represents in East Germany – a Sony Walkman, a Swatch and a pair of Levi's ... He wondered why there were so many different shampoos in the supermarket. Instead of dry, greasy or normal, why isn't there a shampoo for *dirty* hair?'

There were also subtle indications from many quarters that he was not quite hacking it in Britain. In 1987, he performed a cabaret act for the advertising agency J. Walter Thompson, but dried up on stage at the Savoy in front of 500 people – the majority of them fully paid up, red-of-braces Yuppies, and had to pay back half of his £10,000 fee. 'After ten minutes guests started walking out as Connolly told a gruesome joke about vomiting and repeatedly used four letter words,' it was reported. 'When the audience demanded that he say something funny, Connolly responded, "You're just a bunch of arseholes." The comic started shuffling about on the stage and constantly looked at his watch. Silences of over a minute punctuated his act ... Connolly picked up his guitar and sang half a song – and then walked off the stage.' His agent said he'd performed fifty minutes, ten minutes more than required. It was the second time he had dried up – the first being at a finance company's Christmas party for 750 at the Grosvenor House Hotel, when he walked off stage after performing thirty minutes of a forty-minute act.

Only days after Christmas, at Hong Kong's China Fleet Club, Billy was heckled and stormed off stage halfway through his act, even though he had been paid £15,000 for a four-night run. The club manager, Phil Baldwin, commented, 'I would have expected a little more professionalism from Billy. This sort of thing must have happened before. But the heckler obviously touched a raw nerve. He knew something about Billy's past in Scotland and wasn't afraid to shout it out. The audience were furious with Billy and even more angry with the heckler.'

In September 1989 Connolly started rehearsing for *The Big Man*, a film with Liam Neeson and Joanne Whalley about a Scottish bare-knuckle fighter. Filming started at the beginning of October. For the film, he had finally to have a proper haircut and shave his beard off, with his three daughters by Pamela in attendance. 'I don't look like a talking beard anymore.' The girls liked it and thought he looked handsome. 'I had never realized I lived with a man who had a cleft chin as good as Kirk Douglas's,' said Pamela, and this from a woman of whom it was said in the June 1994 issue of *Tatler*, 'The one thing I remember about Pamela Stephenson was her fabulous kneecaps; they were like fragile eggs, absolutely beautiful.' Billy's ever-faithful friend Danny Kyle said that the haircut was a big step for Billy, 'but he can still pull down the walls of the temple'.

On 20 December 1989, aged forty-seven and thirty-nine Billy and

Pamela married, as one does, in Fiji. The invitations were in the form of colourful sarongs which guests were expected to wear. Daisy, five, Amy, three, and Scarlett, eighteen months, were the bridesmaids. 'Our kids are continually asking us to get married,' said Pamela mischievously. Barry Humphries gave the bride away, and the couple tied the knot to the strains of 'You Take the High Road' and the theme tune to 'The Archers', played by Fijian pipers.

'I'm so lucky,' Billy said of his wife. 'She's very bright and reads me better than anyone in the world because we're so similar emotionally. I'm constantly asking her to tell me if I look like a wally. I have such appalling, gaudy taste and I can be arrogant, especially after a tour. You look for "room service" on your home phone. It's so easy to become one of the people you avoid.'

Domestic life was very different from how it had been back in Drymen, or in Drumchapel, for that matter. Billy confessed – or, more likely, boasted – that he cooked and washed up, while Pamela did the accounts, bought houses and organized schooling for the girls.

The wedding prompted Iris to apply for more alimony. In May, with a declared gross income of £600,000 (Pamela's was £180,000), he was taken to court by Iris for more money. Until the divorce, Iris had been paid £1,156 a month, but now she wanted £35,000 a year, including allowances for looking after the children when they were with her. A new contract was negotiated in secret as Billy was signing up for his first American TV sitcom, 'Head of The Class'.

'I would no more have a TV series than put a nail through my forehead. I've never wanted it and I don't want it now,' Connolly had told the *Guardian* as late as February 1989. Now, with a politician's ability to U-turn while smiling, and in what he described as a quite ruthless move to become famous in America – 'I'd have done anything for success' – he had decided to try it. His defence was that he did not ask for a job on TV. 'It was Michael Elias, an executive producer on the series, who met me at a dinner in London and told me he was familiar with my work. They wanted more energy in the series, to change its direction. Howard Hesseman, whom I replaced, is a more technical actor than I am. I'm a comedian. He's an actor. When in doubt, I fall back on energy.'

The route that led to Elias's offer was convoluted. Walt Disney (of all the studios in all the world) became interested in his talent – he had raised some minor ripples in the US after the HBO special with Whoopi Goldberg – and offered him the Robin Williams part in a grim-sounding TV spinoff of *Dead Poets' Society*. 'We did an episode, me and all these schoolboy Americans, young guys, and I thought it was very good, and they did too, but they thought it wouldn't sustain because Americans think in realms of five years for a series. Five is good for a series. Two is the basic: you can't sell it to anyone else if you've less than two. So they didn't think it had five years, and I agreed wholeheartedly. So Disney gave me a Mickey Mouse hat and a watch and some money and sent me on my way rejoicing.'

The word was now out, however, that Connolly was a potential sitcom star. 'Head of The Class' put his name on their list. 'He came highly recommended. We saw the tape and thought, brilliant, the funniest man we had seen in a long, long time,' said Elias. After the London dinner, and having taken advice from Michael Caine as well as Pamela, Billy agreed to do twenty-two episodes. He refused to audition or read for the part, because he regarded that as too demeaning at his age. Elias told him he had the part in the bag, whatever. Billy felt that he had been working in the US for the best part of twenty years, he could fill the Carnegie Hall and the Lincoln Center, receive reasonably prominent reviews, yet still walk home unnoticed. Being left alone by the public, as he wished happened occasionally at home, was one thing, but being a nobody was not very pleasant. The advice he was getting was that, if instant stardom doesn't happen, persistence, being around for years, may pay off, and that TV was the only way to become big. Every city in the US has dozens, even hundreds, of comedy venues, where thousands of frequently quite competent comics ply their trade.

'In England you play a club and word gets around you're good and everyone comes to see you,' he explained to the *Daily News*. 'Suddenly you're known all over the country. It's true in Ireland and Scotland. Play a club in New York and the word doesn't reach Philadelphia and you've entertained more people than you did in Australia. It's the shape of America that makes it important.'

In 'Head of The Class', Billy played an Oxford-educated history teacher Billy MacGregor (it was that curious tendency to cast Billy as

Billy, or at least A Billy, yet again). 'The irony of the Connolly working class motif being worn on the coats of a Glaswegian history teacher who comes to a top high school in America with excellent academic credentials is not lost on Elias,' wrote the *Evening Times* back home. ' "Oh, we slipped that one in," he said with a laugh. "We asked ourselves how we could justify a Scottish teacher here in America. How he got to Oxford was through hard work and sacrifice. We make those points in his character and his history. MacGregor talks about working the shipyards in Glasgow and never denies his working class background." '

'Head of The Class' (which also starred Michael Tyson's ex, Robin Givens) already had a prime-time slot on the ABC network when Hesseman dropped out, achieving a viewership of 37 million. Billy arrived in the US for real, as it were, at the beginning of August, and found himself living in a small house above Sunset Boulevard, feeling alone, isolated, a little scared and anonymous. The first morning in LA, he woke up and rang Danny Kyle, his lifelong friend, at his home in Paisley, where it was four in the morning. 'I panicked,' said Kyle. 'I thought it was an emergency. I said, "What's wrong?" He says, "Nothing. I just wanted to say I was phoning from Hollywood . . . Ah'm away t'ma work noo. Ah'm jist gettin' ma pieces made up." . . . I'm so full of pride for Billy. I'm delighted that one of the lads has finally done it.'

A week later, Pamela and the three girls flew out to join Billy in LA: 'We're going to give Billy some moral support. He's been there for a week. We thought we'd let him get the first episode safely recorded before we joined him,' said Stephenson. They stayed for a month and planned a bi-continental lifestyle because they did not want to uproot their daughters from school. 'My son [Jamie, now twenty] didn't care to come on the trip. He's busy working in Britain. He's a roadie for rock groups [including The Rolling Stones]. I understand him. He's all hairy and trying to buy a car and all that stuff, y'know,' Billy told a mildly interested American press.

Billy Connolly seized his big opportunity with spirit for a man of nearly fifty. He drove by jeep (soon replaced by a Range Rover) down Warner Boulevard each day arriving half an hour early for work on a sound stage at Warner Bros studios in Burbank. There he would park in a place marked 'Reserved for Billy Connolly, Head of The Class'. His on-set Winnebago was smothered with Amnesty and nature conservancy slogans, and a sticker reading 'Lead-free and fart-free'. 'He hangs on to the old scatology as if it were a trusted badge of social menace,' wrote a perceptive visiting journalist.

'I have never met anybody like Billy. He is the first one on the set and the last one to leave. He is so co-operative. His demands are minimal. I mean, I don't think I know what they are. Correction. I don't think there are *any*,' Elias was soon telling the Glasgow *Evening Times'* man who flew over to report on Billy in Hollywood. 'The guy is brilliantly funny. He has a tremendous warmth, and I don't know if you see that aspect of him in his stand-up. But one on one his relationship with the kids is beautiful. Whatever it is, his personality, or the way he delivers the material, he never patronizes them. He treats them like adults and equals and that's refreshing, too.' There was, the paper found, a mad rush on tickets among expatriate Scots for each Friday's live studio taping of the show.

Billy spent all his spare time at home, seldom venturing into LA nightlife, where the prospect of being unknown even in showbiz restaurants (and there is no unknown like being unknown in Los Angeles) must have seemed depressing. He constantly turned down invitations to join Michael Elias for dinner – 'He is always saying he'd rather stay home and work on his lines,' the writer/producer said.

The reaction to Billy's twenty-two episodes of 'Head of The Class', made in four months in LA, was better than conventional wisdom would have it, the proof of the pudding being that Warner Brothers signed him up a few days before Christmas 1990 for an exclusive two-year deal, worth £2m, to star in film and TV projects, which would include a further series of 'Head of The Class', but left open the possibility that the show might be dropped without affecting the contract adversely.

'Billy was just brilliant in the show,' Warner's Harvey Shepherd said. 'We cast him very much as an experiment but it worked out well. He's given the series a new lease of life and we're looking forward to having him back. Billy is just what our scriptwriters and directors have been waiting for. He is going all the way!'

The company held a celebration breakfast for the show, at which Billy, triumphant at having beyond all question achieved what he came to

America to do, spoke without a script, or any notes prepared. 'I started off trying to be nice and say how glad I was to be there, but then I began picking on the cast members and being ruthless with them, and my language was visibly shocking some of them. The head of Warner Brothers TV loved it. But there were others who were just wilting under this physical and verbal assault . . . Oh, it was grand to be unleashed and feel the danger of it.'

No sooner had he signed the most lucrative deal a British TV performer has ever had in the US than huge articles appeared all over the country, falling over themselves to elaborate on just how unknown Billy Connolly – or Billy Who, as some called him – was. The 'Billy Who' furore alone was enough to make him famous in the US – renowned enough to have appeared five times on David Letterman to elaborate on the extent of his unknownness.

Those in the US who admitted he was now a star, likening him to Lenny Bruce and Robin Williams, turned on his accent and personality. The *Washington Post* complained about his 'whiny brogue' and then, in a brilliantly colourful phrase which could be taken either as praise or its opposite, referred to his 'frozen expression of pop-eyed alarm, like a cat with its tail under the rocker'. 'Like Bruce,' wrote one American critic, 'he is prepossessed by breaking down the barriers of hypocrisy, ridiculing man's reticence to accept the inevitability of bodily functions and the baser side of his nature.'

Four months after the celebration breakfast at Warner came what would, were it not for the cushioning effect of Connolly's new contract, have been a catastrophe; 'Head of The Class' was scrapped, the reason given that the cast was too old to play schoolkids convincingly. What should have been a teenage zit-com, you might say, just came across as daft. Billy came out of the business well, however, and was given a new series, 'Billy', made by Michael Elias and the same team. 'Billy' was a TV clone of the film *Green Card*; Connolly played the same character of Billy MacGregor, now a Scottish teacher 'who', wrote the New York *Times*, 'when his work permit expires, moves to maintain his United States residency with a marriage of convenience to a financially strapped divorced woman with three children . . . and, yes, Mom will find herself being charmed against her will.'

Warner spokesmen were now pushing the Billy boat out in spectacular verbal style: 'This is a phenomenal deal for a phenomenal performer. He should be the biggest TV star in the States by the time the series ends. The sky's the limit now he's got his own show and Billy's loving every minute of it.' Billy was now to be at the centre of a ratings war between ABC and NBC, and was receiving, depending on which calculation is accepted, between £20,000 and £40,000 a week for 'Billy'.

The first of thirteen 'Billy' episodes was broadcast on ABC at the plum time of 9.30 p.m. on Friday 31 January 1992. Just before this, the Connollys moved into a five-bedroom, three-bathroom (plus guest apartment and snooker room) home in the Hollywood Hills overlooking the Universal Studios, where the *Psycho* house (and the path leading up to it, known as the Psycho Path) can be clearly seen from the sundeck. A few yards away is David Hockney's blue-and-pink home, a few doors away is the house Errol Flynn lived in. The house the Connollys bought for around £1 million is in a sultry, Mediterranean setting. The only sound is the rustle of cypress and cedar trees in the warm breeze, the noise of distant Los Angeles freeways an even fainter background rush. Discreet notices on every door promise an 'armed response' to intruders. It was all something of an improvement on Kinfauns Drive, Drumchapel.

While the house was being decorated, the family rented the Queen drummer, Roger Taylor's, LA house, and Billy slipped back to Glasgow for a week to help his daughter Cara buy furniture for her flat in the West End of the city (she was at Glasgow University), to see relatives and catch up with Glasgow news. One day, he turned up unannounced at Radio Clyde while cycling to Largs. He did an impromptu interview, and invited himself to lunch with the footballers Derek Johnstone and Ally McQuoist, who happened to be at the station.

Everything was slotting into place for the family. Pamela had just won her green card in the lottery run by the US immigration authorities, which both she and Billy had entered. 40,000 visas are issued from 10 million applications, and Pamela's luck in the draw seemed as good an indication as any that she and Billy – who would now be eligible for a green card too – should make their home in the States. 'We like the way of life and the people here. In America, if you become successful they put your name on the pavement and let people walk on it. In Britain, they don't wait for your name to be engraved, they just walk all over you anyway,' Billy was quoted as saying.

In the first episode of 'Billy', the eponymous hero appeared carrying two suitcases and an aspidistra. 'This is Robert ... plant,' he said. It was one of the last truly funny lines. His wife, Mary, was played by a Texan actress, Marie Marshall. The lack of intimacy between the two of them that was the central tenet of the plot was quickly sketched. Billy/Billy's clichéd Scottishness control was turned up to max from the outset. One minute, Billy was looking distressed when forced to hand his stepson $20; another, he is reading his stepchildren a bedtime story ... 'And they did indeed find a golden haggis and played a plaintive air on the silver chanter of Achiltibuie.'

Criticism of 'Billy' as a show was scathing, but was generous to Billy as a promising actor. *Entertainment Weekly* called it 'feeble', 'resolutely unfunny' and 'totally unfunny'. Under the headline, 'Witty Billy sinks in stupid sitcom setting', *USA Today* wrote: 'When ABC beamed up this Scotty they could do no better than transport him to the land that all but video zomboids forget – Thank God It's Friday Night.' The Washington *Post* called the première 'only numbly amusing'. The New York *Times* said the show's formula was trite, but added tellingly, 'Mr Connolly has a zestful charm that aficionados of this sort of thing may find winning.' The San Francisco *Chronicle* wrote, 'Connolly is a comic of charm stuck in a lame-brain sitcom.' For *Variety*, 'Billy' 'suffers from *déjà vu*-itis and a lack of spark between its leads ... In this opener, some bits are so feeble you get the feeling Connolly's laughing at himself, and the material – not an auspicious start.' But, *Variety* concluded, 'It's obvious this stranger won't stay in the basement – though it's likely the show will end up there if it doesn't cultivate a sharper wit.'

TV Guide – probably more influential than any of the heavy papers with the kind of viewers 'Billy' was aimed at – was kinder. Jeff Jarvis wrote: 'At the least, Billy is a nice show for a Friday night with the family – and that's good. But at its best, Billy could be a launching pad to the big time for one wryly wonderful comedian.' The *Hollywood Reporter* also liked the show, calling it an 'appealing sitcom generating genuine humour'. And the Chicago *Sun Times* critic Ginny Holbert said: 'Billy Connolly, the show's Scottish Star and *raison d'être* is a funny man – debonair and goofy and charming. Although he was fine in the last gasp of Head of The Class, he didn't get to show off one of his finest talents – relating to adorable little kids (Connolly himself has five children). In the pilot episode of 'Billy' he displays his abilities along those lines in a sweet scene in which he and two little girls do their best Mick Jagger imitations while lip-syncing to The Rolling Stones.'

It was all enough to make Billy Connolly an enormously happy forty-eight-year-old man. He may have been aware of the W.H. Auden lines written about left-wing California émigrés fifty years before – 'The tolerant Pacific air/Makes logic seem so silly/Pain subjective' – but nothing was going to stop Billy Connolly feeling free to imagine he was a Beach Boy, Elvis Presley, whoever he wanted to be. The fantasy life of Saturday morning pictures in Glasgow was something near to his day-to-day reality. He drove a 1932 Ford with chrome wheels and a hotrod Chevrolet engine, and would have 'Help Me Rhonda' on the stereo loud every morning as he drove into Burbank. Michael Caine took him to dinners with celebrities like Frank Sinatra and Sylvester Stallone. He delighted in friendships with Sean Connery, Caine and Elton John. He revelled in meeting Clint Eastwood and Robert Redford at dinner parties, and would tell long stories about rather golf-club-ish conversations with them, how Clint approached him and said how funny he is, and that his grandparents were Scottish, how that was funny, because his grandfather (Mr MacLean) lived in Eastwood, and how we all roared. 'A lot of my friends are stars,' he would say quite touchingly, 'and it makes me so happy, having lunch with them.' But he no longer felt, as he had when he made the film *Water* nearly a decade earlier, that he wanted to be a film star. Now he dreamt of being a great comedian; he imagined becoming the new Victor Borge, the brilliant eighty-three-year-old Copenhagen-born pianist and comic who became an American citizen and a millionaire. He admired Borge more than any comic since Chic Murray, who had the chance of becoming big in America, but returned to Scotland because his wife wanted to, and always regretted it.

Danny Kyle came to stay with Billy for his fiftieth birthday, and told friends back in Glasgow of an episode that showed the delight his old pal was taking in his new life. 'One of his wee daughters that Billy had to Pamela had moved to a new school and a schoolteacher suggested to

Billy and Pamela that she should go over to another wee girl in the class for tea,' relates a friend of Kyle. 'The teacher had spoken to the parents and had arranged that the girl's grandfather deliver Billy's wee girl home at 6.30 in the evening. It was all agreed, and at half past six on the button a nice smart car drives up Billy's driveway. Billy's daughter gets out of the car with the grandfather of the other wee girl.

'When Billy opened the door, his daughter was there, and the grand-father was Gene Kelly. Billy recognized him right away and he said "Hello" and all that, and then Gene said, "Mr Connolly, you're a very funny man, I really admire your stuff." So Billy said, "Would you like to come in?" and he did, and had a cup of tea and a bit of a chat about things. After they had left, Billy was sitting there saying he couldn't believe he was with Gene Kelly and Kelly was speaking to him, and he ran to the bathroom, turned on the shower full belt and dived in fully clothed singing the refrain from *Singing In The Rain* with Pam shouting, "You're mad, you're crazy."'

But 'Billy', the series, sadly, was a flop. The show rated only seventy-ninth in America's top 100 programmes, with an audience of just under 12 million. The show was axed in June. ABC said coldly: 'Thirteen episodes of Billy have been screened. The show will not be renewed and there are no future plans ... There are no plans to use Billy Connolly in the future. The shows were poorly rated and failed to attract a significant audience.'

The network's disillusion with the series aside, Billy himself managed to keep his credibility intact. Brian Lawrie, the TV editor of *Variety*, said: 'It's not a death sentence for the future, but you'd have to call it a failure.' Before the announcement that 'Billy' was to be scrapped, Rick Du Brow, TV critic of the Los Angeles *Times*, wrote: 'I like him. I thought he was very good in Head of The Class. He has a vitality about him and in the right spot with the right material he could be a big hit. It's not that "Billy" is wrong for him, it's just that it doesn't make you sit up and take notice.'

Connolly made no pretence that 'Billy' had been a triumph when he discussed it on another flying visit to Glasgow. 'It wasn't successful. Funnily enough, it's still very popular on the streets when I'm touring. People say, "What happened to that thing?" It didn't rate. It's a very dodgy affair. I'm not making excuses here, I'm telling you the truth. But to establish yourself now, to get people to commit a lot of money and the sponsors to be confident in you, you have to rate really well.' He claimed, nevertheless, that 'Billy' 'firmly established' him in America, and there is evidence that this is perfectly true. An October 1992 Chicago *Sun Times* piece on his comedy act – long after 'Billy' was history – opened: 'Now that Scottish comic Billy Connolly has become more familiar to Americans through the magic of sitcoms, it's time for the real Billy to stand up.' He later explained convincingly that the purpose of going to America had not been to become a sitcom star, but to use TV as a lever to getting well-known enough to being a busy, recognized comic, able to play to Americans in towns where previously they had never heard of him.

The real question about the real Billy, however, was this: was the fifty-year-old, 1990s American Connolly the real Billy at all? The *Sun Times* article went on to detail some of the material Billy was presenting to North American audiences. 'He gets riled about some things, like the London tabloids' outrage over Sarah Ferguson. "Fergie topless in St Tropez! Oh the shock! This is written by people afraid to go topless because they look like a tub of lard. Let me tell you, if you don't go topless in St Tropez, they throw you in jail." At a recent concert in Canada,' the piece continued, 'he commented that it was nice to see responsible journalism using formal pictures of the Queen.'

The change in Connolly's outlook over twenty-odd years of stand-up comedy was extraordinary; he strenuously insisted on every occasion he could that he was the wild anarchist he always was, yet like the archetypal golf-clubbing, pal-protecting British comedian, here he was bitterly defending the rich and powerful against the forces of anarchic mockery. A 1974 Billy Connolly would have swooped on, and made merciless, remorseless play of the fact that this topless Fergie was also having her toes sucked by a male friend who was not Prince Andrew. Now, it was as if the unstoppable forces that make us all middle-aged in the end were corroding Billy Connolly's sense of humour. Had he finally, incontravertibly, sold out?

His three-week Hammersmith Odeon show, in June 1991, suggested that, perhaps, he had not yet, unless he was merely, as his friends on the tabloids have been known to, exaggerating one incident that occurred there out of all proportion to preserve his credibility. Carol Thatcher (who had free tickets, along with the usuals, Parky, Barry Humphries and Des O'Connor) walked out of the first night because Billy attacked her mother so ferociously. She claimed she sat through an hour and twenty minutes and was going out to dinner. The next night, Connolly told his audience: 'Carol Thatcher stormed out. Fucking great. Fuck off! I don't blame people for being Tories. If you're doing it right then those buggers shouldn't like it.' (All Ms T. would coolly say in response to this was, 'It seems like a ridiculous fuss. I am amazed he mentioned it. I mean if someone walked out of my show I would not broadcast it to the world.')

If Billy had exploited the Carol Thatcher business to bump up his credibility, the ploy did not quite work for the writer Julie Burchill, who referred to him in relation to the incident as 'that pathetic wreck of a burnt-out, dried-up, sold-out social climber and alleged comedian'. Even a fellow comedian, Jennifer Saunders, lacking quite the same wind in her sails, commented in *Time Out*, 'All that no beard, and don't smoke or drink and jogging in LA and making wholesome TV comedies. I saw one the other day and thought to myself, "What on *earth* has happened to Billy Connolly?" '

The transatlantic Connolly lifestyle continued to be a series of contradictions within enigmas, with, in best Fergie-style, a lot of holidays in between. For fishing, the bottom of the garden in Drymen had been amply replaced by Montana, and by Utah, where he would go on adventurous trips to the Green River that flows into Colorado and has superb trout fishing. At Christmas, when he always used to ensure the family was in Scotland, they went to Aspen. 'I don't ski myself, but the whole family ski so I'll go and look in shop windows until they come back. I couldn't mix with people who wear those damn clothes,' he said. (He rediscovered fishing, US style, when he wandered into a tackle shop in Aspen.) In July, Billy, Pam and the girls went with Fergie to the £120-a-night Cally Palace Hotel in Kirkcudbright, Princesses Beatrice and Eugenie being otherwise engaged. Staff at the hotel were sworn to secrecy, the police checked everything out in advance, but Fergie blew her cover (or at least the Connollys') by window shopping in the nearby village of Gatehouse-of-Fleet. The media descended on the hotel, and the party disappeared for a picnic in the hills.

The problem in Hollywood of what to do with a man who was almost a star but not quite solved itself in small, *ad hoc* ways. Late in 1992, the opportunity came up – and in dramatic style – of a part in the film *Indecent Proposal*, with Robert Redford, Demi Moore and Woody Harrelson. It was, as it turned out, no more than a two-minute cameo, with two lines to speak, as a charity auctioneer in a zoo. Billy, what was more, would be playing nothing more taxing – again – than himself, but they made him feel a star by sending a Lear Jet across the continent to Halifax, Nova Scotia, in Canada, to fetch him for his big moment. The journey was further than Halifax to London, with a refuelling (and peeing – there was no loo on the aircraft) stop at Indianapolis. The role still kept him busy for three days, which gave him the chance to find out what the film was about, as he was only given the two pages of script in which he figured. (The role was a tribute to the powers of Hollywood networking. Billy had only met the British director, Adrian Lyne, once, in an LA restaurant, ten years previously. When he got to the set, he realized that a singer who had been in the restaurant also had a cameo in the film.)

The journeys back to Scotland seemed to be getting more frequent, and in a sense more urgent. Perhaps it was nostalgia, perhaps a desire to be loved as he used to be, but he kept returning, even, in 1994, to do gigs in some of the old folk haunts. In 1993, he was in Glasgow for eleven weeks for Peter McDougall's BBC Scotland play *Down Among The Big Boys*, playing the leading part of gangster Jo Jo Donnelly, which had been written with him in mind. 'The money's crap, but every time you ask for more, they tell you what Bob Hoskins was paid,' he said. McDougall was surprised Billy accepted the part: 'I think he's on that little search for the Holy Grail, to make a bit of peace with himself. You get to the point in your life where you don't know where you belong; where you feel like going back to you roots, looking for a key to it all. I think Billy's doing that.' Connolly, too, was thinking deeply about the draw of Glasgow; he was disturbed by how much he liked going back because his childhood had been so horrid. He readily admitted his career, his life, had been a deliberate attempt to reinvent himself, 'to become this exotic creature you see before you', because he disliked what he was. He was sure, however, that his new persona and identity were the real Billy, and he felt like a ghost wandering about, bumping into old acquaintances in Partick pubs, then having to get away quickly because the gulf had become so wide, and going back to his discreet, smart private hotel in the city centre to field the latest calls from Hollywood.

In June, he was back more involuntarily, for the funeral in Dunoon of his mother, Mary Adams. She died, aged sixty-nine, and Billy turned up for her funeral alone in his green Mercedes jeep. 'Mrs Adams was a popular figure in Dunoon, a devoted great-grandmother and a deeply religious woman,' the local paper reported. 'Her oldest grandchild, Tony Richard, a commercial diver from Louisiana, said: "She was a lovely woman and there was a big turn-out. Things went as well as could be expected." ' Billy Connolly's views were not sought.

He was back yet again later in the year, to present and narrate 'The Bigger Picture', a Scottish art programme for BBC2. He had accepted the faxed (and very low) offer from the producer and booked himself on the next flight out of Los Angeles in less than half an hour; *any* chance to reconcile himself with his roots (and, along the way, to show them a thing or two) was sufficient to drag him away from his poolside. He had some knowledge of art, but, as he said, by the time he wanted to know more, 'I was too famous to go wandering around the galleries . . . I now know there's a great deal more to Scottish art than pictures of the growling mountains of Glencoe on shortbread tins.' He collects paintings by John Byrne, the writer of television's 'Tutti Frutti' and a one-time Glasgow drinking pal, but his main interest was in naive painting – he and Pamela have a collection of Aboriginal art.

In 1994, he even undertook, for the first time in five years, an eight-week tour of Scotland, that took in both big venues like the King's Theatre in Glasgow and clubs and meeting halls in the Highlands and islands. The possibility of a London run was dangled, and in May, he went to the Hammersmith Apollo (formerly the Odeon) for a run that kept being extended almost into June. Although it was repeatedly pointed out that his material was getting a bit dog-eared, it was a very successful tour for him, because it established him once and for all as the ultimate performer of his craft. The beard was history – something that still slightly shocks Britain – and the harlequin stage garb of old replaced by black canvas trousers and a black T-shirt with tails. The gossip columns only reported one harmless incident during the whole tour, when he had a two-inch banjo tattooed on his hand at the parlour of Brian Carville in Windsor. And the critics said all he could have wanted to hear.

Near the start of the tour, in Glasgow, David Belcher wrote in the *Herald*, having, as did all critics, had to buy his ticket – Connolly does not encourage journalists: 'Paying scant heed to what it has read in the papers, Glasgow emerged mob-handed this week for the city's favourite comic soothsayer. Entirely unadvertised, save for a wee mention in the *Evening Times*, Connolly's six shows sold out in hours. For years the papers have insisted that their erstwhile shipyard favourite has got above his station; lost the place; hobnobbed wi' royalty an sellt the jerseys. In truth, he has changed little. What he does now, as then, is reflect every Glasgow face, mankind's face, in the cheeky mirror of his own: truculent, daft, gallus, warm, officious, bullying, stupid, hurt, combative, cruel, incomprehending, kind. And funny.' (One theatregoer in Glasgow grumbled about being 'sore with laughter' on leaving the King's.)

Down in London, a lukewarm *Guardian* review nevertheless concluded that 'Connolly is by far the best comedian to come out of Britain for several generations.' The *Independent*, however, gave him one of the best reviews he has had in years. 'Connolly is still an extremely funny comedian,' said James Rampton. 'Connolly – like David Attenborough's safari suits – just carries on, regardless of the prevailing winds in fashion ... he inundates you with this great big, swamping personality, wave upon wave of Connolly, lapping you into laughter. The experience leaves you happily drained, like a cross-Channel swimmer sprawled on the beach at Calais.' The review concluded, 'So let's forget about the Fergie factor. What other contemporary stand-up could keep a packed Hammersmith Apollo gripped for more than two and a half hours without a break?'

It was, perhaps, the *Independent on Sunday* that produced the mid-life epitaph most delightful to Billy Connolly. Above an appreciative review was the headline: KING OF COMEDY COMES BACK HOME.

CHAPTER 10

Fame

'Should auld acquaintance be forgot, and never brought to mind?'
Robert Burns

Tom Ferrie, Connolly's old friend from Drumchapel, who went on to become a DJ on Radio Clyde, was once telephoned by the *Daily Record* and asked about an evening he had spent with Billy in London. Ferrie chatted briefly about the meeting, mentioned the salubrious surroundings Glasgow's favourite son had earned for himself down south, the butler and waitress serving dinner and so forth, went on to make the perfectly affectionate observation that this was all pretty good going for a former welder, and went on his way. The *Record* slightly misquoted him – not badly enough for him to remember quite how – and as a result, Billy refused to speak to him for six months. Ferrie, now at a radio station in Ayr (and back on the best of terms with Connolly), today steers a wide berth around even the most innocent press inquiry about Billy.

Fame, seek it fervently though he does, has been Billy Connolly's toughest gig. 'I've got the kind of face that people recognize passing the other way on the motorway,' he has complained. 'That kind of fame is a pain in the arse but there's no answer to it. I once asked Noddy Holder of Slade what I should do about it and he said: "Get on with it" … That's the difficulty of fame, the distance that it puts between you and ordinary people and ordinary responses. It gets like the Queen and that wee man with the paint pot who goes ahead of her and paints everything white. The more famous I become the less well I work because it really bothers me, not the audiences and their reaction but the instant recognition away from the stage.'

The change fame brought to people's attitude to him alarmed Connolly as much as the improvement to his bank balance. In 1975 he explained, 'It's made things easier. But what I regret about success and what it does is that a lot of my friends seem to have changed towards me. The other day I went into a pub I've been going to for twelve years, and for the first time, the publican, who is a mate of mine, called me Mr Connolly – and he wasn't sending me up. He meant it. Well, that upset me.' Eventually, of course, he became quite blasé about the reaction in pubs. In 1992, renowned as a non-boozer, he was talking about pubs in Glasgow, and publicans' reactions when he asked for a soda or the alcohol-free Kaliber he advertises on TV. 'They don't mind. They used to say, "It's not a caffee. The caffee's up the road, by the way." They don't say that anymore. Well, not to me.'

For many many of his old friends, he has handled the enormity of his public recognition with exemplary grace. Eddie McCandless, his mate from the army, who went off to be a dustman in Calgary, Alberta, met Billy again, long after he was famous. 'He always approached his old buddies rather than waited to be approached,' McCandless says. 'I was on Glasgow Central Station once, early in the morning, and I heard a loud voice shout out "Eddie!" I didn't think it could be for me, but then I saw Billy running as fast as he could, it must have been 200 yards away down the station, with his banjo over his back. He'd been doing some all-night thing and was on his way home, and we had a long chat. Then in 1980, after the 'This Is Your Life' carry on, when they flew me over from Calgary to be on the programme, Billy took all of us to some amazing Chinese restaurant in London, and he just ordered all this incredible food. I couldn't believe what I was seeing. I'd never seen a place like it.' Even today, every few years, when Connolly does a show in Calgary, he will phone McCandless to arrange a meal together.

Connolly adopts a bluff, no-nonsense approach to fame that belies the fact that he is at once entranced and perplexed by it. On Radio Clyde once, interviewer Sheila Duffy questioned him on fame and wealth. 'The reason I live in a big house with a big wall is because I'm famous,' he replied, 'and when you're famous you don't change any.

You might have mushrooms with your breakfast and drive a Mercedes or something. But that's not really a change. By the following Wednesday you're used to that – it's really easy to get used to that stuff. But the big wall is to keep other people out because people react very oddly to famous people. Some of them are very nice but they want to talk to you all the time about yourself, and it's a very limited subject when it's you. It's like autographs. Autographs are nice but there are few things more boring than writing your name. And I'm prepared to do my bit, but not all day. So I build a big wall and say, "Right, it's my time of day now. Go away." '

The wall at his Maidenhead home was an important symbol for Connolly; it represented his only real defence against intrusion, against the trauma and discomfort that fame, disappointingly, brought him. For the wall to be built needed money, for the money, he needed fame. It was an odd circular argument, and the result was that within a few years of achieving it, Connolly (going a little over the top, but it was an important feeling to him) was beginning to feel fame was 'the saddest thing in the world'.

'The reason for going to private hospitals and schools was the same,' he continued on his discourse on fame. 'You should see the effect. I'd like to take these weary willies of the *Daily Record* with me. And I'll walk into a hospital and you'll see the effect it has on everybody. You see, that's why I go to a private hospital. Because people react very oddly. I went to see Hamish Imlach when he was in hospital, in Motherwell. I had to escape out the window and run across the grounds because people went all wobbly at the end of visiting time. They were all trying to get in the room, and Hamish was sick, so I had to leave out the window – I was like a burglar in reverse. And so that's what happens when you surprise the general public with your famous face. And I don't blame them at all, but that's the way it is. Now the girls don't know anything else. As a matter of fact, Jamie and Cara don't know anything else. I was famous when they were born. And with Jamie and Cara I tried sending them to ordinary schools, and all that, but it's a utopian myth that you can do that ... it's just one of those facts of life. So they now go to schools where they can be protected from it.' ('After the "Welly-Boot Song" became such a hit my career really took off,' he said elsewhere, 'and Jamie had a bit of trouble at school. He was afraid to go without autographs. I had to have a word with the headmistress. Now he is at a little village school. And there I was just a seven-day wonder.')

Billy Connolly is not ordinarily famous. His fame is of the most interesting kind; mention his name, and the reaction will be anything but bland. Vary it may do, from tirades about toilet humour to 'didn't he used to be a docker?', but it will never be just a he's-all-right, he's-got-a-nice-house, I saw it in *Hello!* reaction.

Billy's 'special feeling', that he had been aware of from an early age, was honed into its celebrity success partly by intent and partly by accident. Certainly from the time he saw the attention fame could bring (the story about his girlfriend pointing out a famous singer in the street, and he reflecting sadly that nobody ever said, 'There goes Billy Connolly the welder'), it appealed to him. And, when he first started to experience it for himself in 1974, his response was wide-eyed wonder.

In 1975 – after his first success in London – he said, 'I lie back on the bed and try to convince myself that it's all real; that there's a chauffeur-driven Rolls outside at my beck and call; that my name's up in lights in Piccadilly Circus; that the entire run of my show has been sold out; that Max Bygraves, whom I've never met, has written to me inviting me to join him for dinner any night after the show if I feel like it. Suddenly I'm a celebrity who has the respect of other celebrities. Even Vanessa Redgrave came round canvassing for something or other, but I told them to tell her I'd already left.'

Setting aside the immediate thought – that if being famous meant dinner with Max Bygraves, who would want to be famous? – this account is archetypal off-stage Connolly; the very words he chooses show the enormous inroads success and fame have made into his personality. On the one hand he is endearingly incredulous at his achievement, and dreams of earning peer respect, while on the other, the punchline, he must prove he is still his own man, 'big' enough to make a quip (and not a hundred per cent true one, at that) about not bothering with one of the best British actresses.

In the same interview, he went on to say, 'I'm still coping with the present and trying to work out what suddenly being a star is all about. But what I hope for is to become the best in my field. I want people to look at me and say, "He's the greatest. There's no one like him. He's one for the history books." '

'I'm incredibly popular now in England and in London in particular, which has shocked me,' he said in 1976. 'It's gone beyond anything I imagined. Like taxi drivers shout to me in the street and everything, thump their horns and shout hello, which is a bit beyond what I expected. And wee men who sell papers, there's a wee man in Bond Street, he's got a sort of hut – it's like half a packing case that he sort of leans back inside when it's raining – and he stops me all the time and says, "Great, I've got all your albums." And that kind of level of acceptance was quite staggering for me. I thought I'd get the trendies, but I didn't expect to get the ordinary London people. I thought they liked Charlie Chester and that kind of stuff ... sort of Des O'Connorish kind of comics, the silly English kind of comics. But I think that's all over now, comedy's getting stronger and I think it's all the better for it.

'I've been keeping away from football matches recently because people keep asking me to sign Embassy packets,' he went on. 'I'm a bit brassed off; they ask me to write terrible things on them. And a wee woman came up to me in the street and she had an old muddy Embassy packet that she'd found in the street or something. "Could you sign this?" And I said, "Sure," and I signed it. And she says, "It's going to Australia." And I was imagining her son in Australia, the trendy young executive, opening the envelope and this muddy cigarette packet falling out with my name on it. Probably throw it on the damn fire, think somebody's playing a joke on him.

'When you first get famous you don't feel very famous until famous things start to happen to you, like famous people start turning up to talk to you. And you think, how does he know me? And it suddenly dawns on you that you're famous as well. And you walk along corridors of, say, Television Centre in London, and Reg Bosanquet'll walk out of a door and you'll say, "Hello Reg." And you think, hold on, I don't even know him, and he's going, "Hi, Bill." Two famous people collide in the corridor ... it's the most odd thing.'

Long before he was friendly with members of the royal family, he was learning that several of the younger royals were fans of his. Perhaps it was no surprise: the royals always had a penchant for the bawdy, a thing about Scotland, and at least since John Brown, a soft spot for lippy Scottish courtiers.

Nearly twenty years on, he had a clearer idea of what stardom means, telling the *Telegraph* in 1993: 'Even just being there [America], just walking down the street in New York, I feel like a successful guy.' He still takes, the writer Mick Brown observed, an almost childlike delight in his fame.

In 1993, Connolly was still studiedly disingenuous about having famous friends, as if by sustaining a sort of contrived humility and modesty he will avoid accusations that he has sold out, or is no longer a man of the people, a spokesman for the common man. In Hollywood he lives next to David Hockney and down the road from the late Frank Zappa's pad. 'It's quite breathtaking sometimes,' he said in a *Radio Times* interview. 'You're in the middle of dinner and you stop and think, My God, the last time I saw him I was sitting in a cinema in Glasgow eating popcorn.'

Just how the welder from Govan came to be playing pool with Eric Clapton and Clint Eastwood in Los Angeles, as he did once, is one of the nobody-to-celebrity stories that makes stardom an aspiration anyone can try on for size. But the transition from nobody to notoriety has not, and still does not, sit easily. To complete the process, it is necessary to stop introspecting about it, to stop mooning about your hometown 6,000 miles away, to stop realizing how lucky you have been. And to do all those things, it is necessary to become mindless. It is the fact that Billy Connolly has resisted the need to become stupid that continues to make him attractive to his public, if not to more cynical journalists.

In 1984, on the set of the film *Water* in St Lucia, he said tellingly, 'I do enjoy showbusiness. I find it quite easy.' On fame, he explained, 'I've done it and I love it. It has its drawbacks – you can be the victim of bad journalism – but when it comes to being noticed by people in the street, it's quite lovely. I would hate to have been born, lived and died and nobody noticed. It's a proof you exist, that all the practising with the banjo in your bedroom paid off.'

Yet he does kick up a terrible fuss about what he cannot control and in doing so, gives the best impression he can muster of being terribly self-important. The publicity surrounding the demise of his first marriage, of course, tainted him in this respect, but his identification with the chat-tered-about class was so complete, and so early in his career, as to be quite eerie. A year after the marriage break-up, he mentioned that Edna O'Brien had come to see him backstage in London, and how he had come to admire her. 'I heard her on a radio programme one day destroying Janet Street-Porter, just by being clean and articulate. She totally destroyed her for her book about scandal, and said it was scum. And she was right, of course, because all scandal is scum.'

It was perhaps the most extraordinary passing comment an icon-olclastic icon (if such a clanging oxymoron is permissible) had ever uttered anywhere about anything; if Gore Vidal had said such a thing, his credibility would have nosedived instantly, yet Connolly somehow got away with it. Equally, he waltzed away with cheerful admissions that he had made friends with the kind of people he once would have avoided with horror.

'I've never, ever liked David Owen much,' he said in 1986, 'but I met him recently at a party and I thought, he's a nice bloke. Because he's a fan of mine, and it instantly changes my mind about you if you like me. And actually I liked his wife. I was talking to her for ages ... she's an agent for writers, and she's a really nice and funny girl. And then he came up, and he was saying he was on "Desert Island Discs" and he was trying to choose a track of mine, and he found it awful difficult, for the old desert island. And I thought, that's lovely, what a nice thing to do.'

Six years later, however, he was unequivocal – at least almost – when he was asked if all politicians were scumbags. 'Absolutely, to a man, almost,' said the man who campaigned for Harold Wilson and used to invite the Kinnocks round to lunch. 'I don't like career politicians. I'm an anarchist. Politically I like a bit of anarchy. Anything that frightens them, any time anarchy happens it's a jolly thing.' Either wealth, fame or maturity had finally seen off his socialism. On 'The South Bank Show' in the same year, sitting at lunch with Melvyn Bragg at the Water's Edge restaurant at Bray (he declined to do the interview at his nearby mansion) he said he urged people not to vote these days. 'I don't like socialism any more,' he said.

A lot of his disillusion with the left (although to be honest, he had never been that illusioned with it, supporting only what he called

Brigadoon socialism, fair shares for all) was due to the political correctness that underpinned alternative comedy, and – one suspects – made him feel a bit old. Even though he had once railed against racial jokes, now he lambasted 'the puritans, the new rule book writers. I totally refuse to be part of it . . . those new comedy people who say no racism, no sexism, no that-ism, no this-ism. How dare you? Comedy's been here for thousands of years. How dare you start rewriting the rule book? There is no rule book. Funny is funny is funny.'

Connolly would be happiest if the Fame contract carried an 'as long as' clause. In his dealings with the press, he accepts the agreement conditionally. He is happy being mobbed as long as he can walk away when he chooses to. He is content to be interviewed but not when he disagrees with what is printed. He is pleased that fame brought him into contact with fellow celebrities, the royals and Pamela Stephenson, but not so enamoured with the repercussions when his friendships are criticized and his photograph requested.

Fame has not always been as good as he had hoped. Sometimes, his briefer thoughts on celebrity are more poignant that his wonderful, long, sprawling descriptions and philosophizing. 'I'm alone quite a lot. I think it's a reaction. It's the famous face, I suppose, but when you think of going out you think – is it worth it? – if you go out for dinner and some drunk hassles you.' He knows that without success, the nearest he would ever have got to royalty would have been waving his DIY Union Jack vaguely in the Queen's direction as a child. He is happy to accept that part of it, but not the inevitable flip side of not having everyone jumping for joy for him. 'Yes, I'm one of those "dreadful friends" of Fergie,' he told the *Radio Times*. 'I'm used to vicious, envy-based attacks, but they continue to make me very angry even though they're made by middle-class wallies who would kill to be in my position. I get better tables than them in Indian restaurants, and they know it.'

Fame might have been easier to take on board if Connolly had been middle class, whereby the leap from 'ordinary' to celebrity would have been congratulated and not seen as defecting to the 'enemy' camp. John Cleese, who although a shy man in many ways and not considered a prime candidate for fame in his youth, wears it in middle age with ease, partly because he has nobody snapping at his heels and calling him a class traitor. Whether Billy Connolly still identifies with the working class is not necessarily the issue because circumstance has dictated that 'technically' he is not a member of it.

The kind of criticism levelled at Connolly is dominated by the 'too big for his boots, turning his back on his roots' theme. And it is fuelled by the discovery of early comments such as one in his ancient and forgotten book *Gullible's Travels*: 'Princess Anne,' he wrote back in the early 1980s, 'looks like a horse just shit in her handbag.' What can Connolly say from his Hollywood poolside to the likes of Thomas Lynch, who claimed he used to drink with Connolly at his old pub, the Partick Tavern: 'How can you go from being a socialist to a capitalist and still say you are one of the people? He's forgotten where he's come from.' Or to Garry Hutchieson, a Partick Tavern regular: 'He should get back to where he came from, his own people. What do you hear about him these days? It's all about his wife and his daughters and the royal family and his big house.' Or to Alan Rayte, a Partick policeman: 'I remember him years ago driving his big Cherokee Jeep. He was a bighead then and he's a bighead now.'

Billy correctly defends a welder's right to upward mobility. Even as early as 1976, he was standing up for the moral justice of moving on, grew sick of apologizing, and got angry instead. 'If money changes me, I'll just go ahead and change and be funny that way. I've no ambition to be back where I came from. I've lived there and I don't like it. I get fed up with people talking about the shipyards. I've been in showbusiness longer than I was a welder. I don't want to be know as the comedian who used to be a welder.'

'Some of my old audience would definitely think this [Hollywood] spells sellout,' he continued nearly two decades later. 'But then they resented my getting popular years ago, and had been very possessive. There is that section of my public, and I kind of like them for that. I developed all my early stuff among them. I had a small, cultish band, and then I went and took it into the big outside world. If they don't like me now, it's for the same sort of reason that the Bluesies don't like Eric Clapton or Joe Cocker. Those people don't want progress, and they never did.' (What the more reasoned did argue, it must be said, was that there is nothing essentially objectionable about a star wanting to abandon his roots, but Connolly had done this at the same time as exploiting them on a daily basis for comedy material, and therein lay just criticism.) Above, beyond, behind – who knows? – purist debate about how close a man of the people must stay to them, about how much of a class or musical tradition it is permissible to take in one's baggage on the journey to another social milieu, comes the question of raw envy.

One of the problems that has underpinned and kept alive the envy question is the open secret in Glasgow that Billy Connolly is not unique. Anyone will say – even *he* says – there are hundreds, thousands of Billy Connollys, able for the price of a pint to spin an everyday tale of Celtic life to epic humorous length. Even his friends are adamant that in his youth, Billy was not outstandingly funny. Yet, with neither nepotistic contacts nor financially fuelled hype, nor any real vision of what his future might be (other than the somewhat banal belief that it would be 'big'), it was Connolly alone who felt his way to the limelight.

He had always had that feeling of 'being something special', just like countless lifelong street sweepers have, but the source for this was himself. It certainly, from his own account, did not come from any particularly effective socialization; not from his father (who stretched to recommending he should aspire to a 'little car'), nor the school that advocated engineering as a Holy Grail for one and all.

The drive – and this is what marked Connolly out, and fuelled the envy he suffers from, because other shipyard men may have been funny, but they did not have drive – came from the character that named the school gang after himself; the young man who saw someone famous acclaimed in the street and spent the rest of the evening in the bar, not letting the realization that no one knew who he was evaporate into nothing. It was a feeling that kept Connolly wanting something more than the stability of shipyard life and sent him searching for it – from the TA to Tinseltown.

He had to hold on to the steering wheel tightly at times, even when he started to get famous. Nothing must cloud the opportunistic eye which saw that claiming centre-stage with comedy could push Gerry Rafferty's song-writing talent into the background. Nothing must persuade him to forget that Scotland at that time was not, for practical purposes, where it was at, but that, as he puts it, 'If the Third World War broke out in London they'd tell you it was raining in Oban.' His eye was on the big time and the big world.

Like most celebrities, he feels the press is a monster that takes success from the rich and feeds it to the poor. He would like to believe the poor do not, in their turn, have any desire to consume this success (by mocking and sneering at it), preferring to blame the Tories who run newspapers for feeding their working-class readers a diet of envy. He is faced with the contradiction, however, that the middle-class newspapers, run for broadly the same profit motive, are kinder to him than the likes of the *Daily Record*. Yet it is probably indisputable that *Sunday Mail* readers, and their English counterparts who take the *Sunday People*, lapped up his mother's ghastly whining to reporters, whereas *Daily Telegraph* or *Guardian* types would have recognized them immediately as suspect in the extreme.

He never stops about the press; the *Sunday Mail's* notorious unearthing of his mother, a story which continues to enrage him and his friends (and that many journalists continue to regard as a perfectly OK story) was only one in a series of periodic nadirs as far as Billy was concerned. It has been a constant, unwavering theme since critics first started writing unfavourably about his plays in the mid-1970s. In a *Guardian* interview at this time, in 1976, he was said to be upset about a tip off that a leading Scottish daily was preparing to 'put the boot in', on the grounds that 'we made him and we will destroy him'. He believed the (soon defunct) *Scottish Daily News* never forgave him for refusing to contribute £5,000 to their appeal fund.

The press interest in his divorce astonished him, and he still did not quite seem to understand that journalists started by reading other papers, that an interview he gave to a trusted reporter on a 'nice' paper was not a private confession, to be read only by sympathetic, refined people. He felt he was a star, an artist, a trendy icon, but back in Scotland, to the tabloids, he was the epitome of working class, a robust, pint-o'-heavy and roll-your-own hero and a story that belonged to tabloid readers. 'I was in England,' he explained the year after the marriage break-up, and if I said anything, supposing it was to a journalist who respected me and was decent – and there are many, many of them – and told him the truth about the situation, they would print it. But the story didn't end there.

Then the Scottish end would pick up on the story and run out to Drymen to get Iris's half of the story, plus the ones who were coming round offering money – "My life of hell" stuff. The whole thing has got totally and absolutely out of hand. I've completely and utterly lost respect for them as a breed.'

Connolly had a classic, celebrity misunderstanding of the Scottish press. 'It's the build 'em up, knock 'em down attitude,' he said. 'But they didn't build me up, so how dare they attempt to knock me down?' He was quite right that the press had not made him – he had packaged himself and presented the completed persona as a gift to the media – but wrong if he believed there was a plot to destroy him. There built up, however, a tremendous resentment among the press over his unpleasant behaviour towards them. In that sense, it is arguable that Connolly's problems with the media were self-created. The rider to this, however, was that the bad publicity he received served to keep him famous; a media favourite, always co-operative, ready with a quote and a joke, soon becomes a tired story that slips off the front pages; in many senses, the last thing Billy Connolly needed was privacy.

Some of his best friends, nevertheless, were journalists, even if he did toy with his relationship with them. 'I've got one pal in the Scottish press, Russell Kyle at the *Evening Times*, and I talk to him – he doesn't interview me, I just phone him from time to time,' he said. (It is doubtful that Mr Kyle would be all that pleased by being accused of being a celebrity mouthpiece.) Another time, Billy said on radio that he disliked Duncan Campbell, with whom he had just written a book. 'That was a joke,' he later explained. 'I was trying to get at him via the air waves. He's a great mate of mine. He's an Edinburgh boy. We're very different types. He is middleclass, public-school educated and extremely nice ... also left wing, writes for *City Limits* in London ... We met via another pal of mine, Brian Wilson. Not all journalists are bad. I do like the occasional one.'

Even today, when his battles with the press are barely remembered by the public, he rarely appears on stage without loosing off a joke at a journalist's jugular; if they can use their forum to get at me, he reasons, he can do the same to them. Sometimes he comes close to libelling hacks; he has attacked Ruth Wishart, a highly respected Scottish journalist who has been on his side continually, when she has been in the audience. And in 1994 in Glasgow, he laid into a local journalist, within moments of coming on stage, for reviewing his art programme without, he claimed, seeing it. She must be 'bloody clairvoyant' he snarled. Few of the hacks go so far as Hugh Farmer, who, as an irritating foot-in-the-door reporter for the *Sunday People*, successfully sued Connolly for beating him up.

'I've had a real mauling from the tabloid press,' he says, setting aside the possibility that the converse was equally true. 'A serious mauling. They accuse me of being a hypocrite. But I'm not. I am completely and absolutely comfortable.' It was in the 1980s that he really started to stand up for what he saw as his right to walk around in public on his own terms, without any reporters in attendance. The press coverage of his marriage break-up drove him to distraction and frequent violent attacks. At his Cambridge Theatre show, he addressed the press 'who sit on your roof with a telephoto lens and then call you a publicity seeker'. (There could be no question about it: he was. But he only wanted to choose what publicity he got, having sought it.) He later told Tom Ferrie on air that the Scottish press was 'disgusting' – and his definition was wide. One friend remembers lying at a poolside in Australia with Connolly at the height of his stand-up prowess, and Billy gnashing his teeth with fury over a snarky paragraph that reached him from a folk newsletter in Scotland.

'I remember him [the friend] telling me in Australia the sort of luxurious place that Billy had,' one of Connolly's circle back in Scotland recalls. 'It's a bleak, cold midwinter here, and they're lying in the sunshine on the Gold Coast. And Billy said, totally out of the blue, "You see that bastard Kerry Thompson, I'm going to smack him in the mouth." Thompson is a journalist. There was this little folk sheet, the *Sandy Bells Broadsheet*, named after a pub, which was just a scabby little foolscap thing that was put out to a few hundred people on the folk scene in Scotland, a tiny thing, and Kerry Thompson had seen an album or a video and done a bit of a hatchet job on the crit. There they are, in a millionaire's paradise, he obviously gets Scottish papers wherever he is, and he is really uptight about some little . . . trivia.'

In 1982, at the onset of his Buddhist meditation, he went through a bizarre genial phase with the press. On his return to Heathrow from a

Far East holiday, he smiled at photographers and said to the press, without apparent irony, 'Nice to see you all again ... It's not worth having hassle every time we come through. It's much better to be friends,' Pamela Stephenson added: 'In the past, it was all very unpleasant and unnecessary. But things have improved with time. We've got used to publicity and don't worry now.' This entente cordiale lasted several weeks. When normal four-letter service was resumed, Connolly was at pains to insist that he and Pamela 'didn't ask to be in the gossip columns. It's silly, because we don't live that kind of life, really. If we go out, it's usually to some nice wee restaurant. Or if it's a show, we'll take in a matinée rather than a first night. Most of the time, we just spend quietly at home.'

'Punching photographers is sort of a showbusiness pastime really,' he later joked. His irony now may have been a little nearer the reality of his attitude to the media. An old drinking companion, Bill Barclay, the Edinburgh comedian, later told the Glasgow *Evening Times*, 'He goes through these periods of no publicity, but obviously the guy loves it. He chases the press when they are not chasing him.'

Even as he became more sophisticated in the 1990s, there was still a naivety. By now, he knew all about fame-seeking as the psyche searching for universal approval, but it still irked that the press would provide the fame, but not always the approval. Connolly still, and today still more intensely, brings personal terms into a situation he should be able to deal with by now. He hates the tabloid press, and especially that in Scotland, for daring to take him to task for developing airs and graces along with his fame. (His loathing for the *Sunday Mail* over the discovery of his mother is a special case – although a defensible story that the Press Complaints Commission might well have ruled valid had it been asked to adjudicate, it was a clumsily aimed kick at Connolly's psychological Achilles heel.) The broadsheet press he is suspicious of because it has an (ever-decreasing) tendency to be rude about his art. He has gone on record as saying television contains some of the worst people in the world; and he even complained once at Radio Clyde, his favourite media channel in the world, that he needed the station 'like cancer'. Looked at as a whole, Billy Connolly's relationship with the media resembles a car bitterly complaining about the iniquity of wheels.

In August 1992, Connolly was in Glasgow, revisiting old haunts for

'The South Bank Show', and to publicize a documentary, 'Acoustic Routes', about the guitarist Bert Jansch, for which he had provided commentary. At the preview, he put on 'a shocking display of petulance and bad manners' (said the Glasgow *Herald*) towards the Scottish and other media. He went ballistic against a former entertainments editor of the *Herald*: 'You're the wee bastard who said I didn't make it in America. I was nice to you and that's what you said about me . . .'

After the film's showing was a press conference, amusingly reported by one of the Scottish quality papers. 'The guys from the tabloids had been warned by David Shaw, nervous press officer of the festival. To Tom Grant of the *Daily Record* he whispered: "Don't mention the name of your paper." But the same Mr Shaw was philosophical. Like any good PR, he thinks any publicity is good publicity. "I don't really mind if he turns violent, just so long as the photographers are here," he reportedly said, offering hospitality to the press (provided they paid).' Almost an hour late, Connolly and Bert Jansch came on. Connolly 'skirted the microphones, ignoring an invitation from John Archer, head of arts, BBC Scotland and executive co-producer of the film, to speak. Mr Archer pointed out for the record that the *Scotsman* had got its facts wrong about the film. From the bar, where he had taken position (with a non-alchoholic drink) Mr Connolly took his cue, turning his attention to Scotland on Sunday. "Lying b———" was the punchline he shouted across the gathering after a rant about a rather complimentary piece the paper had carried about his home in Beverly Hills. Mr Connolly then slipped out on the exit line "F—— them all." ' Connolly later sent word through Mr Shaw that he might be prepared to meet some reporters peacefully. 'He was sent a reply quoting his own earlier message. It was in two words, the second of which was "off".'

At Christmas, talking to freelancer Adam Sweeting in New York, he showed no sign of tiring. 'I'll keep slagging them off, those Scottish wankers, cunningly disguised as journalists. Fucking bigots with type-writers. I'm going on television and I'm going to name the ones having affairs, I'm going to tell their girlfriends' names on TV. They have been warned. Journalists have done nothing but fuck me up for twenty years, write shite and lies about me, but they expect me to be nice.'

Unsurprisingly, Connolly reserved special hate for the *Sunday Mail*'s

Jim Lawson, who had written the 'Billy's Secret Mum' story eighteen months earlier; Lawson said he wasn't worried as he'd been happily married for twenty-five years. Sweeting wrote, 'The intensity of what he was saying was unbelievable. The parts of the interview that were about the press were mad.' Andrew Malone (of *Scotland on Sunday*) reckoned the outburst was brought on by Hollywood therapists and 'primal scream counselling', which 'urges people to relieve themselves of in-built anger, often stretching back to childhood'.

A *Sun* photographer, Andy Barr, who tried to take pictures of Billy, Pamela and the children shopping in Glasgow – hardly a gross invasion of privacy – might agree. Barr reportedly asked him to pose for a family picture: 'Fuck off.' Barr took two pictures anyway, and Connolly kicked him in public on the wrist, backside and leg. The *Sun* gleefully reported, its supply of asterisks never more drained, 'As shoppers looked on in amazement Connolly allegedly screamed: "F★★k off – just get to f★★k." And while Pamela and their young daughters looked on he yelled: "You c★★t. F★★k off. Give me that f★★king camera and the f★★king film. Take any more f★★king pictures and I'll stick that f★★king camera up your f★★king a★★e, you c★★t." '

A year later, fired up by accurate but unsympathetic reports of his professional tribulations in Los Angeles, these feelings are intensifying to the point of vendetta. 'I'd like to make a fight of it with some journalists,' he snarled to Andrew Duncan of the *Radio Times*. 'Let's turn up at restaurants where they're eating with their mistresses and expose them for the charlatans they are.'

Connolly's hatred of publicity (except when he loves it) seems to force those who work for him to spout the most humiliating nonsense, unless the example of rubbish unearthed by Nicholas Farrell of the *Sunday Telegraph* in 1991 was a classic. Farrell tried to obtain information for a profile on Connolly from John Reid Enterprises (which also manages Elton John and Viscount Linley). 'To the statement, "We're doing a profile on him", the woman press officer begins with characteristic showbiz blasé. "Billy doesn't do profiles." ' Farrell explained that he just wanted to confirm some biographical details, such as the circumstances of the Fijian wedding, whether Connolly was teetotal, a vegetarian and a Buddhist. 'I'd probably have to ask Billy, and that would be the same as interviewing him and he doesn't give interviews. It is all far too personal,' she told him. As material for a surreal Billy Connolly story, 'The woman who said Billy Connolly doesn't give interviews' would take some beating.

In the mid-1980s, Connolly had said: 'I don't want to be eternally praised, and I don't mind being criticized, although I don't enjoy it. But I hated being lied about.' Just what he means by 'lying' may be the key to understanding his attitude to fame. He has certainly put up with a lot of press rudeness and below-the-belt remarks: 'At a time when the whole world knew my marriage wasn't in great shape, a photographer at Heathrow Airport started to sing my hit song D-I-V-O-R-C-E. That is definitely not allowed. So I belted him one and the taxi queue applauded.'

But Billy's definition of 'lying' can sometimes seem to centre on a discrepancy between how he sees himself and how the press perceive him. His image demands that he always be seen as a rebel, but he relishes the incongruity of being loved by the establishment. 'I'm continually astounded [by my popularity] in a way. I see some of the audience coming into the theatre and think: "They shouldn't like me. They look too *respectable*. Do they realize the strength of what I do?" But I'm always wrong. I've no right to assume anything judging books by their cover. I should know better.' It was hard, indeed, to reconcile these words, in 1978, with the fact that the man speaking them was five years later featured modelling cuddly jumpers in a *TV Times* celebrity knitting book.

Twelve years later, nothing had changed: 'People have knocked me for about six years now. The vast majority of the people who attacked me in the press did so because they didn't know what to do with me any more. They ran out of things to say about me because I'd been a rebel too long for them. But not too long for me. It'll never be too long for me because I've always been an anarchist and I always will be an anarchist.'

Another three, and he was turning the theme on its head, in a Hollywood context: 'They don't begin to understand what I stand for, and neither should they because, according to them, I stand for subversion. I'm the least subversive man on earth. I'd love to be, but they confuse cause and effect. In the same way, I don't think the films of that big, silly Austrian Schwarzenegger make people kill one another.'

He probably best summoned up the true extent of his anarchic-ness in a 1984 *Daily Mail* interview, when he alluded almost in passing to the obvious (but so often overlooked) distinction between what he says on stage and what he is: 'I even cook now and I'm a great deal more settled. I'm still rebellious in my act and way of thinking but in my physical likes I like home comforts. I think I'm just getting older. I don't find being on the road as exciting as I used to. When I'm away from home, I want some of my home comforts with me.' The fact that Connolly includes a lot of true material in his act does not mean that it all carries a warranty.

The confusion between Connolly's self-image and the way he is generally perceived may be a symptom of fame, and being removed from a realistic sense of identity. The progression from blue-collar Glasgow tenement life to million-dollar LA style, with twenty years in the public arena, is bound to have some effect. But the extent to which Connolly has changed is debatable: whether his reinvention of himself is skin-deep or now part of his psyche.

The easiest way to reinvent yourself, superficially at least, is by a sartorial turnaround, and Billy has undergone a series of significant changes in this department that go above and beyond the changing fashion scene. The on-off relationship with his beard is the obvious case in point. He has said he hid behind it for nearly twenty years, but it helped him make his living, and he is duly grateful to it. But clothes have also played a leading role in his image creation. From his early days to the current incarnation (minimalist black on stage and linen suit for 'The Big Picture') his on-stage clothes have leapt from the ridiculous (banana-shaped boots) to the simple. The change can be charted not only by his work (his presentation of 'The Big Picture' may not have been so plausible if he'd worn fruit-shaped boots), but possibly also by his state of mind.

As a young man, he loved the symbolic change from welder's overall to weekend dandy, when he would change into his pride and joy, a Crombie jacket. 'I desperately miss the Friday nights. Coming home all dirty and getting all cleaned up and getting my good gear on.' Later, in his long-haired folk years, he loved encountering public approval in the form of people shouting at him, 'Away and try a bath.' He grew increasingly bold while still in Glasgow, dying his hair 'hooker blonde and once, even lilac'.

His appearance was for a long time based on how many props his body could hold, the only consistency being a beard and looking defiantly mad. Polka-dotted flares in 1974 were followed by the ultimate Big Yin gear: a tour T-shirt in 1975 featured Billy's face which, appropriately enough, after moving the belly backwards and forwards, could be made to look like it was vomiting.

By 1976, however, he was doing more than walking round wearing what looked like a jumble sale after the old folk have taken the good stuff. Connolly went designer, turning up for an interview wearing a 'Tolstoyan blouse' – the interviewer's words. 'It's good, isn't it? It was designed by my friend Chuck Mitchell' (a lecturer at Glasgow School of Art). And a year later he was admitting to an ego. 'Am I vain? Of course I'm vain. Can't you tell from my studied carelessness? You have to think a lot of yourself to step up on a stage. A famous face can be a terrible drag, but I live the life of Riley. And look at me now – starring in a film with Richard Burton [*Absolution*].'

But if he was ever near to being a walking advertisement for fellow Scots' talent, by the 1980s he was fiercely claiming his own identity for himself. 'I don't ever think of my hair as an image. I'm always just me. I don't represent Glasgow or Scotland or my family. I'm just very happy the way I am.' He also felt annoyed by any threat to his originality. 'I buy quite a lot of clothes, but I don't take much interest, except in my handpainted or embroidered jackets, and I always wear cowboy boots – they've got trendy, which makes me angry.'

When his hair was cut for his role as Beefy in *The Beastly Beatitudes*, he abandoned scrubby jeans and T-shirt for more punky, skintight clothes: 'It's the hair! Before, if I tried anything different, I looked like a head transplant case. A cardboard cutout on top o' the wrong body. But I've always dressed to suit myself. First, to look different – I wanted folk to know exactly who was the performer – and second, for fun. I don't look or feel forty, and I'm damn sure I'm no' going to behave forty and order an old man's suit. I'll pick clothes that cheer me up in the morning. And if they give other people a laugh as well, then very good.' His parting of the ways from the beard in October 1989 for his part in

The Big Man could have been viewed as commercial suicide, like Eric Morecambe getting contact lenses or Jack Dee going for jeans and a string vest, but it gave way to an unexpectedly handsome face, to the surprise of even his wife, and so has worked out for the best.

In 1983, he had the considerable honour of being deemed one of Britain's scruffiest figures, along with Patrick Moore, Willie Rushton, Ian Botham, Jim Davidson, Clive James and Harry Secombe, by Harry Rael-Brook of the Mr Harry shirt company; by 1985, he had changed his image again from shabby to flashy: 'I've made myself windswept and interesting. I try to look exotic, but when I buy Cartier sunglasses the police say, "Where'd you get 'em?" '

In the early days, he says, his appearance worked against him; it particularly shocked people when his solo career was starting, and he was hawking around the most insignificant of social clubs and pubs. He was a striking sight, a biblical face apocalyptic enough to rouse the upholders of his Catholic heritage to drown him in holy water, a wild man wearing an ironic kilt on stage. That image did not endear him to some: 'In another old Connolly haunt, Glasgow's Scotia Bar, they resent the fact that he has perpetuated the image of Scots as foul-mouthed drunks with one foot in the gutter and both hands around a bottle of the hard stuff,' wrote a *People* journalist.

In America, he was described as looking like a 'Muppet pirate'. 'I didn't grow my hair for fashion, and I won't cut it for fashion. I just look like a burst mattress,' he told the Chicago *Tribune*. 'When I shaved my beard off, after twenty-seven years, I was fat in the face and had this potato look about me. I've since lost some weight and have gotten down to one chin.' he later told the *Daily News*. 'It was a shock when I shaved it off and found I have a downturned mouth. I thought I had a smiley mouth.'

But the decision to face the audience with bare-chinned cheek had a deeper significance. Mick Brown wrote that Billy's 'transformation – the shearing of his hair, the disappearance of the beard, the fact that he drinks alcohol-free lager – has taken on a mysterious importance. Hair, beard and booze were, after all, totems of the Big Yin, the unruly, iconoclastic Connolly who first came to our attention in the Seventies.'

His wearing of the simplest of (immaculately designer) clothes and shaving off his most identifiable gimmick (which, if he let it grow back now, would be partly white and thereby lack much of its stark early effect) seemed to symbolize increased confidence, as well as moving with the alternative tide. Yet the conservative clothes have, ironically, proved shocking. Although there will always be something essentially wild-man about Connolly that no amount of designer robes can diminish, his cameo in *Indecent Proposal*, to those who have his eclectic image ingrained in their minds, was alarming. Connolly at a Hollywood party with Redford and Demi Moore for an instant looked like the gabalunzie man cleaned up and sneaked into a royal garden party.

The material stuff of fame and wealth has also troubled Connolly. As early as 1977 he was starting to learn that rubbing it in people's noses wasn't going to help his 'man of the people' cause. 'I wouldn't mind having a Rolls-Royce for a while, just to see what it is like,' he said, 'but the public wouldn't like it. They see a Rolls as a two-finger symbol on wheels. I drive a Mercedes station wagon, custom-built because I have two dogs and two children to go in the back.

'The money means more in terms of widening opportunities rather than material possessions. I always used to get ideas from sitting in Glasgow bars listening to other people. The Glaswegian is naturally funny and often doesn't know it. But I can't do that any more. If I walk into a bar they sit and look at me.'

'Scotland thinks I'm too big for my wellies,' he explained to John Heilpern in 1979. 'People who should know me better have now rejected me in Scotland. They assume I must have changed when in my heart I'm pleading to be treated the same. I didn't make it till I was over thirty. I wasn't a seventeen-year-old rock 'n' roll singer. Of course I've got all the trappings of success, but it hurts when friends treat me like some circus freak. I think success and money change other people more than the lucky man who's got them . . . If I identified with Glasgow as severely as I used to, I'd be a phoney. I'd be mimicking them. Because I'm not one of them any more. I have money, a nice house. You might say I've talked myself out of a corner. I'm not a shipyard worker. I've become a different kind of animal. It would be astoundingly pretentious of me to imagine I was the guy I used to be.'

When he went back to Partick, he said eleven years later, he would make a point of going into pubs to see some of the people he grew up with. 'It's a great laugh, but I give it fifteen minutes and then I get out of there. Why? Because I'm rich and it's uncomfortable. For them. Aye, and for me, but that second. It's not just because I've got a lot of money, but because it makes them feel like under-achievers, which they're not. It's just that I do a freaky job, and have been lucky, and am good at what I do, and they're good at what they do but they don't make a lot of money.'

But it is the view of Billy's real friends (and they don't come more loyal) that perhaps provides the most interesting account of the effects of fame on Billy Connolly. On the one hand, Peter McDougall, playwright, fellow working-class hero and old friend, comments on the deep, cor-rosive, psychological effect he suspects fame has had on Billy himself. He said he noted a suspicion in Connolly, brought on by years of fame: 'He has that look that villains have, where he can stare at you and it's completely vacant. I've seen it in pubs – people come up to him and they're either going to start mouthing off or feel compelled to tell him a funny story because he's Billy Connolly, and he'll just blank them. Perfectly polite, but vacant.'

On the other hand, illustrating the fact that the 'hatred' of Connolly in Glasgow is not quite what it seems, BBC drama producer Andy Parks told the *Telegraph*, 'I've got into cabs in Glasgow and had people tell me Billy Connolly's a traitor to his class. But we've been filming in pubs in the east end of Glasgow – all hard tickets, all subject to the bad press he's had here – and it's been, "Whoa, Billy. Good on you. You're always welcome here, pal. We'll look after yer."'

For Danny Kyle, the blank look Billy affects in pubs to ward off over-exuberant strangers is necessary. 'He puts a protective shell around himself – he has to – but he hasn't really changed. He's totally normal; he switches on when he goes on stage but off stage he's quite quiet.' Jimmy Reid, the former communist Clydeside shop steward, and a close mate over the years, explains further, 'Billy's public honesty makes him particularly vulnerable. There are no skeletons in his cupboard, for he has brought them out into the light of day. A few pick over the bones in search of some tasty morsels to chew. The rest of us feel for him and the childhood pain which obviously still hurts. Like everyone else, he is a mass of contradictions. Vulnerable, yet strong ... I've known great talents who were no good as human beings. Billy isn't one. He is a good friend, a good man. When it come to politics, I have always found him on the side of the angels; for the punters, for the poor, against prejudice, racial or religious.'

Billy Connolly is a big man who sincerely wants to be happy. He rejects the idea that all comedians are at heart sad people – the sad clown myth – and thoroughly enjoys his hard-earned fame and wealth. 'I sometimes ask the price of something as a famous guy and hear the answer as a welder,' he says with some pride.

'I pray that somewhere, there's some wee boy whose hero I am,' he once said. 'An ordinary wee guy off the pavement in some wee rotten place in the back of beyond who'll look at me and say: "Well, Connolly did it! Left school wi' sod all, wrote plays, appeared at Carnegie Hall, Madison Square Garden, on the telly, in all the nice papers, the Sunday supplements ... and *wowed* 'em. It *can* be done!" And I'll be his inspiration. When I'm on my deathbed, I'd like to think at least I'd achieved that. It would really be something.'

Casting aside his early bad experience in Australia, he now thinks he might settle there in his old age with Pamela, now his wife of more than five years' standing: 'I think I'd like to live in a warm place that's funny and jolly and happy and optimistic, and I think Australia is that,' he says. 'I would like to write a novel. I would like to write my autobiography properly. I would like to write some more plays. But my brain doesn't work that way yet. I seem to have trouble concentrating for long periods of time ... because I've been on the road for all this time I've been spoiled for so long I think I'm very immature and it affects everything I do. And I think my thinking process has become very immature. I'll have to grow up a bit and sit down and work.'

Billy Connolly is a man of new starts, and a future in Australia, with California left behind, would not be a surprising development. For some years now, Connolly has not felt terribly Glaswegian, or even that Scottish. He spoke on Radio Clyde in 1982 about this feeling that Glasgow was no longer home.

'On Saturday morning I was out with my daughter walking around in Glasgow, and it dawned on me that I don't really belong here any more. It felt strange. But then, when I thought about it I'd been living away from Glasgow for two years, and eight years previous to that I'd been living up in Drymen, so it was like ten years. So to expect to feel at home was a bit naive to say the least. And it'll always be my sort of home, it's where I come from. I'll always have a huge piece in my heart for Glasgow. I do enjoy it very much. I got on the plane last night, which was full of Celtic supporters in Newcastle, and they were giving me a bad time. It was lovely, they were singing and cracking ridiculous jokes and stuff. But it got very turbulent and all the singing stopped and I was very, very grateful. But I'd forgotten how funny they can be, too, how nice.'

If he was a little tired of Glasgow roughnecks, it was not because he found a sudden affinity with the Scottish middle and upper classes – the 'Alistairs and Fionas' he loves to sneer at when he does his act in Scotland (but, one can only imagine, he keeps mum about when he is out and about with the Scotophile royals). His whole attitude to Scotland (and its press, which is so extraordinarily important to him) is as perplexing to the observer as, one suspects, it is to him, too.

As he has never forgotten, the Scottish tabloid press ended up gunning from the hip for him. While most of the Scottish press, and by extension the public too, has gone out of its way to be fair to Connolly, he still has the ability to rile his countrymen, and sometimes does himself no favours when he does so; the reasons for his loathing of the tabloids are understandable, yet the continuation of his campaign against them has been a mistake. Attacking bad journalism *per se* would have been fine, but targeting the Scottish papers so exclusively smacked of hidden agendas. Swearing at journalists at the 1992 press conference for his Bert Jansch film was interpreted by the press as an attack on the Scottish public.

Columnist Allan Laing wrote a blistering attack on Connolly, looking wistfully back at the day when he 'wouldn't demean his country and belittle his working-class background. He wouldn't look for cheap shots to plug his fragile career. He wouldn't come over as a foul-mouthed corner boy, like a man who has been seduced by success and allowed it to go straight to his head... The one abiding memory I have of Billy Connolly in recent years was his appearance on the Clive James Show.

He was being interviewed live from LA and he spent the best part of ten minutes bad-mouthing Glasgow and the Glasgow people.' Connolly had been 'hijacked by the middle class' who 'stole his humour and his personality and turned him into a court jester. They gave him ideas above his station, invited him into their arty-farty world. By doing so they cut off his lifeline to real, human observation.' Was it any wonder, Laing concluded, that, devoid of Glasgow experiences, remote from West of Scotland folk, he was no longer very funny? (The point that might be made about this polemic is that Connolly had always made fun of Glasgow and Glasgow people. He did not leave it until after he emigrated to do so – it was his stock in trade.)

Yet just as, considering the potency of such attacks, Connolly's continuing love for his country is rather touching, the ability of the Scots to empathize with him is equally impressive. As a Glasgow *Evening Times* profile recognized: 'Being a Scottish superstar certainly isn't easy. Either success isn't acknowledged because "Ah kent his faither" or flesh and blood gets turned into a national emblem, and every action is to the glory – or the shame – of Scotland. Heaven help those who leave the country.'

The writer Ian Bell wrote: 'Who would be a Scot making good when your compatriots not only kent yer faither but were on nodding terms with your second cousin's auntie? The phenomenon crushes the spirit and the ambition. It is as though, for many Scots, Connolly's only purpose in life was to confirm their own image of themselves as gallus drolls, taking lip from no-one, living in a little world of limited experiences which must not, at any costs, be disturbed. In Connolly they discovered a man whose honesty always takes precedence over his affections and one who believes, rightly, that the working class are bigger than the stereotypes.'

Yet it is undeniable that a lot of Scots, and not just newspaper writers, but Scots of all sorts, do have a problem with Billy Connolly, and their feelings about him are different from those they display towards other Scottish icons. Perhaps it is the sight of their local hero, with that odd fixed grin in place, battling forth on lacklustre American sitcoms, but, as Jakki Brambles wrote in an article on Connolly in 1992, 'If Billy had been a football player, the Scottish media would have been having a love affair with him these past twenty-five years. Instead, he has been an easy target for some sections of the media. He has been easy prey for the so-called nationalists who believe the Scottish working man should never strive to be anything *but* a working man. What heinous crime is it that Billy Connolly stands accused of? ... Being born with a great talent, working his backside off for twenty-five years and achieving worldwide success! I say we take him outside and shoot him now! Does the fact that he no longer lives in Scotland make him a "traitor"? Does that make Kenny Dalglish, a Scottish hero who has lived in England for the past fifteen years, a "traitor" also? Is Sean Connery a "traitor" because he lives in Marbella and Los Angeles? No, the 007 star gets given the keys to the City of Edinburgh!'

Danny Kyle picked up the point about Connery later, and came up with an interesting theory: 'Why is it that Billy gets this [hostility]? At the moment they're giving Sean Connery the freedom of Edinburgh. Why aren't they treating Billy Connolly like that? He's at the top of the tree but he's never stood on anyone's fingers to get there. I don't know any superstar who *does* live in Scotland. Is it because Billy maintains contact? He's totally in love with Scotland; there's never been a greater ambassador.'

Of course, as he discovered in Brisbane when he was given a hideous reception by expatriate Scotsmen, some of the worst aspects of any nation continue in their undiluted form abroad long after they have disappeared at home. 'The one place in the world I never want to see again is Kearney, New Jersey,' he says. 'An appallingly ugly toilet of a town, where all the exiled Scots live out little fantasies, totally unrelated to the reality of Scotland. I went for a drink in the Kearney Scottish Club, and was almost thrown out because I'm a Celtic fan. It seems Celtic supporters go to the Irish Club, Ranger fans go to the Ulster Club and only Partick Thistle fans attend the Scottish Club.'

He admits to taking a wicked delight in bringing self-denying Scottish expats to task – 'I can't stand jumped-up anything,' he says. 'People with phoney accents can't last when they're talking to me. Mine sort of draws their old one out. And you can see them fighting it. The Adam's apple falling to the side. It's quite extraordinary.'

Billy was once on holiday in Barbados, drinking in the bar of a five-star hotel, when his hackles were raised by a brash Canadian couple who clearly were not as Canadian as they liked to think they were. They asked in (almost) broad Canadian accents if he was the comedian, thinking he was employed by the hotel. So as not to spoil his fun, he went along with them. They had, they claimed, been in Toronto seven years, yet their Scots accents had all but vanished, and they were fraudulently claiming to be hazy about details of Glasgow geography.

Naturally, they knew nothing of comedy, having been big league culture vultures – classical concerts, of course – back in Scotland. They affected not to remember where they used to go to concerts, eventually recalling that it was the St Andrew's Halls. 'But they burned down fourteen years ago, and that's seven years before you left, you dumpling,' Connolly said. Somewhere in the ensuing *froideur*, the woman, having established that the slightly aggressive man with the slightly common accent was not working at the hotel, but was on holiday, asked him bluntly, Scot to Scot, how he could afford it. 'Because I'm loaded,' Billy Connolly replied, equally bluntly, Scot to Scot.

Resentment against Connolly in Scotland, such as it is, often takes the form of a belief that Billy Connolly was funnier when he was a welder; this romantic myth has gained the universality of a proverb, and, like most proverbs, is nonsense.

Connolly's 1994 tour of Scotland was, by any standards, a triumph. He held audiences up and down (and round and round) the country in thrall. He had no reason to be doing the tour other than sheer ego, and that ego must have been satisfied for the time being by the hero's welcome home he was afforded. He is probably not only the most famous Scot alive, but, despite all the fervent words and emotions burnt up in discussing him, the most popular too. There cannot be a Scot under fifty unable to recite his story of the man who kills his wife and buries her bum-up so as to have a place to park his bike.

There is no dismissing his early prowess, but by all accounts his early patter was pretty basic Glasgow humour, and the development of his on-stage comedy has been continual. The 'funnier when he was a welder' theory is a confusion; what a lot of 1990s audiences find is that his reminiscences about childhood and the shipyards are funnier than his modern material, which can lag behind the times – at the start of the

1994 tour, he was still making jokes about East Europeans wearing anoraks, a comic seam that had been exhaustively mined long before. On the other hand, his recall of childhood events seemed to have become funnier than ever; did he know all this stuff twenty years ago and forget to mention it? Or was time and distance helping him see ever funnier angles on everyday events?

Billy Connolly may have been more *fun* when he was boozy and bearded, but it would be hard, ridiculous, indeed, to argue that he has ever been funnier than he is today. Such staying power has been an extraordinary achievement.

Connolly CV

	1972
September	Stage musical: *The Great Northern Welly Boot Show*

	1974
June	Tour: Canada
July	Record: Solo Concert, double album
October	King's Theatre, Glasgow
December	Record: 'Cop Yer Whack For This'

	1975
	Record: 'D-I-V-O-R-C-E' (this and three other records went gold)
10 January onwards	Mini-tour, including:
12 January	One night at the London Palladium
24 August – 21 October	Major one-man tour, UK
13 October	New Victoria Theatre, London
November	BBC TV play: *Just Another Sunday*

	1976
17 March	First play: *And Me Wi' a Bad Leg, Tae*
18 March	Book: *Billy Connolly – The Authorised Version* (Pan)
July – August	Tour of USA with Elton John
5 August	BBC2 documentary: 'Word of Mouth'
3 September	Edinburgh Film Festival: *Big Banana Feet*
September – October	Tour: Australia, three weeks
November	Tour: USA

	1977
	BBC TV play: *The Elephant's Graveyard*
	Extravaganza Tour, UK

214

1978
Tour: USA
Film: *Absolution*
BBC TV documentary: 'My Scotland'

1979
February – April   Big Wee Tour, UK

1980
June   Three-week season of BC's plays, Pavilion Theatre, Glasgow
October   On Your Bike Tour, UK

1981
January   Apollo Theatre, London
Spring   Bite Your Bum, world tour
August   Separation from Iris hits headlines
9 – 12 September   *Secret Policeman's Ball*, Theatre Royal, London
25 November–5 December   *The Pick of Billy Connolly*, Cambridge Theatre

1982
28 June to end August   Theatre: *The Beastly Beatitudes of Balthazar B*
September   Book: *Gullible's Travels*
November – December   Tour: Ireland and Scotland

1983
BBC2: 'Androcles and the Lion'
14 – 24 December   *Jock's Rap*, Apollo Theatre, London
31 December   Daisy born

1984
May   Film: *Water*
October   TV: *Blue Money*
30 December   TV: *A Weekend in Wallop*, LWT

1985
Autumn   Wreck on Tour, UK
26 October   TV: 'An Audience with Billy Connolly'

1986
January   Wreck on Tour, Australia and New Zealand

	1987
March	Mini solo tour: USA
August	Launch and tour: USA
December–January	World tour
	1988
28 July	Scarlett born
	Show at Royal Albert Hall (*Billy and Albert* video)
	1989
July	Tour: US
October	Filmed *The Big Man*
20 December	Marries Pamela Stephenson
	1990
	Film: *The Big Man*
Autumn	TV: 'Head of The Class'
	TV: HBO special with Whoopi Goldberg
Christmas	Benefit concert for underprivileged children in Glasgow
	1991
3 June	Hammersmith Odeon, London, three-week run
	1992
31 January	TV: 'Billy'
6 April	Dome Theatre, Brighton
7, 8 April	Apollo Theatre, Oxford
4 October	TV: 'South Bank Show' special
	1993
	Film: *Indecent Proposal*
19 September	BBC TV play: *Down Among the Big Boys*
September	Tour: Middle East
	1994
January–February	Tour: Scotland
May	Extended season at Hammersmith Apollo, London